Study Guide

for

Woolfolk

Educational Psychology

Tenth Edition

prepared by

Emilie Wright Johnson
Lindenwood University

PEARSON

Boston   New York   San Francisco
Mexico City   Montreal   Toronto   London   Madrid   Munich   Paris
Hong Kong   Singapore   Tokyo   Cape Town   Sydney

CONTENTS

Preface

As a teacher, you will be responsible for making hundreds of independent decisions in your classroom each day. These decisions will impact the learning environment, your effectiveness as a teacher, and the motivation and academic achievement of your students. An understanding of the principles of educational psychology can help you form a basis upon which to make instructional and classroom management decisions. *Educational Psychology, 10th Edition*, by Anita Woolfolk, will provide you with understanding and insights into the human intellectual process and variables that influence teaching and learning. Your text and this study guide encompass a broad spectrum of topics: theories of learning; cognitive, language, and emotional development; classroom management techniques; motivational theories; assessment strategies; and effective teaching practices for reaching all learners.

In an effort to complement your text, I have incorporated in this guide a variety of learning activities to deepen and further your learning. These review and journaling activities are varied in design and format to address individual needs, learning styles and preferences. You will find some of these activities require higher-level thinking, personal reflection and application beyond the university setting. It is my hope these types of activities will prepare you for a future as a reflective classroom practitioner.

Through out this guide you will find activities designed as collaborative exchanges. Through these guided exercises, you will begin to see the value of thoughtful, collegial conversations and dialogue. Collaboration in academic settings is essential to the development of expert teaching skills and is the foundation upon which all effective learning communities are built.

As you work through this guide, you will come to know yourself as a learner, begin to form an understanding of yourself as a teacher, and gain insight into the beliefs, principles and strategies you will bring to your classroom. It is an honor and privilege to guide the learning of young people, may your study of educational psychology prepare you well for the challenges and rewards that await you.

Emilie Wright Johnson, Ph.D.
Associate Professor of Education
Lindenwood University

1

Teachers, Teaching, and Educational Psychology

Teaching After *No Child Left Behind*

On January 8, 2002, President George W. Bush signed into law the *No Child Left Behind (NCLB) Act*. Actually, NCLB was the most recent authorization of the Elementary and Secondary Education Act or ESEA, first passed in 1965. NCLB Act requires that by the end of the 2005-2006 school year, *all* students in grades 3 through 8 must take standardized achievement tests in reading and mathematics every year; in addition, one more exam will be required in high school. Based on these test scores, schools are judged if their students are making *Adequate Yearly Progress (AYP)* toward becoming proficient in the subjects tested. NCLB requires that all students reach proficiency by the end of the 2013-14 school year. The effects on the teacher will be profound according to James Popham, an assessment expert. The law also addresses what makes a *highly qualified teacher*. By the end of school year 2005-6, the NCLB Act reuires that all teachers of core subject must be "highly qualified" according to the Act's definition.

Do Teachers Make a Difference?

For a while, some researchers reorted findings suggesting that wealth and social status, not teaching were the major factors determining who learned in schools (e.g., Coleman, 1966). In fact, much of the early research on teaching was conducted by educational psychologists who refusted to accept these claims that teachers were powerless in the face of poverty and societal problems (Wittrock, 1986). To decie if teaching makes a difference, you could look to your own experience. Were there teachers who had an impact on your life? Perhaps one of your teachers influenced your decision to become an educator.

Teacher-Student Relationships

Researchers have concluded that the quality of the teacher-student relationship in kindergarten predicted a number of academic and behavioral outcomes through the 8th grade, particularly for students with high levels of behavior problems. Even when the gender, ethnicity, cognitive ability, and behavior ratings of the student were accounted for, the relationship with the teacher still predicted aspects of school success.

Teacher Preparation and Quality

Linda Darling-Hammond (2000) examined the ways in which teacher qualifications are related to student achievement across states. Her findings indicated that the quality of teachers-as measured by whether the teachers were fully certified and had a major in their teaching field-was related to student performance.

What is Good Teaching?

Educators, psychologists, philosophers, novelists, journalists, filmmakers, mathematicians, scientists, hisotrians, policymakers, and parents, to name only a few groups, have examined this question; there are hundreds of answers.

Expert Knowledge

Expert teachers: Experienced, effective teachers who have elaborate systems of knowledge for understanding problems in teaching. Their knowledge of teaching processes and content is extensive and well organized. Much of their success comes only through experience and practice! (See Figure 1.1)

THE ROLE OF EDUCATIONAL PSYCHOLOGY

Educational Psychology is the discipline concerned with teaching and learning processes; it applies the methods and theories of psychology and but has its own theories, research methods, problems, and techniques. Educational Psychology differs from other fields of psychology because of its emphasis on understanding and improving education and understanding what teachers and students think, do, and feel within the learning environment. As smart educators, many believe that teaching is merely a matter of common sense, but research findings from the field of educational psychology teach us that as classroom educators, we must put our "common sense" theories and principles to the test. Excellent teachers are classroom researchers. If findings from the classroom repeatedly point to the same conclusions, we can then develop principles about classroom learning, instruction, or behaviors. Example: praising the good behaviors while ignoring the negative behaviors is more effective than reprimands for decreasing undesirable behaviors.

Figure 1.1

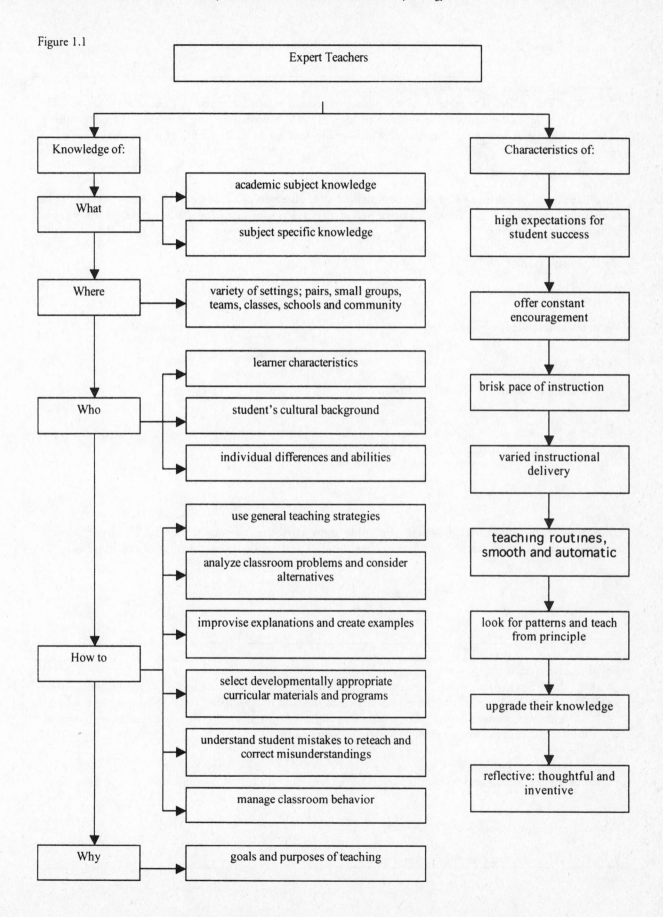

Journaling Activity

This reflective writing activity can help you recognize the strengths, skills, and abilities you will bring to the classroom as a novice teacher. Through journaling, you may express feelings and thoughts, sort out past experiences in your life, and get a clearer picture of your potential as an educator.

Part A:
Think about all the things you have accomplished that give you pride in yourself. Ask yourself: What talents do I possess? What are my positive personality traits and qualities? What have been my most important achievements?

My skills and talents:

My areas of knowledge and experience:

My positive personality traits and qualities:

My most important achievements:

Part B:
Reflecting on the above lists, how will you apply these attributes to your work with children? How will you integrate your talents, experiences, personality and achievements into your teaching?

Collaborative Activity

Interviewing for a teaching position can be exciting, as well as challenging. Teaching candidates are often asked why they have been drawn to the field of education. Find a classmate with whom you feel comfortable and take turns asking and answering the following mock interview questions. Use your notes from your first journaling activity to help you prepare.

<u>Possible Interview Questions:</u>
Teaching is a demanding and rewarding career. What personal and professional qualities do you bring to the classroom?

Why did you want to become a teacher?

Why should I select you over another candidate?

USING RESEARCH TO UNDERSTAND AND IMPROVE TEACHING

Research is conducted for two reasons:
- to **test possible relationships**
- to **combine** the **results** of various studies into theories

Descriptive Studies Educational psychologists design and conduct many different kinds of research studies. Some of these are "descriptive", that is, their purpose is simply to describe events in a particular class or several classes. Reports of descriptive studies often include survey resluts, interview responses, samples of acutal classroom dialogue, or audio and video records of class activities.

Ethnography is a descriptive approach that involves studying the naturally occurring events in the life of a group and trying to understand the meaning of these events to the people involved.

Participant observation is a descriptive technique in which the researcher works within the class or school to understand the actions from the perspectives of the teacher and the students. Researchers also employ **case studies** which investigae in depth how a teacher plans courses for example, or how a student trieds to learn specific material.

Correlation Studies
Often the results of descriptive studies include reports of correlations. **Correlations** range from 1.00 to -1.00. the closer the correlation is to either 1.00 or -1.00, the stronger the relationship.
For example, the correlation between height and weight is about .70 (a strong relationship); the correlation between height and number of languages spoken is.00 (no relationship at all).

The sign of the correlation tells the direction of the relationship. A **positive correlation** indicates that the two factors increase or decrease together. As one gets larger, so does the other. Height and weight are postively correlated because greater height tends to be associated with greater weight. A **negative correlation** means that increases in one factor are related to decreases in the other. Table 1.1 in the text indicated that as the number of teachers without either a major or minor in math increases, student math achievement decreases.

Experimental Studies
A second type of research-**experimentation**-allows educational psychologists to go beyond predictions and actually study cause and effect.
The term **participants** (also called **subjects**) generally refers to the people being studied.

Random means each particpant has an equal chance of being in any group.

In one or more of these groups, the experimenters change some aspect of the situation to see if this change or "treatment" has an expected effect. The results in each group are then compared. Usually statistical tests are conducted. When differences are described as **statistically significant**, it means that they probaly did nothappen simply by chance.

Single-Subject Experimental Designs
The goal of **single-subject experimental studies** is to determine the effects of a therapy or teachingmethod, or other intevention. The goal of **microgenetic** research is to intensively study cognitive processes in the midest of change-as the change is acutally happening.

Longitudinal studies look at changes that occur over time. These studies are informative, but time-consuming, expensive, and not always practical-keeping up with subject over years.

Teachers as Researchers
Research also ca be a way to improve teacing in one classroom or one school. The same kind of careful observation, intervention, data gathering, and analysis that occurs in large research projects can be applied in any classroom.

What is Scientifically Based Research?
No Child Left Behind (NCLB) Act stated that scienfically based research:
- systematically uses observation or experiment to gathe valid and reliable data
- involves rigourous and appropriate procedures for analyzing the data
- is evaluated using experimental or quasi-experimental designs
- makes sure that experimental studies are carefully explained so other researchers can replicate the studies
- has been trhough a rigorous, objective, scientific review bya journal or a panel of independent experts

Theories for Teaching
The major goal of educational psychology is to understand teaching and learning; research is a primary tool. Reaching this goal is a slow process. There are very few landmark studies that answer a question once and for all.

Principle an established relationship between two or more factors-between a certain teaching strategy, for example, and student achievement.

Theory is an interrelated set of concepts that is used to explain a body of data and to make predictions about the results of future experiments.

Becoming a Good Beginning Teacher
Concerns. Beginning teachers everywhere share many concerns, including maintaining classroom discipline, motivating students, accommodating differences amoung students, evaluating student work, dealing with parents, and getting along with other teachers(Conway & Clark, 2003; Veenman, 1984).

Many teachers also experience what has been called "reality shock" when they take their first job because they really cannot ease into their responsiblities. On the first day of their fisrt job, beginning teachers face the same tasks as teachers with years of experience.

STOP/THINK/WRITE
List your concerns for becoming a teacher. Brainstorm a list of people you could go to for support and help in addressing these concerns.

With experience, hard work, and good support, most teachers have more time to experiment with new methods or materials. Finally, as confidence grows, seasoned teachers can focus on the students' needs. At this advanced stage, teachers judge their success by the successes of their studnts (Fuller, 1969; Pigge & Marso, 1997).

Being a Good Beginner. Becoming an expert teacher takes time and experience, but you can start now by becoming a good beginner. You can develo a repertoire of effective princples and practices for your first years of teaching so that some activities quicly become automatic. Yu can also develop the habit of questioning and analyzing these accepted practices and your own teaching so you can solve new problems when they arise.

Diversity and Convergences in Educational Psychology

This last section of every chapter will examine the topic under discussion in relation to student differences in race, ethnicity, family income, disabilities, or gender. Then, we will consider the convergences-the principles or practices that hold well for all students.

Diversity

Trying to address differences in academic achievement for different groups of students was one of the motivations behind the No Child Left Behind Act. This chapter examined the diversity of research methods in educational psychology-from descriptive studies to experimental studies to teachers' action research.

Convergences

Woolfolk believes that educational psychology has much to offer teachers who want to see all students achieve. Merle Wittrock (1992) sums it up well saying "the psychological study of the everyday problems of education, from which one derives principles, models, theories, teaching procedures, and practical methods of instruction and evalution, as well as research methods, statistical analyses, and measurement and assessment procedures appropriate for studying the thinking and affective processes of learners and the socially and culturally complex process of schools."

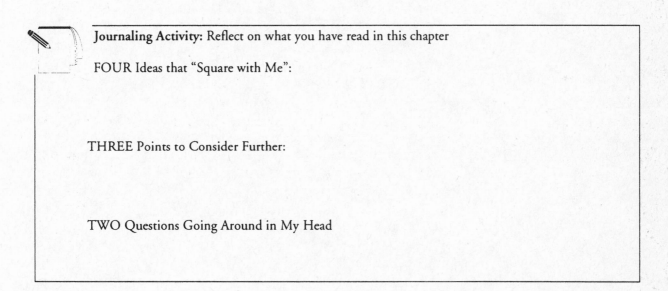

Journaling Activity: Reflect on what you have read in this chapter

FOUR Ideas that "Square with Me":

THREE Points to Consider Further:

TWO Questions Going Around in My Head

MY NOTES

(Use this space to make additional notes for this chapter)

2

Cognitive Development and Language

DEVELOPMENT

Crucial to effective learning and instruction, is developmental readiness. This means that students must be developmentally ready to learn in a cognitive sense, there must be progressive changes in their thinking before they are ready to understand certain ideas and concepts.

Development can be defined as certain changes that occur in humans or animals between conception and death. These changes appear in orderly ways and remain for a reasonably long period of time.

There are many different aspects to human development:

physical development:	changes in the body
personal development:	changes in an individual's personality
social development:	changes in the way an individual relates to others
cognitive development:	changes in thinking
maturation:	changes that occur naturally and spontaneously and to a large extent genetically programmed

An individual's **physical development** is primarily maturation. **Personal, social, and cognitive development** additionally rely upon interaction with the physical and social environment. All changes cannot be defined as development and many would disagree about "why" and "how" it takes place. There are, however, generally agreed upon developmental principles:

- **People develop at different rates. Example:** Some infants may begin speech or walking earlier than others. Cognitive development, such as spatial skills, may develop earlier for some individuals than for others. Girls are said to mature earlier than boys in a social sense. These differences in developmental rates contribute to the individual differences of the students in your classrooms.

- **Rate of development is orderly. Example:** Children will realize that a box has a surface before they realize that it has angles. A child will learn to stand before they will walk.

- **Development takes place gradually. Example:** An infant will not walk the first time he/she stands up but will require a progressive development of balance and coordination. A student will not spontaneously multiply without understanding concepts of number and groupings.

The Brain and Cognitive Development

The part of the brain that is primarily responsible for what we accomplish as humans is called the **cerebral cortex**. It constitutes 85% of the brains weight and covers the greatest number of nerve cells for storing and transmitting information.

Cerebral Cortex: The outer 1/8 inch-thick, wrinkled-looking covering of the brain. It has the following functions:
- receives signals from the sense organs, i.e., visual or auditory signals
- controls voluntary movement
- forms associations

Within the cerebral cortex, different areas have different functions however all of the areas must work together. **Brain Lateralization** also plays an important role in cognitive development.

Brain Lateralization: specialization of the two hemispheres of the brain. The left side of the brain controls the right side of the body and vice-versa.

Application One: Brain Terminology
Identify the areas of the brain that are responsible for the following functions. Check your responses in the answer key. Some of your responses may be used more than once.

a. left hemisphere	b. right hemisphere	c. Wernicke's area
d. Broca's area	e. auditory cortex	f. visual cortex
g. motor cortex	h. myelin coating	i. neurons (nerve cells)

1. ____ receiving language/sound
2. ____ processing language
3. ____ connecting meaning with particular words
4. ____ receiving visual signals
5. ____ setting up grammatically correct ways of expressing an idea
6. ____ processing spatial-visual information
7. ____ handling emotions (non-verbal information)
8. ____ movement on the right side of the body
9. ____ faster and more efficient message transmission
10. ___ store and transfer information

Stop/Think/Write:

Can you be in Pittsburgh, Pennsylvania, and the United States all at the same time? Is this a difficult question for you? Why? How long did it take you to answer?

PIAGET'S THEORY OF COGNITIVE DEVELOPMENT

Jean Piaget, known as the *Genetic Epistemologist* (one who is concerned with the study of the nature of knowledge from a genetic or biological perspective) has made substantial contributions to our understanding of cognitive development. According to Piaget, we constantly strive to make sense of the world and master the environment. This is accomplished through four factors:

1. **biological maturation:** genetically programmed biological changes. **Example:** "learning" to walk.

2. **activity:** interacting with and upon the environment to learn from it. **Example:** A child may know how to walk but learn a different way of walking by shifting balance when walking down a hill. Interactions with the physical environment alter our thinking processes.

Figures 2.1 and 2.2 will help you gain an understanding of the dynamic nature of Piaget's theory.

Figure 2.1

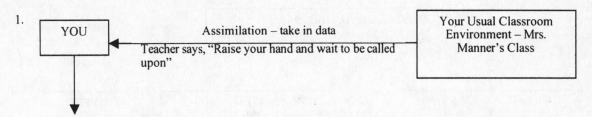

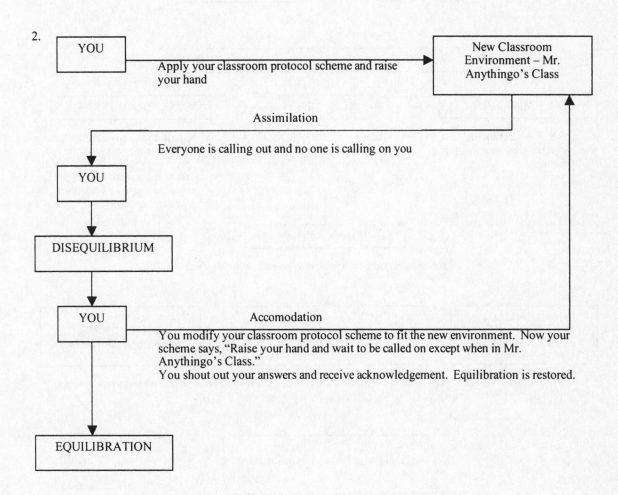

Figure 2.2

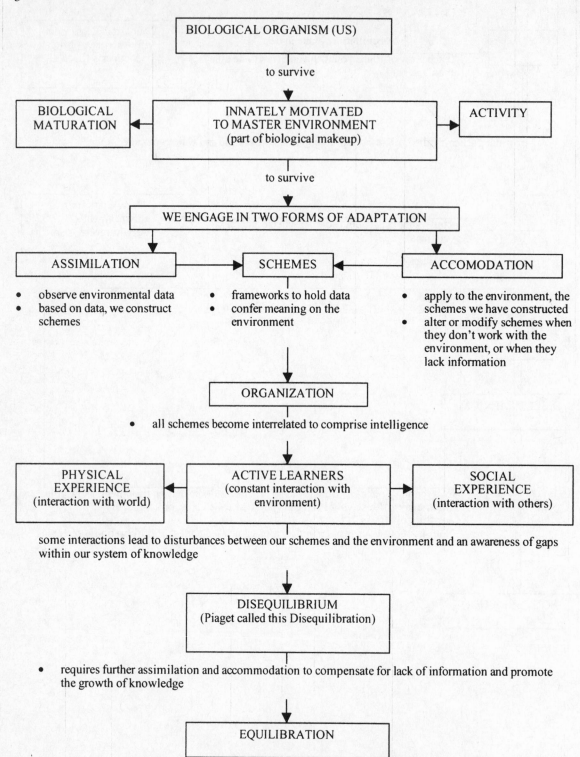

3. social experiences: in addition to physical interaction with the environment, Piaget stated that we need social interaction with others. **Example:** Without social discourse, we would never develop our currently spoken language.

4. equilibration: maintaining a state of balance between our cognitive structures and the environment. **Example:** Correcting the speech of a child when he says "I runnded all the way home" creates an imbalance within his cognitive structure for the past tense of "run." When he modifies his structure to say "ran" his cognitive structure is now in balance with his environment's conception of proper grammar.

These four factors greatly influence cognitive development. As biological creatures, we demonstrate certain basic tendencies in responding to these factors. Two of these basic tendencies are **organization and adaptation.**

Organization: the combining, arranging, recombining, and rearranging of behaviors and thoughts into coherent systems. Simple **structures** of knowing are coordinated and integrated with one another to create a more meaningful system. **Example:** We integrate our **structures** of mathematics with our spatial **structures**, which results in structures called geometry.
Structures =Schemes

Schemes: organized systems or actions of thought that allow us to mentally represent or "think about" the objects and events in our world. Schemes are frameworks we have constructed for understanding the world. According to Piaget, schemes confer meaning on environmental events and transform them into objects of knowing. We "construct" our schemes of knowing based upon our interactions with the environment so children's schemes differ greatly from adult schemes. An adult's scheme for "fun" is probably different from a five-year-old's and unique to the individual. Schemes can be very simple or very complex. **Example:** a simple scheme might be a scheme for strawberries. More complex are our schemes for manners, which might change situationally and culturally.

Adaptation: As biological creatures, in order to survive, we must adjust to our environment. Piaget stated that we engage in two forms of adaptation: **assimilation** and **accommodation.**

Assimilation: occurs when we take in or incorporate environmental data into our schemes of knowing. This is inwardly directed, from the environment into our structures. **Example:** If I tell you that equilibration is the mental equivalent of biological equilibrium, you can assimilate (take in) this information into your biological schemes to make sense of the terminology.

Accommodation: occurs when we apply, modify, or adapt our schemes in accordance with whatever environmental reality we are currently experiencing. This is outwardly directed; you apply what you know to match the situation. **Example:** You have a scheme for how to be recognized in class (classroom protocol scheme), you raise your hand and wait to be called upon. Let's say you go to another class and you **assimilate** that everyone else is calling out and NOT raising their hands. You now must accommodate (modify) your scheme for classroom protocol to meet this particular situation or class, in order to survive in this class.

Disequilibrium (disequilibration): occurs when some of our interactions with the environment result in conflict or an awareness that there are gaps in our structures of knowledge. It is an upset to our equilibration or balance between what we know or think we know and what the environment is telling us. If it were not for disequilibrium, our existing structures/schemes would never be challenged and our need to compensate for the gaps in our knowledge would never exist. Disequilibrium generates the need for us to restore cognitive balance by assimilating new information to correct the conflict or gap. This results in improved knowledge and is at the heart of why we experience intellectual growth. **Example:** A small child sees the sun at her friend's house, and then again when she goes home, and yet again when she goes to school. She **assimilates**

this and constructs a scheme for the sun that says the sun follows her wherever she goes, in addition to being a big yellow ball in the sky. Her mother tells her that the sun does not follow her, which causes **disequilibrium**. Now, to compensate for the imbalance and lack of knowledge regarding the sun, she must **accommodate** her scheme by **assimilating** new information regarding the sun. This will restore **equilibration** and result in an improved scheme.

One must always remember that what children experience and assimilate when constructing schemes, differs greatly from what adults perceive. Adult perceptions are derived from already existing adult schemes and past experiences. Adult schemes are much richer. **Example:** An adult's scheme for conductor may include electrical conductors, orchestral conductors, and train conductors, but a child's scheme for conductors, based on his/her limited experience, may only consist of the man who collects tickets on the train.

To further demonstrate how schemes confer meaning on the environment, read the following situation as related to me by one of my former students. My student was working part-time in a lingerie store to earn some extra money for Christmas. A father came into the store with his two young children to purchase some nightwear for his wife. While the man was being assisted by *my* student, the children had discovered some bawdy-gag lingerie, specifically designed to slip over the male anatomy like a knitted red, white, and green nose warmer. Do you get the picture? Giggles erupted, and much to the father's dismay, he saw that his children had tied the woolly appendages onto their faces like festive Christmas colored elephant noses.

To analyze this from a Piagetian point of view, we can surmise that the children had assimilated (taken in) the featural components of the lingerie (shaped like a nose with strings with which to tie it on like a mask). They accommodated (applied) their scheme for mask to the woolly covering and conferred *their meaning upon it, transforming it into a known object* or something with which they could identify. This operative transformation is the essence of intelligence. This is why Piaget said that "we construct the world" and "the world is as we know it." We uniquely interpret the world through the schemes of knowing that we ourselves have constructed through assimilation and accommodation.

Application Two: Matching Key Terms and Definitions

Select the word from the left column that corresponds to the phrase on the right. Put the number of the matching word in the blank in front of the letters and next to the same letter in the matrix below. If your answers are correct, all numbers across, down, and diagonally, will add up to the same number.

1. Maturation	_2_ a.	When we apply or adapt our schemes in response to the environment
2. Accommodation	_9_ b.	An imbalance between our cognitive cycles and the environment
3. Organization	_4_ c.	When our intellectual structures are in harmony with the environment
4. Equilibration	_7_ d.	When we incorporate environmental data into our structures
5. Schemes	_5_ e.	Mental frameworks of perception and experience
6. Adaptation	_3_ f.	Arranging thinking processes or schemes into larger structures
7. Assimilation	_6_ g.	Adjustment to the environment
8. Development	_1_ h.	Natural, spontaneous, and genetically programmed changes
9. Disequilibrium	_8_ i.	Orderly adaptive changes that occur physically, mentally, and socially

A 2   B 9   C 4

D 7   E 5   F 3

G 6   H 1   I 8

What is the correct number _15_ ?

Four Stages of Cognitive Development
Criteria for Stages

• The order of the stages is fixed; the sequence of concept attainment within each stage appears to be universal.
• It is a **stage** theory and not an **age** theory. Piaget is often criticized because the ages at which children attain the concepts associated with each stage, varies somewhat, but we must take into consideration individual differences in maturation and the quality of cognitive experiences.
• Old structures become part of new structures. Old structures are not abandoned but modified and expanded.
• Concept attainment that corresponds with the end of one stage, is the starting point for concept development within the next stage.

Infancy: The Sensorimotor Stage (approx. 0-2 yrs.)
This stage is aptly named because in the initial part of the stage, all of the knowledge that the infant possesses occurs only while the infant is acting upon the environment in some motoric sense. The infant knows the world NOT through mental thought, but through her actions, her sensory motor actions. Therefore, the infant's first schemes are not schemes of thought but, rather, **sensorimotor schemes.**

Sensorimotor schemes: schemes of knowledge specifically related to motoric action. **Example:** When an infant holds your finger, the infant "knows" your finger as a "graspable" and only while she is grasping it. In other words, objects in the world exist for example, as "see-ables or touchables or taste-ables" and so on. The infant knows the world only through her actions upon it and if she is not performing some motoric action upon an object, then that object ceases to exist. We would say that the infant lacks **object permanence.**

Object permanence: knowledge that an object exists apart from any actions upon it. **Example:** If an infant drops some keys in his lap and you cover the keys with a napkin, the infant who has not attained object permanence will not look for the keys, as these only exist when the infant is seeing, touching, grasping, or tasting them, etc.. If the infant looks for these however, then you know that the keys exist for the infant on a mental plane. Through thinking, he knows that the object exists apart from any action upon it. This is object permanence and Piaget stated that it is the first scheme that occurs on a mental plane. This occurs at approximately nine months of age, but others have argued that object permanence can occur as early as four months of age.

Object permanence occurs due to the repeated coordination of all of the sensorimotor schemes. The rest of the sensorimotor stage is characterized by (1) further refinement and coordination of these schemes, (2) the internalization of the schemes to a mental plane (once object permanence has occurred), and (3) another primary accomplishment, **logical, goal-directed activity.**

Goal-directed actions: deliberate actions toward a goal. The infant has moved from reflex actions to seeking an end to a means. **Example:** Initially when the infant lies in her crib and hits the mobile suspended there, it is fortuitous or by chance. Now the infant sees the mobile, and as she is developing eye-hand coordination, she can reach out, with intention, and touch the mobile *to make it move.*

Early Childhood to Early Elementary: Preoperational (approx. 2-7 yrs.)

Thinking in this stage is characterized by the development of a symbol system for communication and the ability to make actions symbolic through words, gestures, signs, and images. The ability to turn a "chair" into a "train" is called the **semiotic function.**

Semiotic function: The ability to use language, symbols, pictures, gestures, etc., to mentally represent objects or actions. **Example:** A towel can become a crusader's cape. Leaves on a plate can be a salad.
Symbol use has a high frequency in play situations. Children at this stage also play with speech with no real intent to communicate but just to hear themselves talk. This is called **collective monologue.**

Collective monologue: Form of speech in which children in a group talk but do not really interact or communicate.

Language emerges as a means for thinking and problem solving. Thinking that corresponds with this stage is still closely associated with actions or performing what one is thinking. It is thinking that is very tied to the "here-and-now." The child's thinking at this stage tends toward but is not yet fully operational.

Operations: reversible actions a person can carry out by thinking them through instead of literally performing them. **Example:** (a) When holding an empty basket, if you ask a child who is **fully operational**, how many objects would there be in the basket, if he/she first put in an apple and then two pears, the child would respond "three" without actually doing it. (b) If you asked how many objects would be in the basket if the two pears were removed, the child would respond "one" because he is able to reverse his action (operation) mentally. The **preoperational** child could respond correctly to (a) but not to (b) because his mental actions lack **reversibility** and have only one-way-logic.

Preoperational: the stage before a child masters logical mental operations characterized by reversibility.

Reversibility: thinking backward from the end to the beginning. **Example:** mentally going from A to B, and then from B to A.

Because **preoperational thinking lacks reversibility**, the child at this stage is markedly different from children in the next stage. Their lack of reversibility makes them:

- **egocentric**
- not able to **conserve matter**
- not able to **decenter**
- not able to comprehend **identity**
- not able to **compensate**
- not able to **classify**
- not able to **seriate**

Egocentric: Assuming that others experience the world the way you do because you cannot reverse your thinking to understand their position. **Example:** Seated across from a preoperational child, if you asked her to touch your right hand, she would touch your *left* hand because that is the hand which corresponds to *her* right hand. It is not that she is self-centered, it is just that she can only understand her perspective.

Conservation: The principle that some characteristics of an object remain the same despite changes in appearance. **Example:** A conservation of matter task begins with the child asserting the equivalence of water in two identical containers. The experimenter then pours the water from one of the containers into a *shorter but wider* container. The child now asserts that the wider container has more water for four reasons: (1) because the child is incapable of mentally reversing the pouring process which would take her back to the beginning, canceling out the change that has been made, and (2, 3, & 4) she can't **decenter, understand identity, or compensation.**

Decenter: to focus on more than one aspect at a time. **Example:** The child in the above example is focusing on the *width* of the third container but is not taking into consideration the *height*. She feels that since it is wider, it must be holding more water.

Identity: the principle that a person or object remains the same over time. **Example:** If the child in the above example had a complete mastery of identity, she would have realized that if no water had been added or taken away, the amount of water would have remained the same as it was poured into the third container.

Compensation: the principle that changes in one dimension can be offset by changes in another. **Example:** Again, the child in the above example did not realize that changes in the apparent width of the water (making it seem like more) occurred because the water was also shorter.

Classification: grouping objects into categories. Simple classification depends on a student's abilities to focus on a single characteristic of objects in a set and group the objects according to that characteristic. More advanced classification involves recognizing that one class fits into another. **Example:** The preoperational child can understand that a man can be a father and a man can be a policeman, but not that a man can be both a policeman and a Dad. Reversible thinking is necessary for the child to know that both fathers and policemen are subordinate to the higher class of men in general.

Seriation: Arranging objects in sequential order according to one aspect, such as size, weight, or volume.

Example: The preoperational child cannot seriate a bundle of sticks from smallest to largest because to do so would require reversibility. The child must compare larger stick B to smaller stick A on the right, and then reverse the direction of comparison to compare stick B to larger stick C on the left.

> **Stop, Think, Write:** In a class of first-graders there have been several recent incidents of students not giving up their seats at the computers when their turn was over. Describe at least two ways you could encourage these egocentric students to consider the feelings of the children who are waiting to use the computers.
> 1.
>
>
> 2.

Later Elementary to the Middle School Years: The Concrete Operational Stage (approx. 7-11 yrs.)

Concrete operations: Mental tasks tied to concrete objects and situations. At this stage, children's thinking has developed a very complete and logical system of thinking. Children are capable of concrete problem solving and reversibility of operations. They can think through a procedure and mentally reverse the procedure to return to the starting point. Because their thinking is now truly operational and characterized by reversibility, the concrete operational child can conserve matter, seriate, classify, and understands there is a logical stability to the physical world involving principles of identity and compensation. The concrete operational child can also decenter, taking more than one feature into consideration at a time.

Junior and Senior High: Formal Operations (approx. 12 yrs.-adulthood)

All individuals do not attain the level of thought that corresponds with the stage of **formal operations**. **Formal operations**: Mental tasks involving abstract thinking and coordination of a number of variables. Thinking tends toward levels of abstraction, possibility is at the forefront and reality is seen as just one possibility. The focus of thinking shifts from what is to what might *be*. When the individual formulates hypotheses, combines theoretical possibilities through advanced reasoning, and systematically evaluates factors to deduce solutions, this is called **hypothetico-deductive reasoning**.

Problem solving is often approached from an idealistic, "what-if" perspective and adolescents may develop righteous interest in social issues and political causes and dreams of creating "utopias" for future generations.

This stage is also characterized by **adolescent egocentrism**: assumption that everyone else shares one's thoughts, feelings, and concerns. Adolescents perceive themselves as the center of their world, believe their ideas to be better than others', and also believe that "everyone is watching them."
Piaget has stated that not all individuals attain the level of formal operations and that perhaps some people achieve this level only within their fields of expertise. What is important for educators to remember, is that formal operations may in fact be the product of experience, practice in solving hypothetical problems, and using formal scientific reasoning. These abilities may not be taught within all cultures or academic settings. Some students may not be developmentally ready for abstract problems beyond their grasp.

Information-Processng and Neo-Piagetian Views
As you will see in Chapter 7, there are explanations for why children have trouble with conservation and other Piagetian tasks. These explanations focus on the child's developing information-processing skills, such as attention, memory capacity, and learning strategies. As children mature and their brains develop, they are better able to focus their attention, process information more quickly, hold more information in memory, and use thinking strategies more easily and flexibly.

Limitations of Piaget's Theory
Piaget has supplied the world with enormous insights as to how human beings construct knowledge, however his theories have come under criticism with respect to specific aspects of his own research. Some individuals question the concept of separate stages of thinking, suggesting that if stage acquisition is determined by a particular set of operations, then the individual should be able to apply the operation across all conditions, e.g. conservation of number and weight which are acquired in that order and not at the same time. Brain research, however, supports Piaget as brain growth spurts coincide with transitions into stages. Others suggest that some of Piaget's tasks were too difficult or confusing for young children. As a result they may have been more capable than originally thought. There are, alternative explanations for why children have difficulty with some tasks and Neo-Piagetians theories find their bases in the original tenets of Piagetian theory with additional findings from the realm of information processing regarding attention, memory, and strategies for problem solving. Case has suggested that children's thinking develops in stages within specific domains such as number, space, social tasks, motor development, etc. Finally, others pointed out that Piagetian theory tends to focus on tasks that assess the ability to classify within our culture but other cultures may view classification differently. Whatever criteria are used to determine classification, the development of specific cognitive abilities are universally requisite to the ability to classify by whatever system.

VYGOTSKY'S SOCIOCULTURAL PERSPECTIVE
The sociocultural theory emphasizes the importance of the individual's culture in shaping cognitive development by determining "how" and "what" the individual learns. Vygotsky subscribed to the sociocultural perspective relegating greater responsibility to the people and tools in the child's world as

contributors to cognitive development, contradicting Piaget's emphasis on the individual for constructing her own knowledge. He posited that higher mental processes appear between people as they are **co-constructed** during shared activities. Vygotsky believed that the tools of contemporary culture, including language, play a crucial role in determining the paths of our intellectual development. **Example:** A friend confessed to me that he now thinks differently as a result of becoming a computer expert. **A cultural tool** can be an actual tool such as a computer, ruler, or simply a number system that allows certain permutations (unlike the Roman numeral system that is difficult for long division and has no zero, fractions, or positive/negative numbers).

Vygotsky believed that the most important cultural tool is language; an essential for cognitive development. All higher- order mental processes such as reasoning and problem solving are accomplished through the use of language and other symbol systems. He placed great emphasis on what Piaget called "egocentric speech." Vygotsky called this **private speech**.

Private Speech: talking to yourself.

Piaget viewed egocentric speech as another indication that children have little interest in the perspectives of others. As they mature they become more verbally interactive with others. They learn to listen and exchange ideas.

Vygotsky suggested that rather than demonstrating little interest in others, children are actually engaging in private speech for the purpose of "thinking out loud, so to speak to guide their behaviors. Eventually, the self-directed speech loses volume, turning into whispers, and ultimately becoming silent thought. Vygotsky suggested that this linguistic path helps the child to solve problems.

Research supports the notion that children engage in more private speech when encountering difficulties and that as adults, many of us use inner speech to regulate our behaviors, i.e., "let's see, the first thing I have to do is..." Because self-talk is used to guide thought, it is suggested that children be allowed to utilize private speech in the classroom in the form of **cognitive self-instruction**.

Cognitive Self-Instruction: a metacognitive process that students use to talk themselves step-by-step through the process of learning.

Vygotsky also believed that language plays another crucial role in that developing children interact with knowledgeable others who serve as guides and providers of feedback to advance their learning. Therefore, children are not alone in their discovery of conservation or classification. The discovery is mediated through family and peers. Bruner calls this process **scaffolding**.

Scaffolding: Through the interaction with the adult, the child will be supported, assisted and challenged by the adult at each rung of the "cognitive ladder."

Vygotsky assumed that "every function in a child's cultural development appears twice: first, on the social level and later on the individual level; first between people (interpsychological) and then inside the child (intrapsychological)" (Vygotsky, 1978).

Cultural Tools and Cognitive Development

Vygotsky believed that **cultural tools**, including material tools (such as printing presses, plows, rulers, abacus-today, we would add PDAs, computers, the Internet) and psychological tools (signs and symbol systems such as numbers and mathematical systems, Braille and sign language, maps, works of art, codes, and language) play very important roles in cognitive development.

Vygotsky believed that all higher-order mental processes, such as reasoning and problem solving, are *mediated* by (accomplished through and with the help of) psychological tools, such as language, signs, and symbols. Adults teach these tools to children during day-to-day activities and the children internalize them.

STOP/THINK/WRITE List the cultural tools you believe will be important in the cognitive development of the age child you plan to teach:

The Role of Language and Private Speech

Language is critical for cognitive development because it provides a way to express ideas and ask questions, the categories and concepts for thinking, and the links between the past and the future. If we study language across cultures, we see that different cultures need and develop different language tools.

Language and Cultural Diversity

In general, cultures develop words for the concepts that are important to them. For example: How many different shades of green can you name? If you have access to a purse, check out the different shades of lipstick inside. English speaking countries have over 3,000 words for colors. Such words are important in our lives for fashion and home design, artistic expression, films and television, and cosmetic choices-to name a few areas (Price & Crapo, 2002).

Languages change over time to indicate changing cultural needs and values. Vygotsky placed more emphasis than Piaget on the role of learning and language in cognitive development. Vygotsky believed that "thinking depends on speech, on the means of thinking, and on the child's socio-cultural experience" (Vygotsky, 1987, p. 120).

The Zone of Proximal Development

Zone of proximal development: the area where the child cannot solve a problem alone, but can be successful under adult guidance or in collaboration with a more advanced peer. This is where real learning is possible.

Private speech: This occurs when an adult helps a child to solve a problem or accomplish a task using verbal prompts and structuring. This scaffolding may be gradually reduced as the child takes over guidance.

Assessment: Most classroom assessments tell what child can do alone, however, dynamic assessment begins by identifying the student's zone of proximal development and then asks the student to problem solve, all the time supplying prompts to see how he learns, adapts, and uses the guidance. The teacher can then use this information to plan instructional groups, peer tutoring, learning tasks, assignments, etc..

Teaching: Students should be placed in situations where they have to reach to understand but where support is readily available from other students or the teacher. Sometimes the best teacher is another student who has discovered the solution to a problem because they are probably operating in the first student's zone of proximal development. Students need more than to discover on their own but they need facilitation and guidance and encouragement to use language to organize their thinking and to benefit from dialogue.

LIMITATIONS OF VYGOTSKY'S THEORY

There are **three ways** that **cultural tools can be passed** from one individual to another:

- imitative learning--where one person tries to imitate another
- instructed learning--where learners internalize teacher instructions and use them to self-regulate
- collaborative learning--where a group of peers try to understand each other and learning occurs

Assisted learning: guided participation that requires scaffolding-giving information, prompts, reminders, encouragement at appropriate times and amounts, gradually allowing more independent work by students. Listed below are the **strategies** that teachers could utilize for **scaffolding:**

- **procedural facilitators**--teaching students to use signal words such as "who, what, where, when, why, and how to generate questions after reading a passage."
- **modeling use of facilitators**--the teacher would model the generation of questions about the reading.
- **thinking out loud**--the teacher models thought processes, showing choices and revisions.
- **anticipating difficult areas**--during modeling and presentation, the teacher anticipates and discusses potential errors.
- **providing prompt or cue cards**-- procedural facilitators written on cue cards for student use.
- **regulating the difficulty**-- teach skills with simple problems, provide student practice, gradually increase task complexity.
- **provide half-done examples**-- have students work out final solutions for half-completed problems.
- **reciprocal teaching**-- have students and teachers rotate roles. Teacher provides support to students as they learn to lead discussions and ask questions.
- **providing checklists**-- teach students self-checking procedures to help them regulate the quality of their responses.

Interaction between adults and children is particularly beneficial to children when they are at the zone of proximal development.

IMPLICATIONS OF PIAGET'S & VYGOTSKY'S THEORY

By observing how children problem solve we can make many inferences about the level of their thinking (empathic inference). Understanding their level of developmental readiness will guide the curriculum and instruction. There is a wide range of abilities within the classroom and educators must respond to those differences in ways that make learning optimal for all individuals. Students learn most effectively when given opportunities to experiment and construct their own knowledge. Students should encounter disequilibrium and discrepant events at a level that is not too difficult but just challenging enough to promote further investigation and equilibration leading to improved knowledge. Students need the opportunities to apply their constructions, to test their thinking with feedback, and to observe how others solve problems.

THE DEVELOPMENT OF LANGUAGE

An early view of language acquisition proposed that children learn a language through imitating and repeating those utterances that would bring about rewards. Closer examination reveals that children create their language, i.e., "Mommy sock" and "Milk allgone," and phrases never uttered by any adult. Moreover, adults rarely correct children's earliest utterances concerning themselves more with meaning and communication. Adults will simplify their language always staying a bit ahead of the child to advance the child's language development, a form of verbal scaffolding.

Chomsky and others believe that humans have built-in, universal grammars, and a set of rules that limit the range of language learning. It is likely that both biological and environmental factors play a role in language development.

Diversity in Language: Dual Language Development

In 2003, about 15% of school-aged chldren in the United States spoke a language other than English at home. The number grows each year. For example, it is projected that by 2035, about 50% of the kindergarten chldren in California will speak languages other than English at home.

It is a misconception that learning a second language occurs faster for elementary than adolescents or adults. In fact, older students go through the stages of language learning faster than young chldren. However, there appears to be a critical period for learning accurate language pronunciation. The earlier a person learns a second language, the more his or her pronunciation is near-native.

Luckily, learning a second language does not interfere with understanding in the first language. In fact, the more proficient the speaker is in the first language, the more quickly she or he will master a second language (Cummins, 1984, 1994).

Language Development in the School Years

By age five or six most children have mastered the basics of their language leaving aspects of language development for greater refinement.

Pronunciation: Of pronounced sounds, the j, *v, th, and ah* are the last to be mastered. Ten percent of 8-year-olds still have trouble with s, z v, th, and zf more often using the words they can pronounce.

Syntax: word order that corresponds to the rules of grammar. By early elementary school children understand the meaning of passive sentences (they don't use these in normal conversation) and have also mastered basic word order. Understanding of, and then use of, extra clauses, qualifiers, and conjunctions will follow.

Vocabulary and Meaning: Pre-puberty is a critical period for language development, especially for language growth. By the age of 6, average vocabulary is 8000 to 14,000 words, approximating 20,000 by age 11. In the early elementary years children have trouble understanding abstract concepts and may not understand sarcasm or some humor.

Metalinguistic awareness: knowledge and understanding about language itself, beginning at age five.

> **Stop, Think, Write:** What would you say if you were "thinking aloud" for a group of students while modeling the process of tying your shoe?

Diversity and Convergence in Cognitive Development

Research across different cultures has confirmed that Piaget was accurate in the sequence of stages he described, but there is diversity in the age ranges for the stages.

Diversity

Western children typcially move to the next stage about 2 to 3 years earlier than children in non-Western societies. Careful research has shown that these differences across cultures depend on the subject or domain tested and how much the culture values and teaches knowledge in that domain. We have also see that there is diversity in language development. Some children learn two or more languages growing up, others only one. Children in every culture and context learn their native language, but they may learn a different set of rules for language use-pragmatics.

Convergences
In spite of these cross cultural differences in cognitive development, there are some convergences. Piaget, Vygotsky, and more recent researchers studying cognitive development and the brain would probably agree with the following ideas:
1. Cognitive develoment requires both physical and social stimulation.
2. To develop thinking, children have to be mentally, physically, and linguistically active.
3. Play matters. It is the way children and adolescents try out their thinking and learn to interact with others.
4. Teaching what the student already knows is boring.
5. Challenge with support will keep students engaged but not fearful.

Journaling Activity Reflect on what you have read in this chapter .

FOUR Ideas that "Square with Me":

THREE Points to Consider Further:

TWO Questions Going Around in My Head

MY NOTES

(Use this space to make additional notes for this chapter)

3

Personal, Social, and Emotional Development

Physical Development

For most children, at least in the early years, growing up means getting bigger, stronger, more coordinated. It also can be a frightening, disappointing, exciting and puzzling time.

The Preschool Years

Preschool children are very active. Their gross-motor (large muscle) skills improve greatly over the years from ages 2 to 5. However, because they can't always judge when to stop, preschoolers may need interludes of rest scheduled after periods of physical exertion (Darcey & Travers, 2006). Fine-motor skills such as tying shoes or fastening buttons, which require the coordination of small movements, also improve greatly during the preschool years. Preferring the left or right hand for skilled work is a genetically based preference and children should not be made to switch.

The Elementary Years

During the elementary-school years, physical develoment is fairly steady for most children. They become taller, learners, and stronger, so they are better able to master sports and games. Through out elementary school, many of the girls are likely to be as large or larger than the boys in their classes. The size discrepancy can give the girls an advantge in physical activites, although some girls may feel conflict over this and, as a result, downplay their physical abilities.

Adolescence

Puberty marks the beginning of sexual maturity. It is not a single event, but a series of changes involving almost every part of the body. The sex differences in physical development observed during the later elementary years become even more pronounced at the beginning of puberty. One tension for adolescents is that they are physically and sexually mature years before they are psychologically or financially ready to shoulder the adult responsiblities of marriage and childbearing.

The physical changes of adolescence have significant effects of the individual's identity. Psychologists have been particularly interested in the academic, social, and emotional differences they have found between adolescents who mature early and those who mature later. Perhaps the trials and anxieties of matuirng late teach some boys to be better problem solvers (Brooks-Gunn, 1988; Steinberg, 2005).

Adolescents going trhough the changes of puberty are very concerned about their bodies. This has always been true, but today, the emphasis on fitness and appearance makes adolescents even more likely to worry about how their bodies "measure up". For some the concern becomes excessive. One consequence is eating disorders such as **bulimia** (binge eating) and **anorexia nervosa** (self-starvation), both of which are more common in females than in males.

The Brain and Adolescent Development

Along with all the other changes in puberty come changes in the brain and neurological system that affect personal and social development. Teachers can take advantage of their adolescent studens' intensity by helping them devote their energy to areas such as politics, the environment, or social causes (Price, 2005) or by guiding them to explore emotional connections with characters in history or literature.

Other changes in the neurological system during adolescence affect sleep; students need about 9 hours of sleep per night, but many students' biological clocks are reset so it is difficult for them to fall asleep before midnight. Yet in many school districts, high school begins by 7:30, so 9 hours of sleep are impossible and students are continually sleep deprived.

Erikson: Stages of Individual Development
Erik Erikson studied child-rearing practices in many cultures and proposed a psychosocial theory of development.

Psychosocial Theory: Describes the relationship of the individual's emotional needs to the social environment.

Like Piaget, Erikson proposed a stage theory of development where the individual encounters emotional and social developmental crises. How the crises are resolved at each stage, (conflicts between positive versus unhealthy alternatives) will influence the individual's approach and ultimate resolution of future crises. (See Figure 3.1)

Developmental Crises: A specific conflict whose resolution prepares the way for the next stage.

Preschool Years: Trust, Autonomy, and Initative
The infant's first crucial aspect of development depends on whether the infant's needs are met and they develop a sense of security and trust in their environment and the adults who provide care for their well-being. This trust is important, because if the infant feels secure within his environment, then he feels confident to go out and explore the world apart from his secure home base. This positive resolution of the trust vs. mistrust conflict sets the stage for a positive resolution of stage 2, autonomy vs. shame/doubt. **Example:** Bobby is willing to stay at the neighbor's house while his parents go out for the evening because Bobby knows his parents will return. This gives Bobby the chance to have fun at a new household.

Autonomy: independence

If the infant feels secure within her environment, and knows that she has support at home, she will be willing to take **initiative** for exploring the world with a sense of autonomy and a willingness to assume greater responsibility for one's self. Parents need to be supportive of children's efforts and encourage their attempts at independence regardless of the outcomes lest the children **feel doubt and shame** about their abilities to succeed. **Example:** Amber's parents praise her for dressing herself, even when she comes in with her pants on backwards.

If the child has successfully resolved the autonomy crisis and has no doubts about his/her ability to succeed, then the third stage will bring **initiative** to the child. Along with initiative, the child learns that some activities are not allowed and some impulses must be checked. **Example:** To avoid child-guilt, parents must assure children that the children are not "bad" when they engage in certain activities, but rather that the activities are not appropriate.

Initiative: Eagerness to engage in productive work.

Figure 3.1

Erikson's Theory of Psychosocial Development

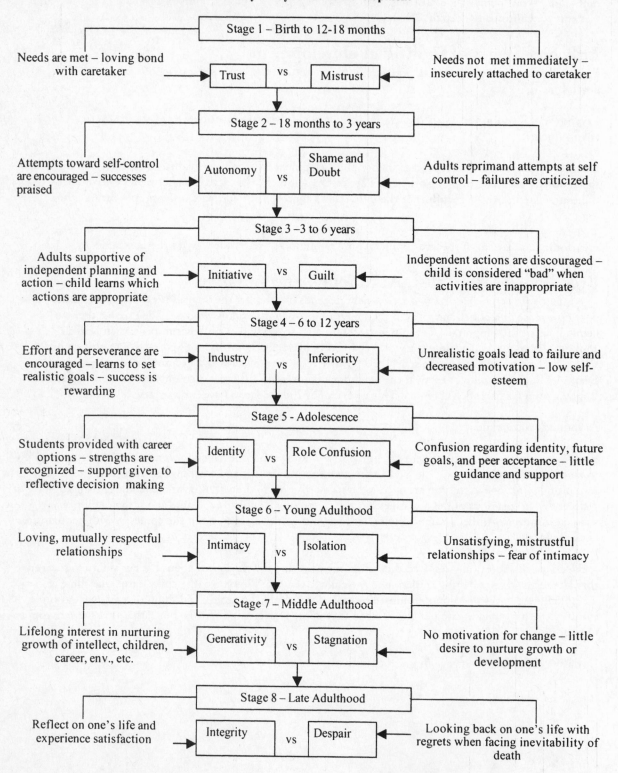

28

Elementary and Middle School Years: Industry vs. Inferiority

Now is the time that demands are being made on children for performance in a work-related sense, either in the form of at-home chores or academic tasks at school. Children who up to this point have met with encouragement and support, will display an eagerness to function and be productive and take initiative to perform and perform well. If the child perseveres and is successful with his or her work efforts, he or she will find this rewarding and **develop a sense of industry**. If the child's attempts at productivity are unsuccessful or met with reproach or criticism, the child may develop a **sense of inferiority** and a decreased likelihood of engaging in productive work in the future.

Industry: Eagerness to engage in productive work. **Example**: Give children tasks within their capacity to perform and reward their efforts when they are successful. Do not give a six-year old your grandmother's china to wash after dinner, lest it backfire. Let your six-year old experience success with the unbreakable dishes.

Adolescence: The Search for Indentity

This stage is marked by the adolescent's struggle to **establish an identity** for herself/himself separate from his/her childhood identities. If conflicts regarding the adolescent's beliefs, abilities, drives, and future goals are not successfully resolved, then the adolescent may experience **role confusion**.

Identity: The complex answer to the question, "Who am I?"

Identity Statuses. Marcia proposed four alternatives to Erikson's Identity vs. Role Confusion. These alternatives are listed below:

1. **Identity Achievement**: Strong sense of commitment to life choices after free consideration of alternatives. **Example**: The adolescent who has explored many options, and been given support and freedom to make decisions, will establish a sense of identity and make choices with which they will be happy.

2. **Identity Foreclosure**: Acceptance of parental life choices without consideration of options. **Example**: Susan is pursuing a medical career because her mother was in medicine, and her mother before her, and she feels that she must carry on the tradition.

3. **Identity Diffusion**: Inconclusive; confusion about who one is and what one wants. **Example**: John doesn't want to think about his future, and prefers to scrape by, day-to-day, doing odd jobs when he can find them.

4. **Moratorium**: Identity crisis; suspension of choices because of struggle; a healthy delay in decision making. **Example**: Juan is not sure if he is ready to enter college because he is not sure of his career interests. He decides instead to take a year to travel around the world to find "himself".

Stop,Think,Write List some of your greatest concerns when you were an adolescent:

Beyond the School Years

Intimacy vs. Isolation: If this conflict is resolved successfully, there is willingness to relate to another person on an intimate level beyond mutual sexual needs. If unsuccessfully resolved, the individual may avoid closeness and intimacy for fear of being hurt and instead may tend toward isolation.

Generativity vs. Stagnation: Sense of concern for future generations. If resolved successfully, individuals seek to nurture the growth of self and others. But if unsuccessfully resolved, the individual stagnates by remaining the same and not seeking to further develop.

Integrity vs. Despair: If successfully resolved the individual develops integrity: sense of self-acceptance, fulfillment, and acceptance of one's inevitable death. If unsuccessfully resolved the individual will look back on one's life with despair and a sense of futility.

> **Stop, Think, Write:** List two ways a teacher could help a painfully shy student?
>
> 1.
>
>
>
> 2.

Bronfenbrenner: The Social Context for Development

Erikson highlighted the role of social and cultural context in personal-social development, but Urie Bronfenbrenner went further to the many interacting social contexts that affect develoment with his **bioecological model** of development (Bronfenbrenner, 1989; Bronfenbrenner & Evans, 2000). The *bio* aspect of the model recognizes that people bring their biological selves to the developmental process. The *ecological* part recognizes the social contexts in which we develop are ecosystems because they are in constant interaction and influence each other. In the microsystem are the person's immediate relationships and activities. The macrosystem is the larger society-its values, laws, conventions, and traditions.

Bronfenbrenner's theory has at least two lessons for teachers:
- Influences in all social systems are reciprocal
- There are many dynamic forces that interact to create the context for individual development

Families

The most appropriate expectation to have about your students' families is no expectation at all. Increasingly, students today have only one or no sibling, or they may be part of **blended families**, with stepbrothers or stepsisters who move in and out of their lives. The best advice is to avoid the phrases "your parents" and "your mother and father" and to speak of "your family" when talking to students.

Parenting Styles. One well-known description of **parenting styles** is based on the resreach of Biane Baumrind (1991). Her work identified for styles based on parents' high or low levels of warmth and control (Berger, 2006):
- Authoritarian parents-low warmth, high control-seem cold and controlling in their interactions with their children.

- Authoritative parents-high warmth, high control-also set clear limits, enforce rules, and expect mature behavior. But they are warmer with their children.
- Permissive parents-high warmth, low control-are warm and nurturing, but have few rules or consequences for the children and expect little in terms of mature behavior.
- Rejecting/Neglecting parents-low warmth, low control-don't seem to care at all and can't be bothered with controlling, communicating, or caring for their children.

Culture and Parenting. Authoritarian, authoritative, and permissve parents all love their children and are trying to do their best-they simply have different ideas about the best way to parent. In broad strokes, there are differences in children associated with these three parenting styles, and cultures also differ in parenting styles.

Divorce. The divorce rate in the United Staes is the highest in the world, over a third higher than the second and third ranked nations, New Zealand and Great Brittain (Berk, 2005). After the divorce, more changes may disrupt the children's lives. Even in those rare cases where there are few conflicts, ample resources, and the continuing support of friends and extended family, divorce is never easy for anyone

Peers

Peers and friendships are central to student's lives. The immaturity and implusiveness of the adolescent brain combined with the power of peer cluture can make peer relationships more difficult.

Peer culture. Recently, psychologists have studied the powerful role of the peer culture in children's development. Peer cultures are groups of studentswho have a set of "rules"-how to dress, talk, style their hair. The group determines which activities, music, or other students are in or out of favor. These peer cultures encourage conformity to the group rules. Beyond the immediate trauma of being "in" or "out" of the group, peer relationships play a significant positive and negative role in healthy personal and social development.

Who Is Likely to Have Problems with Peers? Children and adolescents are not always tolerant of differences. New students who are physically, intellectually, ethnically, racially, economically, or linguistically different may be rejected in classes with established peer groups. Careful adult intervention can correct problems, especially at the late elementary and middle school levels.

Peer Aggression. There are several forms of aggression. The most common form is **instrumental aggression**, which is intended to gain an object or privilege, such as pushing to get in line first. A second kind is **hostile aggression**-inflicting inentional harm. Hostile aggression can take the form of either **overt aggression**, such as threats or physcial attacks or **relational aggression**, which involves threatening or damaging social relationships. Aggression should not be confused with assertiveness, which means to affirm or maintain a legitimate right.

Modeling plays an important role in the expression of aggression (Bandura, Ross, & Ross, 1963). Children who grow up in homes filled with harsh punishment and family violence are more likely to use aggression to solve their own problems (Patterson, 1997). The possible influence of television violence is also a real concern (Timmer, Eccles, & O'Brien, 1988).

Bullies. Aggressive children tend to believe that violence will be rewarded, and they use aggression to get what they want. They are more likely to believe that violent retaliation is acceptable. Helping children handle aggression can make a lasting difference in their lives. Boys (but not girls) who were often physically aggressive in elementary school were at risk for continuing violent andnotfiolent forms of delinquency through adolescence (Broidy et al., 2003). One of the best approaches for preventing problems with aggression later in life is to intervene early.

Relational Aggression. Insults, gossip, exclusion, taunts-are all forms of relational aggression, sometimes called *social aggression* because the intent is to harm social connections. As early as preschool, children need to learn how to negotiate social relations without resorting to aggression.

Victims. Some students tend to be bullies; other chldren are victims. Studies from both Europe and the United States indicate that about 10% of chilren are chronic victims-the constant targets of physcial or verbal attacks. There are two kinds of victims. One kind has low self-esteem and feels anxious, lonely, insecure and unhappy. When they are attacked they generally won't defend themselves and believe they are rejected because they have character flaws. The second type of victim is highly emotional and hot tempered and seems to provoke aggressive reactions from their peers. Members of this group are rejected by almost all peers and seem to have few friends.

Garbarino and deLara (2002) estimate that 160,000 children avoid school every day and thousands more droup out of school altogether "because they are always afraid" at school". See the guidelines in your text for ideans on handing aggression and encouraging cooperation.

Social Skills. Different social skills are important at different ages.

Reaching every Student: Loneliness and Children with Disabilities
Teachers can detect signs of loneliness and notice who is rejected and who plays alone. Teachers should talk to students about their friends and to parents about their child's experiences with peers. In addition, Pavri (2003) suggests that teachers intervene in these ways:
- Provide social skills training for all students
- Create opportunities for interactions through cooperative learning tasks
- Capitalize on lonely students' talents and strengths
- Create an accepting classroom community
- Teach adaptive coping strategies
- Enhance students' self-esteem by giving them responsibilities in class.

Teachers
The first and most important task of the teacher is to educate, but student learning suffers when there are problems with personal and social development, and teachers are the ain adults in students' lives for many hours each week. Teachers have the opportunity to play a significant role in students' personal and social development.

Academic and Personal Caring. When researchers ask students to describe a "good teacher," three qualities are at the center of their descriptions. Good teachers have positive interpersonal relationships-they care about their students. Second, good teachers can keep the classroom organized and maintain authority without being rigid or "mean". Finally, good teachers are good motivators-they make learning fun by being creative and innovative (Woolfolk, Hoe & Weinstein, 2006).

Teachers and Child Abuse. Certainly, one critical way to care about students is to protect their welfare and intervene incases of abuse. As a teacher, you must alert your principal, school psychologist, or school social worker if you suspect abuse. In all 50 states, the District of Columbia, and the US territories, the law requires certain professionals, often including teachers, to report suspected cases of child abuse.

SELF CONCEPT: UNDERSTANDING OURSELVES
Self-Concept and Self-Esteem
Society impacts individual growth and development on personal and social levels. The child's first conceptions of self are concrete, rule-bound, and largely determined by physical appearances. Self-perceptions become more abstract with time, but **self-concepts and self-esteem** develop in accordance with the situations in our lives and how others respond to us.

Self-concept: a cognitive structure of ideas, feelings, and attitudes that people have about themselves. It's who we believe ourselves to be.

Self-esteem: is an affective reaction; an <u>evaluation</u> of who you are. High self-esteem--we like ourselves; low self-esteem--we don't.

The Structure of Self-Concept.
Self-concepts are determined by a number of social-personal factors as well as academic factors. Success in school and social acceptance help to define self-concept and possibly self-esteem, especially for young adolescents. Situational circumstances determine self-concept relative to the comparison group.
The development of self-concept occurs through constant comparisons of self- to- self and self- to- others. Examples of comparisons follow.

How Self-Concept Develops. The self-concept evolves through constant self-evaluation in different situations. Children and adolescents are continually asking themselves, in effect, "How am I doing?" Young children tend to make self-concept appraisals based on their own improvement over time. Thus, the early experiences with the important school task of reading, had strong impact on self-esteem.

During the middle-school years, studens grow more self-conscious. At this age, self-concepts are tied to physical appearance and social acceptance as well as school achievement, so these years can be exceeedingly difficult for students with physical or learning differences.

Self Concept and Achievement> Many psychologists consider self-concept to be the foundation of both social and emotional development. Research has linked self-concept to a wide range of accomlishments-from performance in competitive sports to job satisfaction and achievement in school (Bryne, 2002: Davis-Kean & Sandler, 2001; Marsh & Hau, 2003).

School Life and Self-Esteem
School plays a major role in determining students' self-esteem. Listed below are ways in which school affects self-esteem:

Ma and Kisher (1997) and Marsh (1990) found that:
• students with higher self-esteem are somewhat more likely to be successful in school

Hoge, Smit, and Hanson (1990) found that students' self-esteem was related to:
• students' satisfaction with the school
• interesting classes and caring teachers
• teacher feedback and grades

Diversity and Identity
Another major influence to our self-esteem comes from those groups with whom we associate.

Ethnic and Racial Identity

Many children from different ethnic groups hear messages that de-value their ethnic group. Since community patterns (majority culture) may differ from ethnic patterns (subculture), it may sometimes be difficult for ethnic minority students to establish an identity. Efforts must be made to encourage ethnic pride so that students don't perceive differences as deficits. Students who have adopted the values from both cultures have a greater sense of identity and self-esteem. A great resource for increasing student self-esteem lies with their families.

Ethnic Identities: Outcome and Process. Jean Phinney (1990; 2003) describes four outcomes for ethnic minority youth in serach for identity:
- Assimilation-fully adopting the values and behaviors of the majority culture and rejecting their ethnic culture
- Separated- associating only with members of their ethnic culture
- Marginality-living in the majority culture, but feeling alienated and uncomfortablie in it and disconnected from the minority culture as well
- Biculturalism-(sometimes called integration), maintaining ties to both cultures

Racial Identity: Outcome and Process. William Cross (1991) devised a framework that specifically addresses African American racial identity. The process he calls **nigrescence** has five stages:
- Pre-encounter: In this stage, an African American's attitude may range from ignoring race to feeling neutral about race.
- Encounter-this stage is often riggeed by encountes with overt, covert, or institutional racism.
- Immersion/Emersion: An in-between state -may cause people to be anxious about "becoming the 'right kind" of black person."
- Internalization: Individuals are firmly connected to and secure intheir sense of racial identity.
- Internalization-commitment: This stage is very closed connected with internalization. The main difference is a person's continued interest in and commitment to Black affairs.

Racial and Ethnic Pride. For all students, pride in famkly and community is part of the foundation for a stable identity. Special efforts to encourage **racial and ethnic pride** are particularly important, so that students examining their identities do not get the message that differences are deficits (Spencer & Markstrom-Adams, 1990). Thus, exploring the racial and ethnic roots of all students should foster both self-estemm and acceptance of others (Rotherham-Borus, 1994).

EMOTIONAL AND MORAL DEVELOPMENT

As we seek our own identity and form images of ourselves, we are also learning to cope with emotins and rying to understand the "significant others" around us.

Emotional Competence

Understanding intentions and taking the perspective of others are elements in the development of emotional competence or the ability to understand and manage emotional situations. Social and emotional competences are critical for both academic and personal development.

Theory of Mind and Intention

By 2 or 3 years of age, children are beginning to develop a **theory of mind**, an understanding that other people are people too, with their own minds, thoughts, feelings, beliefs, desires, and perceptions (Flavell, Miller, & Miller, 2002). Children need a theory of mind to make sense of other people's behaviors.

Perspective taking ability

Another aspect of development involves moral reasoning. Piaget called this stage of development **moral realism**. Here children believe rigidly in rules and do not think abstractly about the reasons for rule breaking. Everything is black and white with no shades of gray. Rule breakers should be punished regardless of circumstances.

Moral realism: stage of development wherein children see rules as absolute. As children develop they begin to understand other's perspectives. As Selman suggested, they begin to understand that people have different information and situations and what will work in one situation may not be acceptable in another. A more abstract understanding of rules develops as does morality of cooperation.

Morality of Cooperation: Stage of development wherein children realize that people make rules and people can change them. When the rules are broken, severity of offense and intention are considered.

Kohlberg's Stages of Moral Development

Kohlberg proposed that the development of children's beliefs regarding right and wrong follows a logical sequence. Kohlberg studied the **moral reasoning** of both children and adults by presenting them with **moral dilemmas**.

Moral Reasoning: The thinking processes involved in judgments about questions of right and wrong.
Moral Dilemmas: Situations in which no choice is clearly and indisputably right.

Kohlberg divided moral development into three levels:

Level 1. Preconventional Moral Reasoning-Individuals make decisions based on others' rules and personal needs. There is no real consideration of right or wrong, but rather the individual makes judgments based on whether he/she may be punished for breaking a rule or rewarded for keeping a rule. Judgments are also made on the basis of individual needs. **Example:** Tom finds a wallet with the address of the owner inside but decides to keep the money because he figures no one will ever know who took the money and he could really use it to pay his bills.

Level 2. Conventional Moral Reasoning-Individuals make decisions based on need for others' approval, family expectations, traditional values, the laws of society, and loyalty to country. Judgments are made in consideration of whether or not loved ones and legal structures deem the actions to be right or wrong and whether the individual also subscribes to these beliefs. **Example:** Tom finds a wallet with the address of the owner inside and returns the wallet, because to keep the wallet would be breaking the law.

Level 3. Postconventional Moral Reasoning-Judgments are made based on the belief in socially agreed upon standards of individual right similar to the constitution, and upon individual conscience, involving abstract concepts of justice, human dignity, and equality. Actions are driven more by personal morality than by societies' laws but when personal beliefs take precedence over the laws of society, there is a willingness to accept the consequences of one's actions. **Example:** Tom finds a wallet with no address inside but places an ad in the paper in an effort to find the rightful owner, because Tom believes that it is the right thing to do.

Much of Kohlberg's theory has come under criticism because people exhibit different levels of reasoning in a non-sequential fashion and relative to the situation at hand. Furthermore, Kohlberg's theory doesn't differentiate between social conventions and true moral issues and it has been suggested that Level 3 is biased in favor of Western, male values. Carol Gilligan proposed an alternate theory based upon levels of caring that progress from (1) self-absorbed caring, to (2) caring for certain individuals and relationships, and finally, (3) to caring for all people and humanity. This theory is more consonant with female development. Actual research reveals that both men and women value caring and justice, however, women experience greater guilt when violating caring norms and men experience greater guilt when showing violent behaviors.

MORAL BEHAVIOR

Two influences on the development of moral behavior are, (1) direct instruction, supervision, rewards and punishment, and correction leading to **internalization**, and (2) modeling by caring generous adults who show concern for the rights and feelings of others.

Internalization: when children adopt the moral rules and principles of the authority figures who have guided them. Children are more likely to adopt the external standards as their own if they are given reasons when they are corrected for their actions.

Cheating: Because students cheat, does not mean that they will be dishonest in other situations. Student reports suggest that over 97% of their peers have cheated. Teachers can help to prevent cheating by:
* avoiding placing students in high pressure situations
* helping them to prepare for tests, projects, and assignments
* emphasizing learning, not grades
* providing extra help for those who need it
* highlighting policies on cheating and reinforcing them consistently
* monitoring carefully to prevent cheating

Application 2: Characteristics of Students Who Cheat
Answer true or false to the following statements to assess your knowledge of student cheating. Check your responses in the answer key.

1. ___ Students will cheat because it increases their social acceptance.
2. ___ Students may cheat if the pressure to perform is great.
3. ___ If the chances of getting caught are slim, students are more likely to cheat.
4. ___ College students in the arts and humanities are more likely to cheat than students in engineering, business, and science.
5. ___ High achievers are more likely to cheat than low achievers.
6. ___ Students focusing on learning goals as opposed to performance goals (looking good in front of others) are less likely to cheat.
7. ___ Older and college-age males are more likely to cheat than their female counterparts.
8. ___ Students will cheat because of fear of failure.
9. ___ Students cite being too lazy to study as a reason for cheating.
10. __ Parental pressure for good grades is not related to cheating.
11. __ Students are more likely to cheat when they are behind or cramming for tests.

Aggression: Bold, direct action that is intended to hurt someone else or take property; unprovoked attack. As a classroom manager you will at some point be required to defuse **aggressive** behaviors by your students. Aggression is not to be confused with assertiveness which is affirming or maintaining a legitimate right. Some students are chronic victims of aggression, often falling into one of two categories as either accepting (blaming themselves for the situation) or provoking reactions from students (antagonizing other students by demonstrating high emotions and temper). Modeling is a determining factor in aggressive behaviors. Listed below are some of the places where aggression can be observed:

In the home: Children who observe harsh punishment and violence in the home more likely to use violence to solve problems.

Television: (a.) 82% of programs have some violence, (b) childrens' programs have 32 violent acts per hour; cartoons are the worst, (c) except for sleep, children spend more time watching television than anything else. Violence goes unpunished in over 70% of the violent scenes.

Films and Video Games: violence is frequently depicted by the "hero."

SOCIALIZATION: FAMILY, PEERS, AND TEACHERS

Socialization: ways in which mature members of a society encourage positive development for the immature members of the group. Two important influences on the socialization of children are the family, peers, and teachers.

Characteristics of Today's Students
- More will have one or no sibling
- May be part of a blended family: co-habitation with stepsisters or stepbrothers
- Some will live with "non-parent" adults, one parent, or in foster homes
- 25% of children under 18 live with one parent, usually the mother
- Almost 70% of the women with school-aged children are employed
- There is a growing number of latchkey children
- Experience social pressure to grow up too fast
- Pressured to cope with adult information from the media before they can cope with childhood problems

Divorce

The divorce rate in the United States is the highest in the world. This can possibly be a period of great loss for children:
- loss of parent in terms of residence
- loss of current home for less expensive home
- loss of friends, neighborhood and school due to relocation
- loss of toys, trips, recreation due to fewer finances
- loss of time with parent if custodial parent must work greater hours

Additionally, children may have to cope with parents' new partners or step-parents and step-siblings. The first two years after the divorce are worst for boys and girls. They may blame themselves or engage in behavioral or health disorders. Furthermore, there may be long-term personal and social problems. Teachers need to be receptive to symptomatic changes, avoid insensitive language, be supportive and help students maintain self-esteem. As unbiased individuals who are removed from the home environment, teachers can be wonderful resources to children who are suffering from personal and social problems.

Peer Relations

Peer relationships are central to healthy personal and social development. Rejection by one's peer group can be traumatic and devastating. Consider the findings reported by research:

- Adults who had friends as children, have higher self-esteem
- Adults who had friends as children, are more capable of maintaining intimate relationships
- Having stable, supportive relationships with socially competent, mature individuals promotes social development
- Friends are important during difficult times such as parents' divorce or transition to a new school
- Rejected children are more likely to drop out of school or commit crimes as adults

CHALLENGES FOR CHILDREN

Physical Development: Gross motor skills: voluntary body movements that involve control of the large muscles, improve from the years of 2 to 5. Give ample opportunities to develop physical coordination and balance with plenty of rest. **Fine-motor skills:** voluntary body movements that involve the small muscles are also developing. Experiences such as painting, clay-work, and scissors will refine these skills. 85% of the children will demonstrate right hand preferences but left hand students should be accommodated with special materials.

Throughout elementary school, there is wide variation in physical size, strength, and ability for both boys and girls. Girls may be larger than boys and downplay their physical advantage due to internal conflict. Adolescence is another time for spurts in physical development. The beginning of sexual development is marked by **puberty.**

Puberty: The period in early adolescence when individuals begin to reach physical and sexual maturity. Girls begin puberty about two years ahead of boys and reach their final height by 16; boys will continue to grow until 18. Girls begin to develop breasts between the ages of 9 and 16, menstrual cycles begin between the ages of 11. and 14. For boys, the growth spurt begins between the ages of 12 and 13. Physical changes greatly influence identity. Early maturation has certain advantages for boys, but this is not the case for girls.

Navigating Transitions
To the developing individual, school presents many challenges. Coping with physical, intellectual, academic, personal and social transitions is a tremendous task. What are some of the transitions faced by elementary and middle school students?

Elementary
- Between the ages of 5 & 7, cognitive development is proceeding rapidly. They are moving from preoperational to concrete operational thinking.
- Now, their days are spent in a new physical and social world.
- They must learn to trust new adults.
- They must function autonomously to meet the expectations and rules of the new environment.
- They must demonstrate industry, competency, and work toward new goals, risking failure/comparison.
- They must become part of a group and learn the new role of "student."
- They may be classified in terms of SES and ethnicity by other students and teachers.

Considerations: The way children cope with these transitions can set the stage for future school experiences. Research supports the following findings:
- Two of the best predictors of dropping out of school are low grade point average by third grade and being held back in elementary school.
- Children who do well in first grade are more likely to achieve than those who flounder.
- By 6th grade, the achievement test score differences between students of high and low SES have tripled.
- By third grade, children's performance on achievement tests stabilizes and predicts future performance.
- Quality preschool experiences and full-day kindergarten help children do better in the first grade especially children from low income homes, as do early intervention programs.

Middle Grades
- Once again, cognitive processes are expanding as thinking progresses from concrete operational to formal operational. Thinking becomes more abstract with increased understanding of other's perspectives.
- Physical development is rapidly changing as a result of puberty.
- Sense of self becomes more established but also more differentiated.
- Students must confront a complex society with respect to divorce, morality, and an uncertain economic future if one is uneducated.

Considerations:
- Because of divorce and working parents, adolescents spend less time with adults and more time with TV.
- Adolescents go through puberty earlier and assume adult roles later, therefore they are sexually mature but socially restricted, bombarded by media and conflicting messages.
- Overall self-concept and self-esteem decline in early adolescence as well as assessments of competence in academic and nonacademic areas.
- During middle school, students grow more self-conscious and feelings of self-worth are more closely tied to physical appearance and social acceptance.
- Status and acceptance are extremely important for adolescents.

- Effective middle school strategies include interdisciplinary teachers working with student "pods," integrated curricula that revolve around student interests, teacher/ advisor and student pairings, and special interest exploratory classes. Middle grade schools should have teachers who are knowledgeable about and like young adolescents.

CHILDREN AND YOUTH AT RISK

Child Abuse: Unfortunately, many cases of child abuse go unreported. Parents are not the only people who abuse children, but siblings, other relatives and teachers. Many abusers could change their behaviors if they were to receive help. As a teacher, you must notify your principal, school psychologist, or social worker if you suspect abuse. Understand your state laws for dealing with abuse and your moral responsibility for involvement. At least five children die of abuse or neglect every day in the U.S., often because no one would get involved.

Eating Disorders: Today's standards for beauty and appearance sometimes lead to eating disorders due to excessive concern. Two such eating disorders are:

- **Bulimia:** Eating disorder characterized by overeating, then getting rid of the food by self-induced vomiting or laxatives.

- **Anorexia Nervosa:** Eating disorder characterized by very limited food intake. Anorexics lose 20 to 25% of their body weight and about 5% to 10% literally starve themselves to death. Both of these disorders occur more often with females than with males, but a teacher can be just the person to help with these problems.

Drug Abuse: High percentages of high school seniors (92%) report some experience with alcohol. About 20% of seniors are daily smokers, and 30% have tried at least one illegal drug. Considering the conflicting messages sent to students via media and society, it is no small wonder drug use is increasing among youth. Successful educational programs teach students how to avoid drug usage with no loss of self-esteem and how to make responsible choices.

Suicide: The suicide rate is increasing among adolescents and even youth younger than adolescence. There are certain warning signs that there is trouble:
- changes in eating and sleeping habits
- changes in grades
- changes in disposition, activity level, or friends
- giving away prized possessions
- depression or hyperactivity
- statements indicating that nothing matters or musings about death

If you detect any warning signs, talk directly to the student and take the student seriously. Suicide is often a cry for help, not to be ignored.

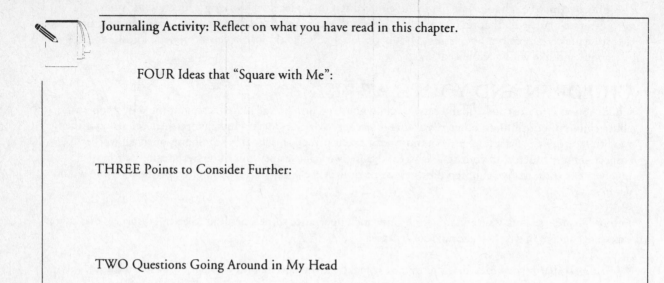

Journaling Activity: Reflect on what you have read in this chapter.

FOUR Ideas that "Square with Me":

THREE Points to Consider Further:

TWO Questions Going Around in My Head

MY NOTES

(Use this space to make additional notes for this chapter)

4

Learner Differences
and Learner Needs

Labeling

As educators, hopefully we will view all of students as exceptional and unique, but as a label, exceptional students comes to mean something very different in terms of their educational needs because their abilities significantly depart from average.

Exceptional Students: Students who have abilities or problems so significant that the students require special education or other services to reach their potential.

The use of labels is controversial. There are both advantages and disadvantages to assigning a label to a student because labels simultaneously help and stigmatize individuals.

As you consider the topic of "labels" you are reminded to be aware of the distinction between the terms **disability** and **handicap**.

Person-First Language. This caution about labeling also applies to many of the common descriptions heard in schools every day. Today, many people object to labels such as "mentally retarded student" or "at-risk student" because describing a complex person with one or two words implies that the condition labeled is the most important aspect of the person. An alternative is "person-first language" or speaking of "students with intellectual disabilities" or "students placed at risk".

STOP/THINK/WRITE
Try rewording thses labels in terms of person-first language. The first one has been done for you.

Limiting Label	**Person-First Language**
Learning disabled student	A student with a learning disability
Special Education Student	_____
An epileptic	_____
A crippled child	_____
Autisitic children or autistics	_____

Disorder: a general disturbance in physical or mental functioning, for example, a communications disorder.

Disability: the inability to do something specific such as walk or hear.

Handicap: a relative term, referring to the difficulties that people with disabilities encounter in some situations. **Example:** a person in a wheelchair is handicapped when trying to ascend a flight of stairs but not when participating in a debate.

The school can help to insure that the physical environment of the school not create handicaps for students with disabilities by providing ramps, elevators, and accessible rooms.

What Does Intelligence Mean?
STOP/THINK/WRITE
Who was the most intelligent person in your high school? Write down a name and he first 4 or 5 words that come to mind when you see that person in your mind's eye. What made you pick this individual?

Definitions of intelligence are as diverse as the mental abilities that comprise intelligence. Psychologists generally debate the structure of intelligence, whether it is a single ability or many separate abilities.

Intelligence: One Ability or Many?
Intelligence: Ability or abilities to acquire and use knowledge for solving problems and adapting to the world. Early notions of intelligence subscribed to one or more of three themes:

- the capacity to learn
- the total knowledge a person has acquired
- the ability to adapt to new situations and the environment in general

Fluid intelligence: mental efficiency that is essentially culture-free and nonverbal.

Crystallized intelligence: the ability to apply culturally approved problem-solving methods.
Today's experts agree that abstract reasoning, problem-solving, and decision making comprise intelligence but still argue as to whether it is one or many abilities. Following are three theorist's positions on intelligence:

- Spearman (1927)- one factor, **g** or **general intelligence** needed to perform any mental task and **s** or **specific abilities** needed to perform specific tasks.
- Carroll (1993)-a few broad abilities and at least 70 specific abilities.

Multiple Intelligence
- Gardner (1983, 1993)-**Multiple Intelligences:** Eight (possibly nine) separate intelligences or abilities:
  1. logical-mathematical: ability to handle logical or numerical patterns and long chains of reasoning
  2. linguistic: sensitivity to sounds, rhythms, word meanings, and different language functions
  3. musical: production and appreciation of rhythm, pitch, timbre, and forms of musical expressiveness
  4. spatial: accurate perceptions of visual/spatial world and mental transformations of initial spatial perceptions
  5. bodily-kinesthetic: skill at controlling bodily movements and handling objects
  6. interpersonal: ability to discern and respond appropriately to moods, temperaments, desires, and motivations of other people
  7. interpersonal: knowledge of one's own feelings, strengths, weaknesses, desires, and intelligence, and ability to utilize this knowledge to guide behavior
  8. naturalist: observing/understanding natural and human- made patterns and systems
  9. (Possibly) existential intelligence: ability to ask big questions about the meaning of life

Research by Gardner and associates suggests that these intelligences may not be as independent as originally suspected but that in the interest of all individuals, these intelligences should be explored and cultivated.

Emotional Intelligence
Howard Gardner's theory of multiple intelligences includes intrapersonal and interpersonal intelligences or intelligence about self and others. Emotional intelligence is a related perspective.

What is EQ? According to Mayer & Cobb, 2000, at the center of **emotional intelligence** are four broad abilities:
- perceiving
- integrating
- understanding
- managing emotions

EQ Goes to School
Some research suggests that programs designed to help students build their emotional competencies have beneficial effects, including an increase in cooperative behaviors and a reduction in anti-social activities such as the use of slurs and bullying. The educational advantages of decreased student aggression and increased empathy are obvious, but these skills also prepare students for life outside the classroom.

Intelligence as a Process

- Sternberg (1985,1990)- **Triarchic Theory of Intelligence**: three processes of intelligence that are common to all people:

  1. Analytic/componential intelligence-involves the mental process of the individual that lead to more or less intelligent behavior.
  2. Creative/experiential intelligence-involves coping with new experiences. Marked by two characteristics:
     a. insight-the ability to deal effectively with novel situations
     b. automaticity-the ability to become efficient and anutomatic in thinking and problem solving.
  3. Practical/econtestual intelligence-highlights the importane of chooosing to live and work in a context where success is likely.

Measuring Intelligence
In 1904, Alfred Binet was commissioned by the French ministry to develop a test that would differentiate between those students who possessed the skills requisite to succeeding in a public school setting from those who would not. Binet and associate, Simon, developed 58 tests for children 3 to 13 for determining the **mental age** of a child.

Mental Age: In intelligence testing, a score based on average abilities for that age group. **Example:** John is four years old, but John can successfully answer the items passed by most six year olds, so John has a mental age of six.

An **intelligence quotient (IQ)** was added to Binet's test after it was brought to the U.S. and revised at Stanford University to compare mental age to chronological age.

$$\text{Intelligence Quotient} = \frac{\text{mental age}}{\text{chronological age}} \times 100$$

In time this formula proved insufficient because mental age does not increase in equal increments. Greater increases occur around the ages of 6 or 7 and then again around the ages of 11 or 12. This prompted the use of the **Deviation IQ**.

Deviation IQ: Score based on statistical comparison of individual's performance with the average performance of others in that age group.

IQ tests should be administered individually by a licensed psychologist as group administered tests are not as reliable. Teachers must be very cautious when interpreting IQ scores based on group tests.

Application 1: IQ Myths and Facts
Read the following statements and determine whether they are myth or fact. Write true or false next to each statement. Check your responses in the answer key.
1. ___ The average IQ score is 115.
2. ___ Approximately 68% of the population scores between 85 and 115.
3. ___ IQ test scores are just as reliable for ethnic, minority groups as for white, native born Americans whose first language is Standard English.
4. ___ Intelligence test scores predict scholastic achievement very well.
5. ___ IQ scores and scholastic achievement are strongly related to success in later life.
6. ___ Individuals' IQ scores remain stable over the life of an individual.
7. ___ If a student scores poorly on an IQ test, he or she lacks innate ability to learn.
8. ___ Student's past experiences and learning have no bearing on IQ test scores.
9. ___ IQ tests provide accurate information about individual's overall intellectual ability
10. ___ IQ tests measure those limited abilities needed to do well in a scholastic setting.

Some theorists feel that intelligence is primarily inherited (nature) while others feel that it is environmental (nurture). Most psychologists believe that intelligence is due to both genetic and environmental factors, although it is impossible to determine the amount that each contributes to IQ.
The problem with adopting a purely genetic approach to IQ is the belief that IQ is stable and not subject to improvement. As educators, we must believe that intelligence can be improved and that compensations can be made for lack of cognitive enrichment within the child's home or scholastic environment.

ABILITY DIFFERENCES AND TEACHING

To adequately teach to the wide range of intellectual abilities within the classroom, many teachers use between class ability grouping.

Between Class Grouping: System of grouping in which students are assigned to classes based on their measured ability or their achievements. This is also known as tracking. **Example:** college prep courses or honors classes, or remedial classes. Research reveals that this may be a good practice for high achieving students, but the problems associated with tracking low ability students are listed below:

- low ability classes receive lower-quality instruction in general
- teachers emphasize lower-level objectives and routine procedures with less academic focus
- there are often more management problems leading to increased stress and decreased enthusiasm
- teachers' negative attitudes may mean low expectations are communicated to the students
- student self-esteem suffers upon assignment to the lower tracks
- attendance may drop with self esteem
- disproportionate number of minority students and economically disadvantaged are assigned to these classes which in effect becomes resegregation
- friendships become limited to students in the same ability range
- assignments to classes are often made on the basis of IQ which is not a good predictor of subject area performance

A more viable alternative are two forms of cross-grade grouping called the **non-graded elementary** school and the **related Joplin Plan.**

Non-graded elementary school/Joplin Plan: Arrangement wherein students are grouped by ability in particular subjects, regardless of their ages or grades. This is more effective as long as the grouping allows the teacher to offer more direct instruction.

Within Class and Flexible Grouping
Another form of grouping frequently used in the elementary schools for reading is called **Within Class Ability Grouping:** System of grouping in which students in a class are divided into two or three groups based on ability in an attempt to accommodate student differences.
(Figure 4.1 at the end of the chapter gives further explanation of the process of adapting instruction to meet the needs of all learners.)

Flexible Grouping: Students are grouped and regrouped based on their learning needs. Assessment is continuous so that students are always working within their zone of proximal development. Arrangements might include small groups, partners, individuals, and even the whole class-depending on which grouping best supports each student's learning of the particular academic content.

LEARNING STYLES and PREFERENCES
Variations in individuals' academic performance may in part, result from certain unique modes of functioning called cognitive styles.

Learning Styles and Preferences: Preferred ways of studying and learning, such as using pictures instead of text, working with other people versus alone, learning in structured or in unstructured situations, and so on.

Another variable that appears to influence student achievement depends upon whether students adopt a **deep-processing approach vs. a surfacing processing approach.** Certainly, situational factors can influence this, but these are tendencies that individuals display.

Deep Processing Approach: when students see the learning materials or activities as a means for understanding some underlying concepts or meanings. These students tend to learn for the sake of learning.

Surface Processing Approach: when students focus on memorizing the learning materials, not understanding them. These students tend to be motivated by external rewards and performance evaluations.

> **Stop, Think, Write:** Suggest one strategy teachers might use to assure that they are meeting the varied learning style needs of their students.

Cautions
Some proponents of learning styles believe that students learn more when they study in their preferred setting and manner (Gunn, Beaudry, & Klavas, 1989; Lovelace, 2005). And there is evidence that very bright students need less structure and prefer quiet, solitary learning (Torrance, 1986). But most

educational psychologists are skeptical about the value of learning preferences. "The reason researchers roll their eyes at learning styles research is the utter failure to find that assessing children's learning styles and matching to instructional methods has any effect on their learning" (Stahl, 2002, p. 99). Some of the teaching ideas may be useful, but not necessarily because they are based on learning styles. So, before you try to accommodate all your students' learning styles, remember that students, especially younger ones, may not be the best judges of how they should learn.

INDIVIDUAL DIFFERENCES and THE LAW

In 1975, **The Education for All Handicapped Children Act (Public Law 94-142)** mandated changes that would influence the appearance of handicapped children within the public school classroom. This law guarantees a free appropriate public education (FAPE) to every child between the ages of 3 and 21 regardless of how seriously handicapped toward full inclusion. Recently, there is a greater move toward the regular education initiative.

Full Inclusion: The integration of all students, including those with severe disabilities, into regular classes.

Regular Education Initiative: An educational movement that advocates giving regular education teachers, not special education teachers, responsibility for teaching mildly (and sometimes moderately) handicapped children.

In the 1990's Public Law 94-192 was amended by the **Individuals with Disabilities Education Act (IDEA)** which replaced the word "handicapped" with "disabled" and expanded the services for disabled students. Also in 1990, further changes were implemented by the **Americans with Disabilities Act (ADA)**.

Americans with Disabilities Act (ADA): Legislation prohibiting discrimination against persons with disabilities in employment, transportation, public access, local government and communications.

Three key points to these laws and amendments are:
1. **Least Restrictive Environment:** Placement of each child in as normal an educational setting possible
2. **Individualized Education Program (IEP):** Annually revised program for an exceptional student, detailing present achievement level, goals, and strategies, drawn up by teachers, parents, specialists, and (if possible) student.
   a. includes student's present level of functioning
   b. goals for the year and measurable instructional objectives
   c. a list of specific services for the student
   d. a description of how fully the student will participate in the regular school program
   e. a schedule for implementation of the above
   f. plans for transitional services to move the student into adult life
3. **Protection of the rights** of disabled students and their parents

The Rights of Students and Families
Several stipulations in these laws protect the rights of parents and students.
- Schools must have procedures for maintaining the confidentiality of school records.
- Testing practices must not discriminate against students from different cultural backgrounds and students must be tested in their native language.
- Parents must consent in writing to the initial evaluation and have the right to see all records relating to their child.
- If they wish, parents may obtain an independent evaluation of their child.
- Parents may bring an advocate or representative to the IEP meeting and parents who can not attend must be assigned a surrogate parent to participate in the planning.
- Parents must receive written notification of changes in their child's placement and have the right to challenge the program developed for their child.

STUDENTS WITH LEARNING DISABILITIES

Learning Disabilities

Learning disabilities is a general term used to describe a broad group of disorders that may manifest as an imperfect ability to listen, speak, do mathematics, write, read, or reason. Most learning disabled students have average or above average intelligence but demonstrate difficulties in one or two subject areas.

Whereas, **students with disabilities are not all alike,** many possess the following characteristics:
• difficulties in one or more academic areas
• attention problems, hyperactivity, and impulsivity
• difficulty organizing and interpreting visual and auditory information
• disorders of thinking, memory, speech and hearing
• difficulty making and keeping friends
• lack effective ways to approach academic tasks; they don't know how to:
  1. focus on relevant information or get organized
  2. apply learning strategies or study skills
  3. change strategies when one isn't working
  4. evaluate their learning
  5. work independently to completion

Early diagnosis is especially important so that those with a learning disability do not develop **learned helplessness.**

Learned Helplessness: The expectation, based on previous experiences with a lack of control, that all one's efforts will lead to failure.

Teaching Students with Learning Disabilities

There is also controversys over how best to help these students. A promising approach seems to be to emphasize study skills and methods for processing informaiton in a given subject such as reading or math. In teaching reading, a combination of teaching letter-sound knowledge and word identificaiton strategies appears to be effective. Maureen Lovett (Lovett et. al., 2000) taught students in Canada with severe reading disabilities to use the four different word identification strategies:
1. word identification by analogy
2. seeking the part of the work that you know
3. attempting diffent vowel pronunciaitons
4. "peelingoff" prefixes and suffixes in multisylabic words.

Students with Hyperactivity and Attention Disorders

STOP/WRITE/THINK If a student is struggling with time management and organization issues, what kind of accommodations would ou provide?

Attention-deficit hyperactivity disorder (ADHD)

Children with ADHD are not only more physically active and inattentive than other children, they also have difficulty responding appropriately and working steadily toward goals (even their own goals). In addition, they may not be able to control their behavior on command, even for a brief period. The problem behaviors are generally evident in all situations with every teacher.

About three to four times as many boys as girls are identified as hyperactive, but the gap appears to be narrowing (Hallahan et al., 2005). Just a few years ago, most psychologists thought that ADHD diminished as children entered alolescence, but now there are some reserachers who believe that the problems can persist into adulthood (Hallowell & Ratey, 1994).

Treating and Teaching Students with ADHD

Today, there is an increasing reliance on drug therapy for ADHD. In fact, from 1990 to 1998, there was a 700% increase in the production of Ritalin in the United States (Diller, 1998). Ritalin and other prescribed drugs are stimulants, but in particular dosages, they tend to have paradoxical effects on many children with ADHD: Short-term effects include possible improvements in social behaviors such as cooperation, attention and compliance. Research suggests that 70%-80% of children with ADHD are more manageable when on medication. But there can be negative side effects such as weight loss, nausea, insomnia, and increased heart rate and blood pressure (Riend & Bursuck, 2002; Hallahan et al., 2005; Panksepp, 1998).

What can teachers do? Teachers can make modifications in the classroom to help students with ADHD. Teachers can shorten some assignments and give smaller portions of the assignment at a time (sometimes referred to as "chunking") with clear consequences for completion. Another promising approach combines instruction in learning and memory strategies with motivational training. The goal is to help students develop the "skill and will" to improve their achievement (Paris, 1988).

Rather than treating the problem child, David Nylund's (2000) idea is to enlist the child's strengths to conquer the child's problems-put the child in control. The focus is on solutions. The steps of the SMART approach are:
- Separating the problem of ADHD from the child
- Mapping the influence of ADHD on the child and family
- Attending to the exceptions to the ADHD story
- Reclaiming special abilities of children diagnosed with ADHD
- Telling and celebrating the new story. (Nylund, 2000)

> **Stop, Think, Write:** List two questions you would ask about any advice for teaching children with ADHD, before using the advice with a child in your class:
> 1.
>
>
> 2.

Students with Communication Disorders

Communication disorders can result from any different sources because many factors contribute to the individual's ability to speak, i.e., hearing, inadequate language at home, or emotional problems. One form of disorder is speech impairment.

Speech Impairment: Inability to produce sounds effectively for speaking. Two forms of speech impairment are **articulation disorders** and **voicing problems**.

Articulation Disorders: Any of a variety of pronunciation difficulties, such as the substitution, distortion, or omission of sounds. **Example:** "I thought I thaw a putty tat," Elmer Fudd.
Stuttering: Repetitions, prolongations, and hesitations that lock flow of speech. **Example:** "I wa wa wa want some wa wa water."

Voicing Problems: Inappropriate pitch, quality, loudness, or intonation. **Example:** When I worked with children at a psychiatric institute, there was a girl who spoke in a monotone and was perceived as quite frightening by the other children there, when she stated, "I don't want to play with the children" in a deep-voiced monotone.

Language Disorders: Markedly deficient ability to understand or express language, compared with other students of the same age and cultural group. **Example:** When students seldom speak, use few words or short sentences, or rely only on gestures to communicate, this may be a language disorder.

Students with Intellectual Disabilities

Some differences in your students' intellectual functioning will be more extreme. About 1 to 1.5 percent of the population meets the AAMD's definition of **mental retardation.**

Mental Retardation: Significantly below-average intellectual and adaptive social behavior, manifest before the age of 18. Below average intellectual functioning is an IQ score less than 70 -75. This alone is not sufficient for diagnosing mental retardation, because in the past, a disproportionate number of minority individuals were diagnosed as mentally retarded due to low IQ scores but they showed no deficits in adaptive functioning and could survive quite well in society. Their IQ scores more likely reflected linguistic difficulty and cultural differences.

As a regular teacher, you will probably work with mildly retarded children. In the early grades, these children will appear slow, but by third or fourth grade, they will fall behind their classmates. By junior and senior high school there should be greater emphasis on vocational and self-care skills that will enable the individual to become self-sufficient. One such program is transition programming.

Transition Programming: Gradual preparation of exceptional students to move from high school into further education or training, employment, or community involvement.

Students with Emotional or Behavioral Disorders

Students with emotional and behavioral disorders can be mong the most difficult to teach in a regular class, and are a source of concern for many prospective teachers (Avramidis, Bayliss, & Burden, 2000). Behavior is considered to be a problem when it deviates so far from normal that it interferes with the intellectual growth and development of the student and others.

The language in IDEIA describes *emotional disturbances (ED)* that involve inappropriate behaviors, unhappiness or depression, fears and anxieties, and trouble with relationships. The American Psychological Association and the medical community refer to *mental disorders* (Friend, 2006). The range of possible emotional and behavioral disorders is wide. And students with other disabilities may have emotional or behavioral problems. Methods from applied behavioral analysis (Chapter 6) and direct teaching of social skills (Chapter 3) are two useful approaches.

Suicide/Drug Abuse/Prevention

Up to 10% of adolesents have attempted suicide at some point, but even more have considered it. Native American and rural students are more likely to commit suicd. There are four general risk faxtors and they seem to apply to both male and female African American, Latino, and White adolescents: depression and substance abuse, history of suicide in the family, being under stress, and family rejection or confict.

Although drug abuse is not always associated with emotional or behavioral problems and people without these challenges may abuse drugs, many adolescents with emotinal problems also abuse drugs. Experiementation and abuse are not to be confused. The best way to help students who have trouble saying no appears to be through peer programs that teach them how to say no assertively.

Providing information or "scare" tactics such as the DARE drug prevention prgram seem to have little positive effect and may even encourage curiosity and experimentation (Dusenbury & Falco, 1995; Tobler & Stratton, 1997). The most effective prevention programs include:
- developmentally appropriate language and concepts;
- teach students to resist social pressure;
- provide accurate information about rates of behavior;
- use inteactive teaching methods such as role-playing;
- provide training in skills that help in many situations such as the 6-step problem solving strategy described in Chapter 12;
- give thorough coverage of the topic with follow-up; and practice cultural sensitivity.

LESS PREVALENT PROBLEMS/MORE SEVERE DISABILITIES
Students with Health Impairments

Some students must have special devices such as braces, special shoes, crutches, or wheelchairs to participate in normal school programs. **Two health impairments** you may encourter are **cerebral palsy and seizure disorders.**

Cerebral Palsy and Multiple Disabilities: Damage to the brain before or during birth or during infancy can cause a child to have difficulty moving and coordinating his or her body. The problem may be very mild to sevee. The most common form of cerebral palsy is characterized by **spasticity**-overly tight or tense muscles.

Seizure Disorders (Epilepsy): a cluster of behaviors that occurs in response to abnormal neurochemical activities in the brain.

Gerneralized or tonic clonic seizures: accompanied by uncontrolled jerking movements that ordinarily last two to five minutes, possible loss of bowel or bladder control, and irregular breathing, followed by a deep sleep or coma.

Absence seizures: student just loses contact briefly. The student may stare, fail to respond to questions, drop objects, and miss what has been happening for 1 to 30 seconds.

Students Who Are Deaf
Hearing Impaired: the deaf community prefers the terms deaf and hard of hearing. Signs of hering problems are turning one ear toward the speaker, favoring one ear in conversation, or misunderstanding conversation when the speaker's face cannot be seen.

Students with Vision Impairments
Low vision: students can read with the aid of a magnifying glass or large-print books.

Educationally blind: students must use hearing and touch as the predominant learning channels.

Autism Spectrum Disorders
In 1990, **autism** was added to the IDEA list of disabilities qualifying for special services.
Autism is defined as "a developmental disability significantly affecting verbal and nonverbal communication and socail interaction, generally evident before age three, that adversely affects the child's educational performace" (34 Federal Code of Regulations 300.7)

A preferable term may be **autism spectrum disorder** to emphasize that autism includes a range of disorders from mild to major.

Fron an early age, children with autism spectrum disorders may have difficulties in social relationships. They do not form connections with others, avoid eye contact, or don't share feelings such as enjoyment or interest with others. Communication is impaired. About half of these students are nonverbal; they have very few or no language skills. They may obsessively insist on sameness or routine in their environment and may repeat behaviors. They may be very sensitive to light, sound, touch, or other sensory information.

Asperger syndrome is one of the disabilities included in the autistic spectrum. These children have many of the characteristics described above, but their greatest trouble is with social relations. Language is less affected. Their speech may be fluent, but unusual, mixing up pronouns of "I" and "you" for example (Friend, 2006). Many students with autism may have mild-to-severe intellectual disabilities, but those with Asperger syndrome usually have average-to-above average intelligence.

Theory of Mind One current explanation for autism and Asperger syndrome is that children with these disorders lack a theory of mind-an understanding that they and other people have minds, thoughts, and emotions. They have difficuluty explaining their own behaviors, appreciating that other people might have different feelings, and predicting how behaviors might affect emotions.

Interventions Early and intense interventions that focus on communication and social relations are particularly important for children with autism spectrum disorders. As they move into elementary school, some of these students will be in inclusive settings, others in specialized classes, and many in some combination of these two.

STUDENTS WHO ARE GIFTED AND TALENTED

Stop, Think, Write: List two of the challenges you anticipate facing when teaching gifted students in a regular education classroom:

1.

2.

Greater recognition is now being given to the fact that 50% of gifted students are not achieving to their potential and schools are not adequately meeting their needs.

Gifted Students: Very **bright, creative, talented students** with the **following characteristics:**
- significantly above average intellectual functioning (Renzulli and Reis, 1991)
- a high level of creativity (Renzulli and Reis, 1991)
- high level of task commitment and motivation to achieve in certain areas (Renzulli and Reis, 1991)
- larger, stronger, and healthier than the norm (Terman, et.al., 1925, 1947, 1959)
- walked sooner and were more athletic (Terman, et.al., 1925, 1947, 1959)
- more emotionally stable than their peers (Terman, et.al., 1925, 1947, 1959)
- better adjusted adults than the average (Terman, et.al., 1925, 1947, 1959)
- lower rates of delinquency, emotional difficulties, divorces, and drug problems (Terman, et.al., 1925, 1947, 1959)

Problems the Gifted Face
Even though these findings seem to indicate that gifted children are well-adjusted and superior in many ways, they still encounter problems.

Many gifted children experience boredom and frustration in school as well as ridicule from their peers and a sense of isolation.

They may demonstrate great impatience when others do not share their interests and may place great expectations on themselves for peak performances.

The greatest adjustment problems are found with those students who have IQs above 180. Furthermore, sex-differences in social adjustment and self-esteem favor gifted males over females with gifted girls perceiving their abilities lower than even non-gifted boys and girls.

Teaching the Gifted
Some educators believe that gifted students shoud be accelerated-moved quickly through the grades or through particular subjects. Other educators prefer enrichment-giving the students additional, more sophisticated, and more thought-provoking work, but keeping them with their age-mates in school.

Teaching methods for gifted students should **encourage abstract thinking** (formal-operational thought), creativity, reading of high-level and original texts, and independence, not just the learning of greater quantities of facts. One approach that does *not* seem promising with gifted students is cooperative learning in mixed abilities groups. Gifted students tend to learn more when they work in groups with other high abilitiy peers.

In working with gifted students, **the teacher** must be **imaginative, flexible, tolerant, and unthreatened** by the capabilities of these students. The teacher must ask:
• What do these children need most?
• What are they ready to learn?
• Who can help me to challenge them?

Diversity and Convergence in Learning Abilities
Diversity
Even though there are many good tests and careful procedures for making special education placement decisions, racial and ethnic minority students are overrepresented in the disability categories and underrepresented in gifted programs. For example, almost 20% of all student defined as having disabilities under IDEIA are African American, but only 15% of all students are African American. 34% of all students identified as having intellectual disabilities/mental retardation and 27% of students identified as having emotional disturbance are African American—twice as many as we would expect based on the percentage of African American students in the United States. In contract, African American and Latino students make up only 8% of the students identified as gifted and talented (Friend, 2006).

For almost four decades, educators have struggled to understand the causes of these over- and underrepresentations.

Convergences
This chapter is about diversity-the many differences among individuals in abilities and disabilities, learning styles and preferences, strengths and challenges. But even with this diversity, differences among individuals are vey small compared to all the characteristics we share.

Journaling Activity: Reflect on what you have read in this chapter.

FOUR Ideas that "Square with Me":

THREE Points to Consider Further:

TWO Questions Going Around in My Head

Figure 4.1

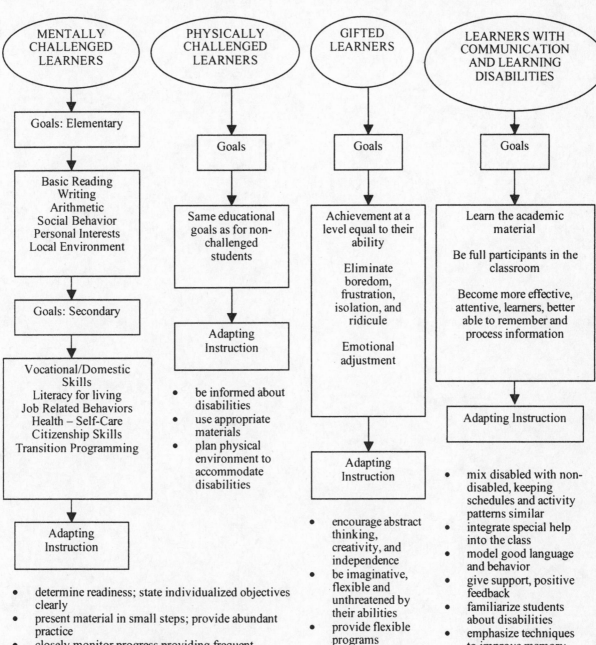

ADAPTING INSTRUCTION FOR LEARNER DIFFERENCES

MENTALLY CHALLENGED LEARNERS

Goals: Elementary

Basic Reading
Writing
Arithmetic
Social Behavior
Personal Interests
Local Environment

Goals: Secondary

Vocational/Domestic Skills
Literacy for living
Job Related Behaviors
Health – Self-Care
Citizenship Skills
Transition Programming

Adapting Instruction

- determine readiness; state individualized objectives clearly
- present material in small steps; provide abundant practice
- closely monitor progress providing frequent feedback, help, and reinforcement
- vary materials and present in a variety of ways to make connections for students
- have students overlearn, repeat, and practice more than non-challenged students
- teach students how to learn and how to study

PHYSICALLY CHALLENGED LEARNERS

Goals

Same educational goals as for non-challenged students

Adapting Instruction

- be informed about disabilities
- use appropriate materials
- plan physical environment to accommodate disabilities

GIFTED LEARNERS

Goals

Achievement at a level equal to their ability

Eliminate boredom, frustration, isolation, and ridicule

Emotional adjustment

Adapting Instruction

- encourage abstract thinking, creativity, and independence
- be imaginative, flexible and unthreatened by their abilities
- provide flexible programs
- continually assess students' needs

LEARNERS WITH COMMUNICATION AND LEARNING DISABILITIES

Goals

Learn the academic material

Be full participants in the classroom

Become more effective, attentive, learners, better able to remember and process information

Adapting Instruction

- mix disabled with non-disabled, keeping schedules and activity patterns similar
- integrate special help into the class
- model good language and behavior
- give support, positive feedback
- familiarize students about disabilities
- emphasize techniques to improve memory, attention, and study skills

MY NOTES

(Use this space to make additional notes for this chapter)

5

Culture and Diversity

Today's Diverse Classrooms
Individuals, Groups, and Society
Our country is more culturally diverse than it has ever been since its inception. The immigrant influx during the past decade was larger than the total amount of immigrants to enter this country in the past century. One of the characteristics of today's immigrants is its youth with an average age of 13 to 41 years. This means today's immigrants are primarily in their prime working and prime child bearing years. This will have a major impact on the amount of minority students in the public school system. This will present new challenges to classroom educators because many minority students demonstrate lower academic achievement.

In the beginning of the 20th century, the immigrants who entered the country were expected to enter the **cultural melting pot** and to adopt the language, ways, and mores of those who had come before.

Melting Pot: A metaphor for the absorption and assimilation of immigrants into the mainstream of society so that ethnic differences vanish.

In the past few decades, educators suggested that because they had not become part of the melting pot, minority and poor students were culturally disadvantaged in school; hence poorer performance results. This is explained by the **cultural deficit model**.

Cultural Deficit Model: A model that explains the school achievement problems of ethnic minority students by assuming that their home cultures are inadequate and does not prepare them to succeed in school.

Today this notion is rejected and it is believed that no culture is deficient but instead, it may be incompatible with the school culture. During the 60s and 70s, there was an increasing awareness of ethnic pride and a desire to become part of mainstream society while retaining cultural identity.

Multicultural education is one way to address ethnic pride.

Multicultural Education: Education that teaches the value of cultural diversity through the expansion of educational curricula that includes the perspectives, histories, accomplishments, and concerns of non-European people and grants educational equality to all.

STOP/THINK/WRITE
Take a quick break from reading and turn on the television. Find a channel with commercials. Listen to about 15 commercials. For each one, is the voice male or female? Old or young? Economically privleged or poor? What is the character's ethnicity or race? Do a quick tally of how many instances you observe in each category.

Culture and Group Membership
Groups create culture. Groups can be defined along regional, ethnic, religious, racial, gender, social class, or other lines. As each of us belong to many groups, we are also influenced by many cultures. Sometimes, the ideas and beliefs of one culture are incompatible with another.

Culture: The knowledge, values, attitudes, and traditions that guide the behavior of a group of people and allow them to solve the problems of living in their environment.

Two cultural cautions are:

1. Much of the available research focuses on social class, gender, and ethnicity but real children are complex beings who belong to and are influenced by the many groups to which they belong.

2. Membership in a certain group does not determine behavior but makes certain behaviors more likely.

Figure 5.1

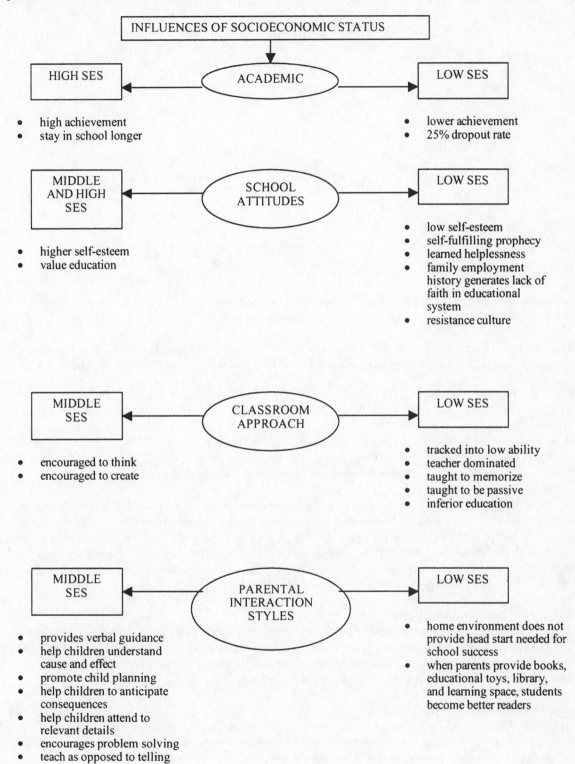

INFLUENCES OF SOCIOECONOMIC STATUS

ACADEMIC

HIGH SES
- high achievement
- stay in school longer

LOW SES
- lower achievement
- 25% dropout rate

SCHOOL ATTITUDES

MIDDLE AND HIGH SES
- higher self-esteem
- value education

LOW SES
- low self-esteem
- self-fulfilling prophecy
- learned helplessness
- family employment history generates lack of faith in educational system
- resistance culture

CLASSROOM APPROACH

MIDDLE SES
- encouraged to think
- encouraged to create

LOW SES
- tracked into low ability
- teacher dominated
- taught to memorize
- taught to be passive
- inferior education

PARENTAL INTERACTION STYLES

MIDDLE SES
- provides verbal guidance
- help children understand cause and effect
- promote child planning
- help children to anticipate consequences
- help children attend to relevant details
- encourages problem solving
- teach as opposed to telling

LOW SES
- home environment does not provide head start needed for school success
- when parents provide books, educational toys, library, and learning space, students become better readers

ECONOMIC AND SOCIAL CLASS DIFFERENCES

Stop, Think, Write: List three ways that teachers might effectively work with low-income parents to help the children of these parents achieve in school.

1.

2.

3.

SOCIAL CLASS AND SES

Socioeconomic Status (SES) has been categorized by four levels (upper, middle, working, and lower) although no single variable, not even income, is an effective measure of SES.

Socioeconomic Status (SES): Relative standing in the society based on income, power, background, and prestige. Social class is a strong character uniting like individuals even beyond ethnic differences.

POVERTY and SCHOOL ACHIEVEMENT
Characteristics of the poor:
• one in six Americans under the age of 18 lives in poverty
• poverty level is $19,350 for a family of four living in an urban area
• US has the highest rate of poverty for children of all developed nations
• the poverty rate is five to eight times higher than most other industrialized countries

In 2003, the absolute number of children living in poverty was about the same for non-Hispanic White children (4.2 million), Latina/o children (4.1 million), and Black children (3.9 million). But the rate of poverty is higher for Black and Latino children-34% of Black and 30% of Latino children lived in poverty in 2003, while 12.5% of Asian and 9.8% of non-Hispanic White children were poor. Contrary to many stereotypes, more poor children live in suburban and rural areas than in central cities, and poor families have only 2.2 children on average (Children's Defense Fund, 2005).

Health, Environment, and Stress
Many factors are associated with low-SES: lower achievement, poor health care for mother and child, low expectations, self-esteem, and learned helplessness. Limited resources, low paying jobs, exposure to violence, overcrowding, homelessness, family stress, interruptions in schooling, and other factors lead to school failures. Also, low-SES students may become part of a **resistance culture**.

Peer Influences and Resistance Culture
Resistance Culture: Group values and beliefs about refusing to adopt the behaviors and attitudes of the majority culture. To succeed in school, many low-SES students believe that they must act "middle class" which may mean cooperating with teachers, studying, etc., and in effect, "selling out".

Tracking: Poor Teaching
Two other explanations for the lower achievement of low-SES students is that they (1) experience **tracking** and are actually taught differently, i.e., taught to be passive and memorize, and (2) childrearing styles that do not adequately prepare them for school.

Tracking: Assignment to different classes and academic experiences based on achievement.

ETHNIC AND RACIAL DIFFERENCES
Ethnicity: A cultural heritage shared by a group of people. This can be based upon common nationality, culture, language, religion or race.

Race: A group of people who share common biological traits that are seen as self-defining by the people of the group.

People often mistake the term **minority group** to mean particular ethnic or racial groups.

Minority Group: A group of people who have been socially disadvantaged-not always a minority in actual numbers. Sociologists use this term to label a group of people who receives unequal or discriminatory treatment.

The Changing Deomographics: Cultural Differences
There are visible and invisible signs of culture. The visible signs are things such as costume, music, food, etc.. The invisible differences may include rules for conducting interpersonal relationships. For **example**, people from some cultures get very close to one another when conversing, but if you are from a culture that places greater distance between its members, then you might take affront at someone "invading your body space". Cultural conflicts are usually about the subtle, or invisible signs of culture, because when cultural differences meet, misunderstandings occur and members from different cultures may be perceived as rude, ignorant, or disrespectful.

It is a well established finding that some ethnic groups consistently achieve below average. We can look to cultural differences, discrimination, and the result of growing up in a low-SES environment as causal factors. Even after the *Brown v. the Board of Education of Topeka* ruling and the declaration that segregation is illegal there still appears to be other subtle forms of segregation. Too often, minority group students are placed in low ability tracks even in integrated schools. However, when minority group students are placed in high quality schools with a predominance of middle-class students, achievement and future outcomes improve.

Cultural Conflicts
The United States is a racist society, but education may be one of the best ways to combat **prejudice**. If schools emphasize acceptance and teach the value of all ethnic groups, attitudes may change.

Prejudice: Prejudgement, or irrational generalization about an entire category of people. Prejudice may take many forms: racial, ethnic, religious, political, geographic, gender, and sexual orientation.

Application 1: Understanding Differences

Which of the scenarios listed below is consistent with what we know about ethnic and minority groups? When your decision is "inconsistent", explain your decision. Check your responses in the answer key.

1) The school counselor was working with a student from a different cultural background. The counselor was discussing career options, but upon receiving no acknowledgment from the student, repeated all of the information. Again, no response was forthcoming from the student, so the counselor assumed that the student was slow or just didn't care.

2) Oh Carter's mother is from the Republic of China. Joan Smith's mother is from Iowa. Both are discussing their children's school failures and the probable causes. Hoe's mom blames the school system whereas Joan's mom states that Joan just doesn't put forth enough effort.

3) Danika is a five-year-old Black child. When she was told to choose between a white doll and a black doll, but that she should pick the one that is prettier and smarter, she chose the black doll because that is the one with which she was able to identify.

4) A group of non-Hispanic Americans living in LA were asked whether they believed that Hispanic Americans preferred to live off of welfare and the majority of the respondents stated that they disagreed and it was a ridiculous notion.

5) Teachers from the science and mathematics department surveyed their students about career goals in math and science. To their relief, they discovered that the majority of their students who planned to pursue careers in these areas were African American and Hispanic American

6) Nate Johnson's favorite television show was "All in the Family". One of his favorite authors is Rush Limbaugh. Nate's children frequently instigate racial conflict.

7) Jacque Renault is a high achieving, white male. His teacher gives him a tremendous amount of attention in class.

8) In Cali and Nick's reading group, the girls said they wanted to read a story about a boy for a change.

9) The school guidance counselor was extremely upset when Jennifer, who in her senior year would become valedictorian, stated that she did not want to take any more math and science courses.

10) Nicole Graham is an only child who comes from a white middle-class family. When asked what they value in Nicole, her parents respond "achievement, competitiveness, and emotional control".

The Development of Prejudice

There are several theories as to why prejudice develops but several factors have been shown to relate to the appearance of prejudicial attitudes. It is generally thought to be a combination of personal and social factors. Children may develop prejudices as a result of familial attitude, friends, media, advertising, and the entire environment around them.

We use schemas to structure and make sense of the world. Our experiences help us to construct our schemes of knowing, and as with everything we know, we also construct schemes about different groups of people, based upon characteristics we have encountered or what others have told us, called **stereotypes.**

Stereotypes: Schema that organizes knowledge or perceptions about a category.

When schemas result in negative stereotypes, then **discrimination** can ensue. Discrimination is prevalent within our society toward women and ethnic Americans. **Discrimination** can cause many problems for ethnic and minority groups because they must reconcile their identity with their ethnic group while trying to fit in with mainstream America.

Discrimination: Treating particular categories of people unequally.

Stereotypes can generate an emotional and cognitive burden of worrying that your performance in an academic situation might confirm a stereotype that others hold about you. This is called **stereotype threat.** Fear that you might confirm a stereotype, i.e., girls are inferior to boys in math, has been shown to induce anxiety and decrease performance. Long-term effect of **stereotype threat** is that in order to protect their self-esteem about academics students disidentify with academics, a phenomenon more associated with African Americans than Whites.

Collaborative Activity
  Brainstorm ideas to combat prejudice in the classroom. What activities would you plan to help students change their current schemas?

For what age group would this activity be most appropriate?

What subject areas?

What positive outcomes can be expected from the activity?

Are there any negative outcomes to be concerned about?

Would you, as a teacher, feel comfortable using this activity? Why/why not?

Girls and Boys: Differences in the Classroom
Sexual Identity
The word *gender* usually refers to traits and behaviors that a particular culture judges to be appropriate for men and for women. In contrast, *sex* refers to biological differences (Brannon, 2002; Deaux, 1993).

Sexual identity includes gender identity, gender-role behaviors, and sexual orientation (Patterson, 1995).
  • *Gender identity* is a person's self-identification as male or femal.
  • *Gender-role behaviors* are those behaviors and characteristics that the culture associates with each gender.
  • *Sexual orientation* involves the person's choice of a sexual partner.
Relations among these three elements are complex.

Sexual Orientation
During adolescence, about 8% of boys and 6% of gilrs report engaging is some same-sex activity or feeling strong attractions to same-sex individuals. Fewer adolescents actually have a homosexual or bisexual orientation-about 4% of adolescents identify themelves as gay, lesbian, or bisexual. This number increases to 8% for adults (Savin-Williams & Diamond, 2004; Steinberg, 2005).

Scientists debate the origins of homosexuality. There are quite a few models describing the development of sexual orientation. Most focus on how adolescents develop an identity as gay, lesbian, or bisexual. Generally, the models include the following or similar stages (Berk, 2005; Yarhouse, 2001):

- *Feeling different*-Beginning around age 6, the child may be less interested in the activities of other children who are the same sex. Some children find this troubling and others do not.
- *Feeling confused*-In adolescence, as they feel attractions for the same sex, students may be confused, upset, lonely, unsure of what to do.
- *Acceptance*-As young adults, many of these youth sort through sexual orientation issues and identify themselves as gay, lesbian or bisexual.

Gender Role Identity

Gender-role identity is the image each individual has of himself or herself as masculine or feminine in characteristics.

Differences do exist between men and women and these differences are biological and environmental. Early on, interactions with our parents help to shape our notions of what it is to be male or female known as **gender schemas**.

Gender Schemas: Organized networks of knowledge about what it means to be male or female. **Example:** My friend's three year-old insisted that their postman was a woman because he had long hair and an earring. His appearance was inconsistent with her gender schemas. Gender schemas help children to make sense of the world and guide their behavior. Little boys may avoid playing with dolls because it is inconsistent with their gender schemas about boy behaviors. Gender schemas help individuals to develop notions of **gender-role identity**.

Gender Bias in the Curriculum

During the elementary school years, children continue to learn about what it means to be male or female. Unfortunately, schools often foster these **gender biases**.

Gender Biases: Different views of males and females, often favoring one gender over the other.

A major source of gender bias can be found in textbooks where both females and males are portrayed in sexually stereotyped ways:

- Most of the textbooks produced for early grades portrayed both sexes in stereotypical ways. (before 1970)
- A study of 2,760 stories from 134 books found the total number of stories dealing with males or male animals to be four times greater than the number dealing with females or female animals. (1975) Females tended to be shown in the home, behaving passively and expressing fear or incompetence. (1975)
- Males were usually more dominant, adventurous, and rescued females. (1975)
- Girls portrayed as more helpless than boys. (1990)

Still, another source of gender bias stems from classroom teachers' interactions with their students.

- Teachers interact more with boys than with girls
- Teachers ask more questions of males, give males more feedback (praise, criticism, and correction)
- Teachers give more specific and valuable comments to boys
- By college, men are twice as likely to initiate comments as women
- From preschool through college, girls receive 1,800 fewer hours of attention and instruction than boys
- Minority-group boys, like girls receive less teacher attention
- Boys are questioned 80% more than girls in science classes
- Boys dominate the use of equipment in science labs

Sex Differences in Mental Abilities

In the 1970's, research showed that males outperformed females on all tests of spatial ability and in mathematics. This has changed somewhat in the past 20 years. Sex differences favoring males still exist on spatial tests that require mental rotation of a figure in space, prediction of the trajectories of moving objects, and navigating. The differences in mathematics are diminishing with males still maintaining a slight edge over females but African-American females outperform their male counterparts in math and Asian-American females perform as well as Asian-American males in math and science.

Sex differences in mathematics are greater among academically talented students. One explanation for the apparent differences may be due to the fact that girls take fewer mathematics courses than boys. When previous number of courses are equated, differences virtually disappear, except for high achieving boys and girls, that is. Academically qualified girls do not take advanced math and science courses, limit their college and career opportunities in these areas, hence, only 15% of the scientists, mathematicians, and engineers are women. Evidence indicates that teachers, are in part responsible for instilling in girls the belief that they aren't cut out for mathematics.

In schools where no gender differences in mathematics were found, teachers had strong backgrounds in mathematics, engineering, or science, not just general education. The brightest students, male and female were grouped together for math and there was a heavy emphasis on reasoning in the classes.
Culture and Community

LANGUAGE DIFFERENCES IN THE CLASSROOM

Culture affects communication. Children from different cultures and ethnic backgrounds experience many confusions in the classroom and one of the largest areas of confusion can stem from language and **dialect** differences.

Dialects
Dialect: Rule-governed variation of a language spoken by a particular group.
Each dialect within a language system is logical, complex, and conforms to as many rules as **standard speech** but these rules will differ from dialect to dialect.

Standard Speech: The most generally accepted and used form of a language.

The best teaching approach when one's students speak with a dialect is to accept their dialect as valid and a correct language system but to teach standard speech. To cope with linguistic diversity in the classroom, teachers:
- need to be sensitive to their own possible negative stereotypes about children who speak a different dialect
- should ensure comprehension by repeating instructions using different words and by asking students to paraphrase instructions or give examples
- check your chapter for further guidelines

Bilingualism

Bilingualism is a topic that sparks heated debates and touches many emotions. One reason is the changing demographics discussed earlier in this chapter. About 18% of the United States populations speaks alanguge other than English at home-half of these families speak Spanish. By 2050, about one-fourth of the entire United States population is expected to be Latina/o (Yetman, 1999).

Bilingualism: Speaking two languages fluently. Two associated terms are:

English as a Second Language (ESL): Designation for programs and classes to teach English to students who are not native speakers of English.

Limited English Proficiency (LEP): Descriptive term for students who have limited mastery of English.

Reaching Every Student: Recognizing Giftedness in Bilingual Students

To identify gifted bilingual students, you can use a case study or portfolio approach in order to collect a variety of evidence, including interviews withparents and peers, formal and informal assessments, samles of student work and performances, and student self assessments. This checklist from Castellano and Diaz (2002) is a useful guide.

Watch for students who:

- learn English quickly
- take risks in trying to communicate in English
- practice English skiils by themselves
- initiate conversations with native English speakers
- do not frustrate easily
- are curious about new words or phrases and practice them
-

CREATING CULTURALLY INCLUSIVE CLASSROOMS

Sheets (2005) uses the term "culturally inclusive" to describe classrooms that provide culturally diverse students with equitable access to the teaching-learning process.

The goal of creating **culturally inclusive classrooms** is to eliminate racism, sexism, classism, and prejudice while adapting the content and methods of instruction to meet the needs of all students.

Culturally Relevant Pedagogy

Ladson-Billings developed a conception of teaching excellence. She uses the term **culturally relevant pedagogy** to describe teaching that rests on three propositions. Students must:

- experience academic success
- develop/maintain their cultural competence
- develop a critical consciousness to challenge the status quo

Fostering Resilence

In any given week, the 12% to 15% of school-age children who have urgent needs for social and emotional support are not getting help. Community and mental health services often don't reach the students who are at the highest risk. But many children at risk for academic failure not only survive-they thrive.

Resilient Students

People vary in their capacity to be resilient. Students who seem able to thrive in spite of serious challenges are actively engaged in school. They have good interpersonal skills, confidence in their own ability to learn, positive attitudes toward school, pride in their ethnicity, and high expectations (Borman & Overman, 2004; Lee, 2005).

Resilient Classrooms

There is some evidence that changed in classrooms-succh as reducing class size and forming supportive relationships with teachers-have a greater impact on the academic achievement of African American students compared to Lation and White students (Borman & Overman, 2004). Borman and Overman (2004) identified two characteristics of schools associated with academic resilience: a safe, orderly environment, and positive teacher-student relationships. Doll and her colleagues (2005) describe the characteristics of resilient classrooms. They assert that there are two strands of elements that bind students to their classroom community. One strand emphasizes the self-agency of students-their capacity to set and pursue goals; the second strand emphasizes caring and connected relationships in the classroom and the school.

Diversity and Convergences

Diversity in Learning

Roland Tharp (1989) outlines several dimensions of classrooms that reflect the diversity of the students. These dimensions can be tailored to better fit the background of the students:

- social organization
- cultural values
- learning styles
- sociolinguistics

Cultural Values and Learning Preferences

Rosa Hernandez Sheets (2005) describes three characteristics of teaches who design culturally inclusive classrooms. The teachers:

1. recognize the various ways all their students display their capabilities;
2. respond to students' preferred ways of learning; and
3. understand that a particular group's cultural practices, values, and learning preferences may not apply to everyone in that group.

Sources of Misunderstandings

Some children are simply better than others at reading the classroom situation because the participation structures of the school match the structures they have learned at home. They know the unwritten rules. Some students from different cultural backgrounds may have learned participation structures that conflict with the behaviors expected in school. The source of misunderstanding can be subtle sociolinguistic difference, such as how long the teacher waits to react to a student's response. It seems that even students who speak the same language as their teachers may still have trouble communicating, and thus learning school subjects, if their knowledge of pragmatics does not fit the school situation.

Digital Divide

One area of teaching that often places students at risk is the use of technology. Many students have limited access to technology at home or in their communities while families with higher family income have a greater percentage of access to the internet. This split in access to technology has been called the **digital divide**.

> **Stop, Think, Write:** Describe one way you will strive to make sure each of your students is aware of the participation structures, or communication rules, in your classroom.

Journaling Activity
If you were a high-school English teacher planning for your second-year American literature class, what information about your students' ethnic backgrounds might be useful to you in choosing reading assignments? How would you go about finding out what you'd like to know, in a way that would not make students fear stereotypes or misunderstandings?

Convergences

The goal of this chapter is to give you a sense of the diversity in today's and tomorrow's schools and to help you meet the challenges of teaching in a multicultural classroom. Here are three general teaching principles to guide you:

- **Know your students-** Before you can engage in effective teaching, you must be able to understand your students' cultures, parents, home, and community environments. Try to bring parents into the classroom and don't wait until a student is in trouble before you meet with the family member. Watch how they interact in groups and spend non-teaching time with them.
- **Respect your students-** Acceptance is an important first step toward helping your students develop self esteem. Once you know your students' strengths and accomplishments, you can help them to increase pride by highlighting their accomplishments and integrating their culture into the classroom.
- **Teach your students-** Acceptance is an important first step toward helping your students develop self esteem. Once you know your students' strengths and accomplishments, you can help them to increase pride by highlighting their accomplishments and integrating their culture into the classroom.

And finally, teach students directly about how to be students.

Application Four: Creating Culturally Compatible Classrooms
Research has provided us with generalized findings regarding ethnic differences in social organization, learning styles, and sociolinguistics. Read the learning style statements to match the corresponding ethnic group. Some statements may require more than one response. Check your responses in the answer key.

    a. Hispanic Americans   b. African Americans
    c. Native Americans   d. Asian Americans   e. Mexican Americans

1) ____ tend to be field dependent
2) ____ preferring holistic, concrete, social approaches to learning
3) ____ possess visual/global learning styles
4) ____ reason by inference rather than by logic, a tendency to approximate numbers, space, and time.
5) ____ show strong preferences for learning privately
6) ____ learn best in cooperative settings
7) ____ value teacher approval and work well in structured, quiet learning environments where there are clear goals
8) ____ tend to be more passive
9) ____ show greater dependence on nonverbal communication
10) ____ prefer energetic involvement in several simultaneous activities rather than routine, step-by-step learning
11) ____ dislike being made to compete with fellow students

Journaling Activity: Reflect on what you have read in this chapter

FOUR Ideas that "Square with Me":

THREE Points to Consider Further:

TWO Questions Going Around in My Head

MY NOTES

(Use this space to make additional notes for this chapter)

6

Behavioral Views of Learning

LEARNING: A Definition

Most of us, if asked, could probably offer a definition of **learning**. As educators, we want to learning to continue long after our students leave the hallowed halls.

Learning: Process through which experience causes permanent change in knowledge or behavior.

This change may be intentional or not, good or bad, but brought about by the environment. These changes are not due to maturation. Temporary changes such as hunger or pain, are not learned responses either. Psychologists appear to embrace two separate notions regarding learning:

Behaviorists: believe that learning is evidenced by a change in behavior. Learning is observable.

Cognitivists: believe that learning is evidenced by a change in knowledge. Learning is not directly observable.

Behavioral Learning Theories: Explanations of learning that focus on external events as the cause of changes in observable behaviors.

EARLY EXPLANATIONS OF LEARNING: CONTIGUITY AND CLASSICAL CONDITIONING

One of the simplest forms of learning occurs through association. This is called **contiguity**. After repeated pairings an association is formed between two events. When one event or sensation (**stimulus**) occurs, it triggers recall of the other event (**response**).

Contiguity: Association of two events because of repeated pairings. **Example:** If a friend comes up to you and says, "Knock, knock", you respond, "Who's there?" Repeated pairings over time causes you to respond to the stimulus "knock, knock" with the age-old response, "who's there?".

Stimulus: Event that activates a behavior. **Example:** "knock, knock" Response: Observable reaction to a stimulus. **Example.** "who's there?"

Contiguity learning is a basic component of the next three forms of learning that will be discussed from a behavioral perspective. The first of these is **classical conditioning**.

Classical Conditioning: Association of automatic or involuntary responses (**respondents**) with new stimuli. **Example:** An involuntary response is one that we cannot control, such as sweating.

Respondents: Responses (generally automatic or involuntary) elicited by specific stimuli.

Classical conditioning occurs when we respond involuntarily to something that wouldn't normally bring about that response. When asked to go in front of a room full of people, a three year old would not automatically break into a sweat, but an older student, who has repeatedly paired public appearances with uncontrolled nervous reactions, may break into a sweat at the mere mention of an oral report. Aspects of classical conditioning are easily understood by examining Pavlov's experiments with salivating dogs.

Pavlov is thought of as the father of classical conditioning and although he won the Nobel for his work on the digestive system, he is most widely remembered for his work with salivating dogs. Pavlov noticed that not only were the dogs salivating at the appearance of meat powder but also when Pavlov himself entered the room. To explain this phenomenon, Pavlov began his experiment.

a. Pavlov enters room and sounds a tuning fork, to which the dog made no response.
Neutral Stimulus: stimulus that does not automatically elicit a response. **Example**: tuning fork

b. Pavlov sounds fork and then presents food. The dog salivates at the presence of the food, constituting the food as an **Unconditioned stimulus (US)**: Stimulus that automatically produces an emotional or physiological response (respondent). **Example**: the food.

The salivation to the food is an **Unconditioned Response (UR)**: Naturally occurring emotional or physiological response (respondent). **Example**: salivation to the food This is where contiguity learning comes to play. Repeated paired associations of the tuning fork and food eventually result in the following scenario. The tuning fork is sounded, the dog is reminded of the food through paired associations, and salivates to the tuning fork before the food is presented.

c. Pavlov sounds the tuning fork and the dog salivates. The tuning fork is no longer a neutral stimulus but through **contiguity learning** has become what we call a **Conditioned Stimulus (CS)**: Previously neutral stimulus that evokes an emotional or physiological response after conditioning. **Example**: tuning fork.

d. The dog salivates but this time, the salivation is in response to what was previously a neutral stimulus. Now, the salivation is known as a **Conditioned Response (CR)**: Learned response to a previously neutral stimulus. **Example**: salivation to the tuning fork, and salivation to Pavlov.

Three other processes are involved in classical conditioning:
- **Generalization**: Responding in the same way to similar stimuli. Example: When we hear the police siren behind us, we respond in the same way regardless if the siren has a slightly different pitch. We pull over to the side of the road and we probably get a queasy feeling in our stomachs.
- **Discrimination**: Responding differently to similar, but not identical stimuli. Example: Hearing an air raid siren would not produce the response of pulling over to the side of the road, but instead, you would probably continue to drive until you had located a fall-out shelter.
- **Extinction**: Gradual disappearance of a learned response. In classical conditioning, this is accomplished by presenting the conditioned stimulus without the unconditioned stimulus. Example:Let's say that you started walking to college past a house with a vicious dog who charges at you baring his teeth, growling, and barking. Luckily, his chain does not reach the sidewalk. Every time he barks and growls, you tremble, sweat, and your heart rate increases. After awhile, as soon as you approach this house, you begin to sweat and have fear reactions. The growling dog is the UCS, house is the CS, and your reaction is the CR. To get you over your fear, we must present the CS (house) without the UCS (scary dog) and eventually, the CR (your fear of the house) will be extinguished.

Emotions can influence classroom learning, especially when these emotions are negative. Think about how you would handle a child who developed panic reactions everytime she had to take an exam. How would you work to eliminate the fear, anxiety, and embarrassment of a student who is afraid to do oral presentations in front of the class. How would you use principles of extinction to eliminate these involuntary responses?

Stop, Think, Write: List some concerns you have about using behavioral learning techniques as a teacher?

How will you overcome these concerns?

OPERANT CONDITIONING: TRYING NEW RESPONSES

The second type of behavioral learning that incorporates contiguity learning is called **operant conditioning**. Whereas classical conditioning involves involuntary responses called respondents, operant conditioning involves voluntary responses to stimuli called **operants**.

Operant Conditioning: Learning in which voluntary behavior is strengthened or weakened by consequences or antecedents.

Operants: Voluntary (and generally goal-directed) behaviors emitted by a person or an animal.
With operant conditioning, an **antecedent** or stimulus occurs to which people choose to respond or not. If a person responds, this operant response is followed by consequences that will serve to determine the likelihood or unlikelihood of that person responding again. We can change behaviors by changing the antecedents or changing the **consequences** or both. We can't always tell which antecedents or stimuli cause behaviors, so to change behaviors, more often then not, we need to change behaviors through consequences. Two forms of consequences are **reinforcement** and **punishment**.

Antecedents: Events that precede an action. **Example:** see below A B Cs of operant conditioning

Consequences: Events that follow an action. **Example:** see below A B Cs of operant conditioning

Reinforcement: Use of consequences to strengthen a behavior. Reinforced behaviors increase in frequency or duration. **Example:** Receiving a paycheck (**reinforcer**) at the end of the week increases the likelihood that you will return to work.

Reinforcer: Any consequence that strengthens the behavior it follows.

Punishment: Process that weakens or suppresses behavior. **Example:** Getting a pink slip at the end of the week decreases the likelihood that you will return to work.

Below, the **A-B-C's of operant conditioning**.
Many of the findings from the field of behavioral psychology come from work done by Thorndike and B.F. Skinner (more commonly known as the father of behavioral psychology). Their experiments with cats, rats and pigeons placed in **Skinner Boxes** showed how animals' behaviors could be shaped by the chance reinforcements they encountered when acting on their environments.

Skinner Box: Experimental chamber designed to isolate stimulus-response connections.

There are two forms of reinforcement, **positive reinforcement** and **negative reinforcement**.
Positive Reinforcement: Strengthening behavior by presenting a desired stimulus after the behavior.
Example: Positive reinforcement occurs when a student earns an "A" for effective study habits OR when a student is given attention when he or she is acting inappropriately in the classroom. Do Not confuse reinforcement with reward. A teacher may reprimand a child in class but if that child was "acting out" in order to receive attention, then the teacher actually reinforced the "acting out" behaviors. Remember, reinforcement is anything that increases a behavior, *either good or bad.*

Negative Reinforcement: Strengthening behavior by removing an aversive (irritating or unpleasant) stimulus.
Example: Students in Ms. Tullen's class have to do homework every night, even on the weekends. Ms. Tullen tells her students that if they study hard and improve on the next exam, then they won't have to do homework on the weekends.

There are also two forms of punishment, **presentation punishment** and **removal punishment**.
Presentation Punishment: Decreasing the chances that a behavior will occur again by presenting an aversive stimulus following the behavior; also called Type I or positive punishment. **Example:** The teacher hands out detentions to students who are late to class.

Removal Punishment: Decreasing the chances that a behavior will occur again by removing a pleasant stimulus following the behavior; also called Type II or negative punishment. **Example:** The teacher tells the class that the next student who is caught fighting will lose recess privileges for the next month.

Always remember, **both reinforcement and punishment are defined by effect!** If it doesn't increase behavior it is not reinforcement. If it doesn't decrease behavior, then it isn't punishment.

Stop, Think, Write: List the steps that would be involved for a first-grader to learn to use one of the class computers to play a reading game.

How can the student be reinforced for learning each step in the process?

Reinforcement Schedules

The best way for people to learn a behavior is when they are **continuously reinforced.** Once the new behavior has been mastered, it is better to reinforce **intermittently** so that skills can be maintained without the expectation of constant reinforcement. Eventually, we would like for our student's successes to be reinforcement enough, without some additional, external reward.

Continuous Reinforcement Schedule: Presenting a reinforcer for every appropriate response.

Intermittent Reinforcement Schedule: Presenting a reinforcer after some but not all responses. Two types of intermittent schedules are interval and ratio.
- **Interval Schedule:** Based on the amount of time between reinforcers.
- **Ratio Schedule:** Based on the number of responses between reinforcers.

Either of these schedules may be either **fixed** (predictable) or **variable** (unpredictable).

Fixed Interval	Reinforcement after a set period of time	Pizza party every Friday
Variable Interval	Reinforcement after varying lengths of time	Fishing
Fixed Ratio	Reinforcement after a set number of responses	Three news reports = 10 pts
Variable Ratio	Reinforcement after a varying number of responses	Recess whenever the teacher feels that the students have completed enough work

When the reinforcement schedule is fixed and students know when it is coming, they will work rapidly and steadily until reinforced and then productivity will drop after reinforcement. When students don't know when the reinforcement is coming, they will work steadily in anticipation of reinforcement and maintain the level of productivity since reinforcement may be coming again at any time or after any amount of responses. Variable schedules are best for maintaining steady levels of productivity.

Application 1: Modifying Behaviors

Read the following scenarios and decide whether positive reinforcement, negative reinforcement, presentation punishment, or removal punishment is being applied and state how it is influencing the behaviors.

1) Trish wants to extend her bedtime from 9:00 to 9:30. Every night she argues with her mother and delays her bedtime procedure so that by the time she finally gets into bed it is 9:30.
2) Moira's newborn cries loudly. Moira tries changing her diaper, cuddling her, feeding her, and rocking her. When Moira hits upon the right behavior, the crying stops.
3) Richard Hutchings never gets any attention at home unless it is negative attention. His parents tell him he is a bad seed and will never amount to anything. When he goes to class, he makes rude noises to make everyone laugh and when his teacher says he sounds like a hog, he oinks loudly. His classmates laugh and tell him he is the "baddest dude in town."
4) Carrie obtained a copy of her science exam prior to the exam. She shared the exam with all of her friends and they all obtained "A's". Her science instructor has not changed his exam in 10 years so many copies are in circulation throughout the school.
5) Mr. Barkley told his class that if they behaved during assembly, his wife would bring in oatmeal scotchies for everyone to eat. The students had eaten the scotchies before and equated them with cardboard. When they went to assembly, Mr. Barkley's students started a near riot.
6) Whenever it is time for Pablo to give an oral report in class, he goes to the nurses office where she allows him to lie down for the remainder of the period.
7) Shirley Friedman uses cooperative learning structures in her classroom. When students' scores improve on their tests, the average amount of improvement scores determine the prizes awarded to each group.

---

8) Tim Thompson was student teaching in Mr. Brown's history class. Everytime Mr.Brown left the class a spitball fight erupted and chaos ensued. Mr. Thompson never sent the unruly students to the office fearing a bad evaluation about his ability to discipline the class.

9) Principal Gonzales decided to offer an incentive program to all of the students in the high school. Any student who showed improvement in GPA from the first to the second quarter or obtained a GPA of 3.00 or above would be allowed to attend a school-wide camping trip.

10) The student teacher in Cali's classroom taught the students the bones of the body by having them play Simon Says "touch your clavicle, Simon Says touch your femur, etc." and offered small pumpkins to the winners as it was close to Halloween.

Whereas extinction can be applied in classical conditioning by presenting the conditioned stimulus without the unconditioned stimulus, it can also be used in operant conditioning. If the reinforcer is withheld, the behavior will disappear. How long do you think you would continue to go to your job if they withheld your paycheck and gave you a pat on the back instead? Sometimes, antecedents will provide cues as to what behaviors will be reinforced. This is called **stimulus control**.

Stimulus Control: Capacity for the presence or absence of antecedents to cause behaviors. **Example:** The teacher sets a timer (cue) and if the students get lined up before the buzzer goes off, they can have 10 extra minutes of playtime on the playground. The students are under stimulus control.

Antecedents and Behavior Changes

Cueing: Providing a stimulus that "sets up" a desired behavior. **Example:** In the above example, the timer is the cue.

Prompt: A reminder that follows a cue to make sure the person reacts to the cue. **Example:** In the above example, if after the teacher sets the timer, he says, "Now what are you supposed to do when I set the timer?", then his question becomes a prompt.

One of your primary teaching responsibilities will be to maintain classroom discipline and this can be effectively accomplished through **Applied Behavior Analysis.**

Applied Behavior Analysis: The application of behavioral learning principles to understand and change behavior. Applied Behavior Analysis is often equated with Behavior Modification .

Behavior Modification: Systematic application of antecedents and consequences to change behavior. **Example:** When the teacher sets the timer to give the students one minute to line up, that is the antecedent. When they successfully line up within a minutes time, they experience the reinforcing consequence of 10 extra minutes of recess. If they do not line up before the buzzer goes off, they will experience the punishing consequence of losing 10 minutes of recess time.

Methods for Encouraging Behaviors

Praise and Ignore Techniques: Research has shown that teachers can improve student behavior by ignoring rule breakers and praising students who are following the rules. Of course, this will not work in all situations and some behaviors just cannot be ignored.

Premack Principle: Principle stating that a more-preferred activity can serve as a reinforcer for a less-preferred activity. **Example:** "If you finish your math problems, you may read the book of your choice".

Shaping: Reinforcing each small step of progress toward a desired goal or behavior. **Example:** The first grade class is learning to write the alphabet. Instead of waiting until each student has perfectly mastered the letter "S", Ms. Harris circulates around the room, giving corrective feedback, and praising every slight improvement in form. A component of shaping is **task analysis.**

Task Analysis: System for breaking down a task hierarchically into basic skills and subskills. **Example:** Writing a research report requires that a student , (a) pick a topic, (b) go to the library (c) read the articles (d) summarize the articles, etc. At each step of the report writing, the teacher can reinforce its successful completion.

Positive Practice: Practicing correct responses immediately after errors. **Example:** The students entered the classroom pushing and shoving so Mr. Waters had them line up and practice going in and out in an orderly fashion.

Coping with Undesirable Behavior

Negative Reinforcement: Strengthening a behavior by removing an aversive stimulus. Although this is usually used to increase a positive behavior, very often the increase of a positive behavior means the decrease of a negative behavior. **Example:** Let's say the students aren't studying. We want to decrease "their not-studying - behaviors" and increase their studying behaviors. Therefore, we might introduce an aversive stimulus such as a "weekly quiz" and when the students demonstrate improved study skills, the weekly quizzes will be removed.

Satiation: Requiring a person to repeat a problem behavior past the point of interest or motivation. **Example:** The students were throwing spit wads every time the teacher's back was turned. The teacher would turn around to discover a sea of wads on the floor. She decided to have the students make and throw wads for the next 30 minutes. They lost interest after 10 and never made another wad again.

Reprimands: Criticisms for misbehavior; rebukes. The most effective reprimands are those which are soft and private as opposed to loud and public and humiliating. **Example:** Mr. Slemmer walked over to Jason's desk and tapped him lightly on the shoulder, quietly telling him to get back on task.

Response Cost: Punishment by loss of reinforcers. **Example:** To stop their fighting, Mrs. Ortez gave Carrie and Stephanie each five circles. Everytime they fight, they lose a circle. When all of the circles are gone, they won't be allowed to go on the class trip.

Social Isolation: Removal of a disruptive student for 5 to 10 minutes. **Example:** Mr. Ross asked Matt to take his work into the "time-out" room so that he could complete it without distracting everyone around him.

Time Out: Technically, the removal of all reinforcement. In practice, isolation of a student from the rest of the class for a brief time. **Example:** Jackie was loving all of the laughter and attention from the class each time she fell out of her chair. Her teacher took her chair away and made her stand and sit on the floor for the rest of the day.

Whenever, you use punishment, make it part of a two-prong attack; stop the negative behavior and provide a positive alternative so that the individual doesn't replace one negative behavior with another.

Application 2: Matching Key Terms and Definitions Operant Conditioning

Select the word from the left column that corresponds to the phrase on the right. Put the number of the matching word in the blank in front of the letters and next to the same letter in the matrix below. If your answers are correct, all numbers across, down, and diagonally, will add up to the same number.

1. Prompt

2. Positive Practice

3. Response Cost

4. Social Isolation

5. Satiation

6. Task Analysis

7. Reprimands

8. Cueing

9. Shaping

____ a. Practicing correct responses immediately after errors

____ b. Reinforcing each small step of progress toward a desired goal or behavior

____ c. Removal of a disruptive student for 5 to 10 minutes

____ d. Criticisms for behavior; rebukes

____ e. Requiring a person to repeat a behavior past the point of interest

____ f. Punishment by loss of reinforcers

____ g. System for breaking down a task hierarchically into basic skills and subskills

____ h. A reminder that follows a cue to make sure the person reacts to the cue

____ i. Providing a stimulus that "sets up" a desired behavior

A	B	C
D	E	F
G	H	I

What is the correct number _____?

Reaching Every Student: Functional Behavioral Assessment and Positive Behavior Support

Group Strategies for Behavior Management

Teachers in both regular and special education classes have had success with a new approach that begins by asking, "What are students getting out of their problem behaviors-what functions do these behaviors serve?" The reasons for problem behaviors generally fall into four categories (Barnhill, 2005; Maag & Kemp, 2003). Students act out to:

1. receive attention from others-teachers, parent, or peers.
2. escape from some unpleasant situation-an academic or social demand.
3. get a desired item or activity.
4. meet sensory needs, such as stimulation from rocking or flapping arms for some children with autism.

If the reason is known, then the teacher can devise ways of supporting positive behaviors that will serve the same "why" function.

Postive Behavioral Supports

The Individuals with Disabilities Improvement Act (IDEIA, 2004) discussed in Chapter 4 requires positive behavioral supports (PBS) for students with disabilities and those at-risk for special education placement. **Positive behavioral supports** are interventions designed to replace problem behaviors with new actions that serve the same purpose for the student. The process of understanding the problem behavior is known as a **functional behavioral assessment (FBA)** "a collection of methods or procedures used to obtain information about antecedents, behaviors, and consequences to determine the reason or function of the behavior" (Barnhill, 2005, p.132).

Group Consequences

Stopping misbehaviors may be accomplished subtly without calling the attention of everyone in the class to the situation. Frequent reprimands do not translate to mean the best behaved classes. Some effective ways are (1) to make eye contact or move in closer proximity to the offender, (2) remind students of the correct procedure if they are not following it correctly, (3) ask students to state the correct rule and then follow it, and (4) tell the student in a clear, assertive, and unhostile way to stop the misbehavior.

Many classroom management procedures are aimed at the global behavior of the class. Many of Cali's teachers would give points for good behaviors and when they accumulated enough points they would have a pizza party. This is an example of the **good behavior game**.

Good behavior game: Arrangement where a class is divided into teams and each team receives demerit points for breaking agreed-upon rules of good behavior. The team with the least marks at the end of the period receives a special reward. If both teams receive less marks than the previous period, both teams receive a reward.

Without dividing the class into teams, you could also use **group consequences**. Peer influences can be a positive form of support for establishing appropriate behaviors but cautions must be taken lest a single troubled student is held responsible for the majority of his or her team's penalties, potentially creating even further problems for that individual. Teachers should show students how to give each other constructive feedback and support.

Group Consequences: Rewards or punishments given to a class as a whole for adhering to or violating rules of conduct.

Another system in which students are reinforced for appropriate behaviors are **token reinforcement systems**. Here, all students are provided with the opportunity to earn tokens that provide the students with purchasing power.

Token Reinforcement System: System in which tokens earned for academic work and positive classroom behavior can be exchanged for some desired reward.

Once again, cautions must be exercised because extrinsic rewards are replacing intrinsic satisfaction. Once a system is working well, tokens should be distributed on an intermittent schedule and saved for longer periods of time before they are exchanged for rewards. Token reinforcement systems should be used in only three situations:

- to motivate students who are completely uninterested in their work and have not responded to other situations
- to encourage students who have consistently failed to make academic progress
- to deal with a class that is out of control

Some students benefit from token economy systems more than others. Students who are slow learners or mentally challenged, children who frequently fail, and children who have few academic skills and behavior problems, all respond to token systems yet teachers must re-evaluate their curriculum, material, and teaching practices before resorting to token systems.

Contingency Contract

Another special program that fosters active goal setting, self-management, and independence is called a **contingency contract**. Contracts may be used for any subject area, any topic and at any age. They teach the very valuable lesson of time management and breaking a large long-term project into short-term do-able tasks. What helps to make this effective, is that students receive reinforcements throughout the project, rather than waiting to be reinforced only upon project completion.

Contingency Contract: A contract between the teacher and an individual student specifying what the student must do to earn a particular privilege or reward.

RECENT APPROACHES: SELF MANAGEMENT

As educators, one of our goals is to have students assume responsibility for their own learning. One way to accomplish this is through the behavioral approach called self-management.

Self-Management: use of behavioral learning principles to change your own behavior. Important components of self management include goal setting, recording and evaluating progress, and also self-reinforcement.

Self-Reinforcement: Providing yourself with positive consequences, contingent on accomplishing a particular behavior.

Cognitive Behavior Modification: Procedures based on both behavioral and cognitive learning principles for changing your own behavior by using self-talk and self-instruction.

Self-Instruction: Talking oneself through the steps of a task.

Criticisms of Behavioral Methods

Some psychologists fear that rewarding students for all learning will cause them to lose interest in learning for its own sake (Deci, 1975; Deci & Ryan, 1985; Kohn, 1993, 1996; Lepper & Greene, 1978; Lepper, Keavney, & Drake, 1996; Ryan & Deci, 1996). Studies have suggested that using reward programs with students who are already interested in the subject matter, may, in fact, cause students to be less interested in the subject when the reward program ends.

Ethical Issues

The ethical questions related to the use of the strategies described in this chpater are similar to those raised by any process that seeks to influence people. What are the goals? How do these goals fit with those of the school as a whole? What effect will a strategy have on the individuals involved? Is too much control being given to the teacher?

Diversity and Convergence in Behavioral Learning

Diversity

There is great *diversity* in the learning histories of students. Every person in your class will come to you with different fears and anxieties. Different activities or objects will serve as reinforcers for some students, but not for others. The research and theories presented in this chapter should help you understand how the learning histories of your students might have taught them to respond automatically to tests with sweaty palms and racing hearts-possible classical conditioning at work.

Remember, what works for one student may not be right for another. In addition to providing a diversity of reinforcers, teachers, classrooms, and schools should provide a diversity of models because students learn through observation.

Convergences

Even though your classroom will be filled with many different learning histories, there are some convergences-principle that apply to all people.

1. No one eagerly repeats behaviors tha have been punished or ignored. Without some sense of progress, it is difficult to persist.
2. When actions lead to consequences that are positive for the person involved, those actions are likely to be repeated.
3. Teachers often fail to use reinforcement to recognize appropriate behavior; they respond instead to inappropriate behaviors, sometimes providing reinforcing attention in the process.
4. To be effective, praise must be a sincere recognition of a real accomplishment.
5. Whatever their current level of functioning, students can learn to be more self-managing.

Figure 6.2

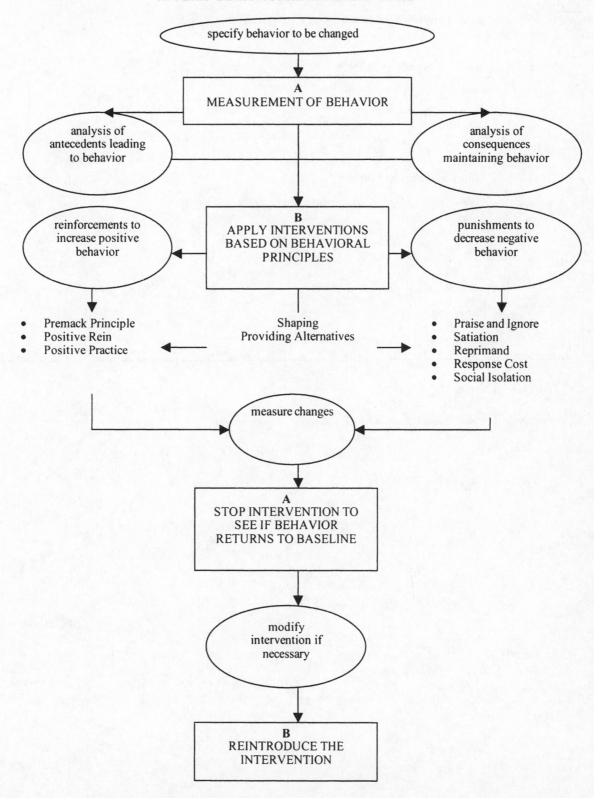

APPLIED BEHAVIORAL ANALYSIS - ABAB

specify behavior to be changed

A
MEASUREMENT OF BEHAVIOR

analysis of antecedents leading to behavior

analysis of consequences maintaining behavior

reinforcements to increase positive behavior

B
APPLY INTERVENTIONS BASED ON BEHAVIORAL PRINCIPLES

punishments to decrease negative behavior

- Premack Principle
- Positive Rein
- Positive Practice

Shaping
Providing Alternatives

- Praise and Ignore
- Satiation
- Reprimand
- Response Cost
- Social Isolation

measure changes

A
STOP INTERVENTION TO SEE IF BEHAVIOR RETURNS TO BASELINE

modify intervention if necessary

B
REINTRODUCE THE INTERVENTION

Journaling Activity: Reflect on what you have read in this chapter

FOUR Ideas that "Square with Me":

THREE Points to Consider Further:

TWO Questions Going Around in My Head

MY NOTES

(Use this space to make additional notes for this chapter)

7
Cognitive Views of Learning

The cognitive perspective had its origins in the philosophies of the ancient Greeks. Since that early time, educators and philosophers have been interested in how people think, learn concepts, and solve problems.

Cognitive View of Learning: A general approach that views learning as an active mental process of acquiring, remembering, and using knowledge.

Assumptions about the cognitive perspective:
- Knowledge is learned, and changes in knowledge make changes in behavior possible.
- Reinforcement is seen as a source of feedback about what is likely to happen if behaviors are repeated. Feedback is a source of information.
- People are seen as active learners who initiate experiences, seek out information to solve problems, and reorganize what they already know to achieve new insights.
- New cognitive approaches stress the construction of knowledge.
- Already acquired knowledge determines to a large extent what we will pay attention to, perceive, learn, remember, and forget in the future.

According to the cognitive perspective there are different kinds of knowledge.

General Knowledge: Information that is useful in many different kinds of tasks; information that applies to many situations. **Example:** How to add or subtract or make change, skills that are useful both in and out of school.

Domain Specific Knowledge: Information that is useful in a particular situation or that generally applies to only one specific topic. **Example:** Knowledge that a "roux" is a butter and flour mixture used in cooking.

Declarative Knowledge: Verbal information; facts; "knowing that" something is the case. **Example:** Information that can be taught through lectures or acquired through books, verbal exchange, Braille, sign language etc. This is a broad category ranging from, the date of my brother's birthday, to mathematical rules, to knowledge of how to grow vegetables.

Procedural Knowledge: Knowledge that is demonstrated when we perform a task; "knowing how." **Example:** We may know what ingredients go into a cake (declarative knowledge) but how to combine them to make the cake is procedural knowledge.

Conditional Knowledge: "Knowing when and why" to use declarative and procedural knowledge. **Example:** You may know what a kokanee is (declarative knowledge) and you may know how to catch one (procedural knowledge) but knowing under what conditions you should fish shallow or deep is conditional knowledge.

Application 1: Behavioral and Cognitive Approaches

Read the following situations and decide whether each is more consistent with the behavioral or cognitive approach. Check the correctness of your responses in the answer key.

1. _____ Learning is the result of our attempts to make sense of the world.
2. _____ Reinforcement strengthens responses.
3. _____ Reinforcement is seen as a source of information.
4. _____ Learning can best be thought of as a stimulus-response paradigm.
5. _____ Our existing knowledge influences how and what we learn.
6. _____ People are passively influenced by environmental events.
7. _____ Much of the research in this area has been conducted in controlled laboratory settings.
8. _____ Experts in this area study a wide range of learning situations.
9. _____ People are active learners who initiate experiences.
10. ___ Their goal is to identify a few general laws of learning that apply to all higher organisms.

THE INFORMATION PROCESSING MODEL

Information processing views of memory rely on the computer as a model. Like a computer, the mind takes in data, stores the data, retrieves the data to work with it when necessary, and adapts and modifies the data. The whole system is guided by control processes that determine how and when the information will flow through the system.

Information Processing: Human mind's activity of taking in, storing, and using information.
for a concept map of Memory Stores.

SENSORY MEMORY

All kinds of stimuli from the environment bombard our **receptors**. **Sensory Memory** is the initial processing that identifies these incoming stimuli so we can make sense of them.

Receptors: Parts of the human body that receive sensory information. **Example:** When you tap your arm, sense receptors detect the sensation. The sensation is held very briefly in the sensory memory also called the sensory register and then the sensation fades.

Sensory Register: System of receptors holding sensory information very briefly. The capacity of the sensory register is very large and it contains almost an exact image of the information as it occurred but we have no use for the retention of all stimuli exactly as seen, heard, smelled, felt, or tasted so this information lasts but a split second. **Example:** Look around the room and close your eyes. You can retain an exact image of everything you saw but just for a second. Would you want to retain all of this information forever? It would be rather useless, don't you think? Some of this information, however, we do wish to retain by moving it into working memory.

The content of sensory memory resembles the sensations from the original stimulus. **Perception** and attention are critical at this stage.

Perception: Interpretation of sensory information. **Example:** How we interpret what we perceive is largely based on our past experiences and existing knowledge. For example, if you shout out the word "love" to a tennis pro, the pro will probably first perceive this as a zero score in tennis versus a deep emotional attachment.

Explanations of perception derive from **Gestalt** theorists who state that we tend to perceive things in their best form or most "meaningful whole". More current explanations of perception are **bottom up processing** and **top down processing.**

Gestalt: German for pattern or whole. Gestalt theorists hold that people organize their perceptions into coherent wholes.

Bottom-Up Processing (feature analysis): Perceiving based on noticing separate, defining features and assembling them into a recognizable pattern. **Example:** / \ / \ From my keyboard, this is back slash, forward slash, back slash, and forward slash. But for you to organize this into a meaningful whole, you probably perceive this as the letter "M" or perhaps a mountain range in Switzerland.

Top-Down Processing: Perceiving based on the content and the patterns you expect to occur in that situation. **Example:** If your were to fleetingly perceive a winged creature fly past the window of your house, even though it was a partial glimpse, you would probably perceive it as a "bird" and not a "bat" or a "fairy" because a bird would be more consistent with your interpretation of the global perception. You may be wrong, it could be a fairy, but to specifically determine that it was a fairy would require greater attention to the scene.

Attention: Focus on a stimulus. Example: **The first step in learning is ATTENTION!!** Did that get your attention? Without attention, no perception, no interpretation, no learning would take place. When teaching your students, employ the guidelines from your chapter for gaining and maintaining attention, that are briefly summarized below:

- Use signals to direct student actions and inform them of what's coming.
- Make sure the purpose of the lesson or assignment is clear to students.
- Emphasize variety, curiosity, and surprise to maintain attention and **KEEP YOUR STUDENTS AWAKE AND ANXIOUSLY ANTICIPATING YOUR NEXT MOVE!**
- Ask questions and provide frames for answering to help students focus on how they plan to study, what strategies they'll use and why the material is important. Help them attend to their own errors.

WORKING MEMORY

The second component of the multistore theory of memory is **short term memory** which is synonymous with **working memory.**

Short Term Memory: Working memory, holding a limited amount of information briefly. Short term memory holds the information from the sensory register that your brain (after sifting through all of the sensory perceptions and selecting what is important based on past experience and knowledge) has interpreted and stored.

Working Memory: The information that you are focusing on at a given moment. The capacity of working memory is limited to five to nine separate units of new information. This is why after meeting someone, and being told many units of information about that person, you very often have to ask "What's your name again?" The capacity for new information has been exceeded and unless you keep repeating that person's name over and over again, the most recent incoming information will push the other new information right out of working memory.

Another factor that influences the functioning of short term memory is its duration. Information can only be held for approximately 20 seconds without **maintenance rehearsal.**

Maintenance Rehearsal: Keeping information in working memory by repeating it to yourself. **Example:** Her name is Roberta, her name is Roberta, Roberta, Roberta, Roberta. As long as you say the name, it is in active use in working memory. The name "Roberta" is short enough that it fits the limitation of the articulatory loop.

Articulatory Loop: A rehearsal system of about 1.5 seconds.
Another form of rehearsal for keeping information in working memory and moving information from working to long term memory is **elaborative rehearsal.**

Elaborative Rehearsal: Keeping information in working memory by associating it with something else you already know. **Example:** When you meet Roberta, you don't need to engage in maintenance rehearsal because your mother's name is Roberta and by making the association, you can also move Roberta's name into long term memory. Another strategy for "expanding" the capacity of working memory is called "chunking".

Chunking: Grouping individual bits of data into meaningful larger units. **Example:** Our-social security numbers are nine digits in length which is the maximum amount contained within working memory, but when given large strings of numbers, we usually chunk single digits into larger units. The social security numbers 1 *2*8*2*5*3*6*9*8 becomes 128-25-36-98. That's four chunks instead of nine. Try to remember the number sequence both ways to determine which way is more effective.

Information in working memory can be lost or forgotten due to decay. Exceeding 20 seconds without rehearsal will cause the new information to be forgotten and exceeding the 5-to-9 units will ensure that some of the information will be forgotten. Forgetting is important because we need to empty working memory to make way for new information. Also, we would never want to retain every sentence we've ever read.

Decay The weakening and fading of memories with the passage of time. **Example:** Your 20 seconds are up. What was the social security number written above? Unless you've been rehearsing the number all of the time, decay has probably removed the number from your working memory.

LONG TERM MEMORY
The final memory storage system from the multi-store theory is called **long term memory.**
Long Term Memory: Permanent store of knowledge. **Example:** You can remember your telephone number because it is stored permanently in long term memory.

Long term memory is said to be high in **memory strength** or more durable and well-learned. The capacity of long term memory is virtually unlimited and once information is in long term memory, it is there permanently. When you're trying to recall information from long term memory when you're taking an exam, you may have your doubts as to the permanence of the information. It really is in there, however, the difficulty really lies with retrieval.

Several theories exist as to how information is stored in long term memory. Paivio suggested that information is stored as visual images, verbal images or both. But this theory is insufficient for explaining our memory of emotions, sounds (can you hear a melody in your head) and smells (can you smell chocolate brownies baking in the oven). Schunk suggests that images would occupy too much space in memory. He posits that images are actually stored as verbal codes and then translated into a visual image when needed. Today, most psychologists distinguish between three categories of long term memory: **semantic, episodic, and procedural.**

Explicit Memories: Semantic and Episodic

Semantic Memory: Memory for meaning. These memories are stored as propositions, images, or schemas.

Propositions and Propositional Networks: Set of interconnected concepts and relationships in which long term information is held. A proposition is the smallest unit of information that can be judged to be true or false. A propositional network is comprised of interconnected propositions. **Example:** Washington D.C. is our nation's capital. You may have constructed a network that includes the capital, our president, the Washington Monument, cherry blossoms, etc. Recall of one proposition may influence recall of another and so on.

Images: Images are representations based on perceptions of the structure or appearance of the information. Images are not exact copies because perceptions are based on experiences or knowledge. **Example:** We can all construct an image of a flower, but our images and constructions differ greatly.

Schemas: Basic structures for organizing information; concepts. **Example:** A schema for justice is complex and could not be adequately represented by either images or propositional networks.
Several types of schemas provide us with structures to help us perform and respond. Two such schemata are called story grammars and scripts.

Story Grammar: Typical structure or organization for a category of stories. **Example:** A typical story grammar for a love story might go like this, boy meets girl, boy and girl fall in love, misunderstanding occurs between boy and girl, boy and girl make up , everyone lives happily ever after.

Script: Schema or expected plan for the sequence of steps in a common event or everyday situation.

Up to this point. we've been discussing aspects of memory that relate to the meaning of things and knowledge about many things. Some memories focus not so much on the meaning of the content but rather memory surrounding events at different times and different places, called **episodic memory** and memory for how to perform things, called **procedural memory**.

Episodic Memory: Long term memory for information tied to a particular time and place, especially memory for the events in a person's life.

Flashbulb Memory: Memories that are vidid and complete of dramtic or emotional moments in your life.

Implicit Memories

Procedural Memory: Long term memory for how to do things. **Example:** No matter how old, you never really forget how to ride a bike. Procedural memories are comprised of condition-action rules sometimes called productions.

Productions: The contents of procedural memories; rules about what actions to take, given certain conditions. **Example:** When riding your bike around a corner, you must slow a bit and lean into the curve. The more practiced the procedure, the less you consciously think about these rules.

Priming: Activating information that already is in long-term memory through some out-of-awareness process.

STORING AND RETRIEVING INFORMATION IN LONG TERM MEMORY

You might ask how we store information; creating semantic, episodic, and procedural memories. A key contingency for saving information is how we learn, process, and connect the new information with already existing knowledge, to begin with. Several strategies for encoding information are discussed below.

Elaboration: Adding and extending meaning by connecting new information to existing knowledge.

Material that is elaborated when first learned will be easier to recall later. Another effective strategy, is to arrange information in such a fashion that it is logically grouped within your cognitive **organization**.

Organization: Ordered and logical network of relations. **Example:** To learn the bones of the body, you might teach your students all of the bones from the shoulders up, then those in the torso region and so on.

Context: The physical or emotional backdrop associated with an event. **Example:** The room in which you study becomes part of the associative structure of memory. As you are thinking about Pavlov, if you are looking at the clock on your wall, then the clock becomes part of the memory. If you see a similar clock on the wall while you are taking your exam, that clock will serve as a trigger for your recall of Pavlov.

An alternate theory, called the **Levels of Processing Theory**, suggests that how deeply you process information in the first place will influence later recall. **Example:** Level 1-I learn what a hammer is. **Level 2**-1 learn what a hammer is and what it looks like. **Level 3**- I learn what a hammer is, what it looks like, and names for different types of hammers, i.e., ball peen, claw hammer, rock hammer, mallet. If I learn something to the depth of Level 3, I'll have an easier time accessing the information from long term memory.

RETRIEVING INFORMATION FROM LONG-TERM MEMORY

Accessing information from long term memory is sometimes conscious, other times, automatic. Information is retrieved into working memory through **the spread of activation**.

Spreading Activation: Retrieval of pieces of information based on their relatedness to one another. Remembering one bit of information activates (stimulates) recall of associated information.

Retrieval: Process of searching for and finding information in long term memory. A sometimes less accurate method of retrieving information than spread of activation is called **reconstruction**.

Reconstruction: Recreating information by using memories, expectations, logic, and existing knowledge. This is a problem solving process that makes use of logic, cues, and other knowledge to construct a reasonable answer by filling in any missing parts. **Example:** People at crime scenes often reconstruct inaccurate reports because logic, cues, and their own schemata would often lead them to make the wrong conclusions.

Forgetting and Long-Term Memory

When information is lost in working memory, it's lost for good and must be re-entered. Many psychologists believe that all information can be eventually retrieved from long term memory given the right cues. More recent research indicates that time decay and interference can erase some memories. New memories may interfere with old memories and old memories may interfere with new memories.

Interference: The process that occurs when remembering certain information is hampered by the presence of other information. **Example:** When the new year changes, how many of you continue to write the old year's date on your checks?

Long term memory is still the most important memory. Research supports the notion that teaching strategies that encourage student engagement and lead to higher levels of initial learning (such as those listed below), are associated with longer retention.

- frequent reviews and tests
- elaborated feedback
- high standards
- mastery learning
- active involvement on learning projects

> **Stop, Think, Write:** One disadvantage of storing long-term memories in schemas and scripts is that new information which does not fit the schema may not be remembered or may be distorted in memory. Describe one way that you, as a teacher, can help students accurately remember information that does not fit well into their schemas.

METACOGNITION and REGULATION

To explain individual differences in why some people learn and remember better than others may be a function of their **executive control processes.**

Executive Control Processes: Processes such as selective attention, rehearsal, elaboration, and organization that influence encoding, storage, and retrieval of information in memory. Sometimes these executive control processes are called **metacognitive skills** because they can be used intentionally to regulate cognition.

Metacognition: Knowledge about our own thinking processes.

Cognitive Monitoring: People's awareness and monitoring of their own thinking and learning strategies.

Metacognitive knowledge helps us to regulate thinking and learning by employing the following three skills:
- **Planning:** involves how much time to give to a task, which strategies to use, how to start, what resources to gather, what order to follow, what to skim and what to give intense attention, and so on.
- **Monitoring:** on line awareness of "how am I doing?" and "is this making sense?".
- **Evaluation:** making judgments about the processes and outcomes of thinking and learning. Is this paper sufficient, should I get help, should I change strategies, etc.

"Reaching Every Student" Metacognitive Strategies for Students with Learning Disabilities

For students with learning disabilities, executive processes such as planning, organizing, monitoring progress, and making adaptations are especially important, but often underdeveloped (Kirk, Gallagher, Anastasiow, & Colemen, 2006). It makes sense to teach these strategies directly. Some approaches make use of mnemonics to remember the steps. For example, teachers can help older students use a writing strategy called DEFENDS (Deshler, Ellis, & Lenz, 1996):

- Decide on audience, goals, and position
- Estimate main ideas and details
- Figure best order of main ideas and details
- Express your position in the opening
- Note each main idea and supporting points
- Drive home the message in the last sentence
- Search for errors and correct

Development of Declarative Knowledge

To learn declarative knowledge is really to integrate new ideas with existing knowledge and construct an understanding. First, students need a good base of knowledge to build upon with further information. Strategies for accomplishing this are discussed below.

Make it Meaningful

Meaningful lessons are presented in vocabulary that makes sense to the students. New terms are clarified through ties with more familiar words and ideas. Meaningful lessons are well organized, with clear connections between the different elements of the lesson. Finally, meaningful lessons make naural use of old information to help students understand new information through examples of analogies.

Visual Images and Illustrations

Richard Mayer (1999a, 2001) has found that the right combination of pictures and words can make a significant difference in students' learning. Mayer's cognitive theory of multimedia learning includes three ideas:

- *Dual Coding:* Visual and verbal materials are processed in different systems
- *Limited Capacity:* Working memory for verbal and visual material is severely limited
- *Generative Learning:* Meaningful learning happens when students focus on relevant information and generate or buld connections.

Mnemonics: Systematic procedures for improving memory; also the art of memory. Many of these strategies use imagery. Examples of different types of mnemonics can be found below.

Loci Method: Techniques of associating items with specific places. **Example:** If you need to purchase a variety of items at the store, take an imaginary walk through your house and imagine the eggs in the fireplace, the celery coming out of the toilet, milk coming out of your faucet, and a cake in the bathtub, well you get the picture. And the picture or image will really help you with recall.

Peg-type Mnemonics: Systems of associating items with cue words. **Example:** This is similar to the loci method however, instead of memorizing furniture or rooms in your house, you would memorize pegs such as one is bun, two is shoe, three is tree. When you want to remember your grocery list you would envision a carton of eggs in a hamburger bun, grapes spilling out of a shoe, steaks hanging from the branches of a tree.

Acronym: Technique for remembering names, phrases, or steps by using the first letter of each word to form a new memorable word. **Example:** SCUBA -self contained underwater breathing apparatus. To help Cali remember the planets in order from the sun, I taught her the sentence My Very Eloquent Mother Just Sat Upon Nine Puppies. The first letters, MVEMJSUNP stand for Mercury, Venus, Earth, Mars, Jupiter, Saturn, Uranus, Neptune and Pluto.

Chain Mnemonics: Memory strategies that associate one element in a series with the next element.

Keyword Method: System of associating new words or concepts with similar sounding cue words.

Mnemonics can be helpful but one problem is that many of them require self-generated imagery which may be difficult for younger children. Younger children would probably benefit more from chain mnemonics or mnemonics that you, as the teacher, provide. All in all, the best method for helping students to learn material is to make it meaningful so that they can process the material at a deep level versus reliance on rote memorization.

Rote Memorization: Remembering information by repetition without necessarily understanding the meaning of the information. **Example:** Sometimes, the material to be learned has no inherent meaning, e.g. the capitals of all the states in the United States, so memorization requires repeated practice versus semantic comprehension.

When you try to remember a long list of words, you may find your recall subject to the **serial position effect.**

Serial Position Effect: The tendency to remember the beginning and the end but not the middle of the list. **Example:** If you had to remember the names Bertha, Hubert, Hermione, Francis, Julietta, and Simone, you would probably remember Bertha and Simone best.

One way to combat the serial position effect is through the use of **part learning** and when combined with another strategy, **distributed practice**, more effective learning occurs. Unfortunately many students engage in **massed practice**.

Part Learning: Breaking a list of rote items into shorter lists. **Example:** Bertha and Hubert would be on list one. Hermione and Francis would comprise the second and Julietta and Simone would be on the third list.

Distributed Practice: Practice in brief periods with rest intervals over time. **Example:** If your test is on Friday you would start to study Monday and then again Tuesday, Wednesday, and Thursday.

Massed Practice: Practice for a single extended period also known as cramming. **Example:** If your test is on Friday, you crack the book for the first time on Thursday night.

Distributed practice is the best strategy for a few reasons. The first of these is that distributed practice allows for deep level processing versus surface level processing where little other than memorization of definitions takes place. Distributed practice affords students the time to reflect and organize the new information and connect it to already existing knowledge. Massed practice does not afford students the time necessary to accomplish this. Secondly, with massed practice, once studying has ended, forgetting begins, and then it's test time. But with distributed practice once studying ends, forgetting begins, but when you start studying again, this constitutes relearning and relearning is more efficient.

Stop, Think, Write: Create an initial-letter mnemonic device to help students remember the following four key parts of a research paper: Thesis, Literature Review, Support, and Conclusion.

Stop, Think, Write: Use the same strategy to create a device to help you remember a key concept of this chapter.

List three steps you, as a teacher, could take to help students remember important information by avoiding interference.

1.

2.

3.

BECOMING AN EXPERT: DEVELOPMENT OF PROCEDURAL AND CONDITIONAL KNOWLEDGE

Experts in a field possess great declarative, procedural, and conditional knowledge. Experts also have **automated basic skills.**

Automated Basic Skills: skills that are applied without conscious thought. **Example:** When you first learned how to ride a bike, you had to think about every step, but after awhile, you could jump on and ride away without much thought except to the traffic around you. Most psychologists have identified three stages in which behaviors become automated:

- **Cognitive Stage:** The initial learning of an automated skill when we rely on general problem-solving approaches to make sense of steps or procedures. **Example:** When learning to ride a bike, we make take each action step-by-step. We may pedal and try to keep our balance. We probably won't try to navigate a turn until we have good balance and even when we first try to turn the corner, we may stop pedaling
- **Associative Stage:** Individual steps of a procedure are combined or "chunked" into larger units. **Example:** Back to the bike example, now when you turn the corner you can also simultaneously pedal or brake, but you're still concentrating on all of the processes.
- **Autonomous Stage:** Final stage in the learning of automated skills. The procedure is fine tuned and becomes "automatic". **Example:** Now you can pedal, turn, brake, ring the bell, and you don't really have to consciously concentrate on what you're doing.

An important aspect of making skills automatic is providing plenty of practice. Practice in real contexts helps students learn not only how to do a skill but *why* and *when*. *All* practiced actions do not become completely automatic and nor should they be. Some strategies should be consciously applied as is the case with **domain-specific strategies.**

Domain Specific Strategies: Consciously applied skills to reach goals in a particular subject or problem area. **Example:** Once your bicycling has become autonomous, your maneuvers when changing lanes may be automatic but your decision was conscious and based on the traffic conditions around you.

Diversity and Convergence in Cognitive Learning

Many of the concepts and processes discussed in this chapte-the importance of knowledge in learning; the sensory, working, and long-term memory; metacognition-apply to all students. But there are developmental and individual differences in what students know and how their memory processare used.

Diversity: Individual Differences and Working Memory

There are both developmental and individual differences in working memory.

Developmental Differences
Research indicates that young children have very limited working memories, but their memory span improves with age. Recent research shos that the three components of working memory-the central executive, phonological loop, and visualspatial sketchpad-all increase in capacity from ages 4 through adolescence (Gathercoe, Pickering, Ambridge, & Wearing, 2004). It is not clear whether these differences are the result of changes in memory *capacity* or improvements in *strategy* use.

Individual Differences
Besidese developmental differences, there are other individual variations in working memory, and these differences have implicaitons for learning. Some people seemto have more efficient working memories than others (Cariglia-Bull & Pressley, 1990; Divesta & Di Cintion, 1997; Jurden, 1995), and differences in working memory may be associated with giftedness in math and verbal areas.

Diversity: Individual Differences and Long-Term Memory
The major individual difference that affects long-term memory is knowledge. When students have more *domain specific declarative* and *procedural knowledge,* they are better at learning and remembering material in that domain (Alexander, 1997). People also differ in their abilities to use images in remembering. There are both developmental and individual differences. Children are more likely than adults to use images. Because people grow up in different cultural contexts, they have different funds of knowledge.

Individual Differences in Metagcognition

Some differences in metacognitive abilities are the result of development. Not all differences in metacognitive abilities have to do with age or maturation. There is great variablitity even among students of the same developmental level, but these differences do not appear to be related to intellectual abilities. In fact, superior metacognitive skills can compensate for lower levels of ability, so these metacognitive skills can be especially important for students who often have trouble in school (Schunk, 2004; Swanson, 1990).

Convergences: Connecting with Families

The last several sections of your chapter described many ideas for helping students become knowledgeable- memory strategies, mnemonics, metacognitive skills such as planning or monitoring comprehension, and cognitive skills. Some students have an advantage in school because they learn these strategies and skills at home. One way to capitalize on this diversity is to connect with the family in support of the child's learning.

Application 2: Fill in the Blanks

Read the following statements and fill in the blanks with the best word or words to complete the sentence.

1) I am trying to memorize a long list of terms for my anatomy test, but when I test myself, I find that I remember the first and last words from the list. This is an example of the
   Serial Position Effect.

2) Since my short term memory can hold only 5 to 9 units of information, I try to combine the single units into larger units which is called _Part Learning_.

3) The term for my long-term memory for events connected to a particular time and place in my life is called _____

4) The long term memory that holds information for "how to do things" is called
   Procederal memory.

5) When I use NASA to remember National Aeronautic Space Administration, this is a good example of
   Acronim.

6) I just met my new, next- door neighbor and so that I can remember her name, I'm going to repeat it over and over again. This is called _____

7) To combat the serial position effect, I'm going to take the long list that I have to memorize and break it into several shorter lists. This is called _____

8) Sets of interconnected concepts and relationships in which long-term knowledge is held are called
   _____

9) As I follow my everyday sequence of events by walking to the College of Education, climbing the stairs, opening my office, getting my mail, answering my voice mail, and answering my email, I am reminded that "I'm just a character in the play of life"; following one of its

   _____

10) When you are able to play your computer games without hardly thinking about what you're doing because you've done it thousands of times, this is called _____

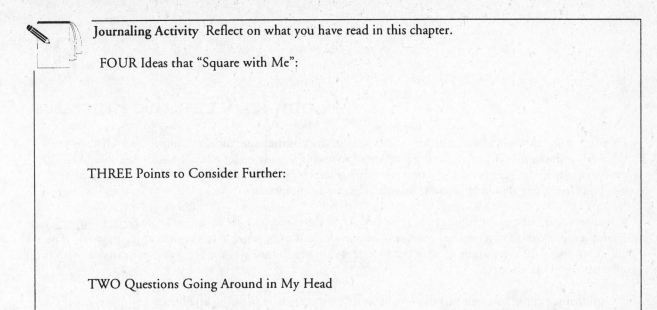

Journaling Activity Reflect on what you have read in this chapter.

FOUR Ideas that "Square with Me":

THREE Points to Consider Further:

TWO Questions Going Around in My Head

MY NOTES

(Use this space to make additional notes for this chapter)

8

Complex Cognitive Processes

Of great importance to all of us who are or will be educators, is that our students comprehend what we teach them beyond rote memorization for the purpose of achieving a grade on an exam. Ideally, they should be able to understand and remember information to routinely apply it outside of the school setting. This involves a good understanding of **concepts** and relationships among concepts.

Concept: A general category of ideas, objects, people, or experiences whose members share certain properties. **Example:** An example of a concept is a *bird*. Concepts help us to organize vast amounts of information. There are many, many different kinds of birds but by categorizing birds into 10 or more groups we can deal with the diversity within this concept.

Traditionally, people have believed that members of a concept share **defining attributes**.
Defining Attributes: Distinctive features shared by members of a category. **Example:** A defining attribute for the concept *bird* might be that they all have wings.

When teaching students about concepts you will generally help them to understand the concepts by giving them the example of a **prototype**.

Prototype: Best representative of a category. **Example:** For the concept *bird,* the best representative may be a "robin".

Another way to explain concept learning is to identify members of a category by referring to its **exemplars**.

Exemplars: A specific example or memory of a given category that is used to classify an item. **Example:** You may have an exemplar of a swimming pool, like the one in your backyard, against which you make comparisons of any other swimming pools you will encounter.

Prototypes are probably built from experiences with many exemplars. Eventually, all of the memories of every swimming pool you have ever encountered will blend together over time creating the swimming pool exemplar. We also recognize concepts through our schematic knowledge attached to that concept. We may have schemes that say "swimming pools can be indoors/outdoors, above ground/below ground, inflatable, plastic, concrete, etc."

STRATEGIES FOR TEACHING CONCEPTS

Concept-Attainment Lesson
Whereas children most readily learn about concepts on the basis of best examples and defining attributes, teaching of concepts utilizes both of these through hypothesis testing. To teach a concept you will need the following four components:
- name of the concept
- definition of the concept
- examples and non-examples (to set the boundaries, e.g. a bat is not a bird)
- relevant and irrelevant attributes

Furthermore, whenever you are teaching concepts, you will achieve greater success when. you can graphically represent the concept which you are trying to teach. See Application One for an example of how this works.

Start your lesson with a prototype to help students establish the category. Along with a definition include less typical examples to prevent **undergeneralization** and nonexamples to prevent overgeneralization.

Undergeneralization: Exclusion of a true member of a category; limiting a category. **Example:** Some students may not think to include "ostrich" within the concept of *bird* since ostriches can't fly.

Overgeneralization: Inclusion of nonmembers in a category; overextending a concept. **Example:** Some students may think a "bat" is a *bird* since it has wings and can fly.

As students examine examples and non-examples (positive and negative instances) they should be forming hypotheses about the concepts much as you did in the exercise in Application One. Ask your students to reflect on their problem solving processes and document their findings. This will help to develop their metacognitive strategies. A useful strategy for students above the primary grades is **concept mapping**.

Concept Mapping: Student's diagram of his or her understanding of a concept.

Teaching Concepts through Discovery

Jerome Bruner's work examined instructional approaches designed to promote concept learning with an emphasis on activity and inductive reasoning in learning. According to Bruner, students will learn the most when they focus on the subject structure and coding system of the area under study. Bruner suggests that students must be active in order to grasp the subject structure and they must identify key principles for themselves rather than blindly accept teachers' explanations. This can be accomplished through discovery learning.

Subject Structure: According to Bruner, the fundamental framework of ideas, the essential information.

Coding System: A hierarchy of ideas or concepts.

Discovery Learning: Bruner's approach, in which students work on their own to discover basic principles. **Example:** Some of my students employed a lesson in discovery learning to help kindergarten children learn their secondary colors. See the description of the lesson below.

> "My students wanted a group of kindergarten children to discover for themselves which primary colors combined to make the secondary colors. The K children already knew their primary colors; red, yellow, and blue. Here is where the fun began. My students went into the classroom dressed as clowns with multi-colored clown wigs and costumes. Using themselves as color models, they asked the K children to identify each color by pointing to their own costumes and wigs. Having established that the children knew the primary colors, my students brought forth a number of flasks containing colored water; red, blue, and yellow. They placed empty flasks on a table and while the K students observed, combined red and blue water into an empty flask and asked the children if they could tell them what was happening. The children shouted out their observations, "Red and blue make purple! ". The children then took over the lesson, experimenting with combinations and recording their data via a color chart in which, for example, a yellow piece of paper and a red piece of paper were placed and made to equal an orange piece of paper. The children continued in this fashion until they had completed a color chart with all of the combinations they had observed. They were very proud of their discoveries and the lesson ended with all of the children decorating iced cupcakes with varying combinations of colored sugar. Their learning was fun and rewarding!"

In a discovery lesson, the teacher provides examples and the students work with these examples to "discover" the underlying principles and rules. This type of reasoning is known as inductive reasoning and as it is sometimes called, Eg-Rule Method. This method requires intuitive thinking on the part of students.

Inductive Reasoning: Formulating general principles based on knowledge of examples and details.

Eg- Rule Method: Teaching or learning by moving from specific examples to general rules.

Intuitive Thinking: Making imaginative leaps to correct perceptions or workable solutions.

Unfortunately, traditional education often discourages intuitive thinking tending more toward coming up with one correct answer, safe and uncreative. Whereas, in Bruner's discovery learning the teacher organizes the classroom so that students can make intuitive guesses and discoveries, sometimes this may occur within too haphazard a situation. When more guidance and structure is required for learning to take place, **guided discovery** would be more appropriate.

Guided Discovery: An adaptation of discovery learning, in which the teacher provides some direction. **Example:** The "color" lesson on the previous page is a good example of guided discovery.

Teaching Concepts through Exposition

Whereas there are many advantages to discovery learning, it is not appropriate for every situation. For example, how long do you think it would take you to "discover" the theory of relativity? Some topics can be learned more efficiently and much quicker when they are taught directly which brings us to Ausubel's theory of **Expository Teaching/Reception Learning.** According to Ausubel (see also Figure 8.1) people acquire knowledge through reception rather than through discovery. By reception, Ausubel does not mean rote memorization but rather the connection of information, ideas, and the relationships among ideas through meaningful verbal learning. Exposition is taken to mean explanation and presentation of materials in a carefully organized, sequenced, and usable form. This type of learning relies upon deductive reasoning and is sometimes called the Rule-eg method.

Expository Teaching: Ausubel's method-teachers present material in complete, organized form, moving from the broadest to the most specific concepts.

Meaningful Verbal Learning: Focused and organized relationships among ideas and verbal information.

Deductive Reasoning: Drawing conclusions by applying rules or principles; logically moving from a general rule or principle to a specific solution.

Rule-Eg Method: Teaching or learning by moving from general principles to specific examples.

The best learning occurs when there is a connection between what the student already knows and the material to be learned. To help accomplish this, always begin a lesson with an **advance organizer.**

Advance Organizer: Statement of inclusive concepts to introduce and sum up material that follows.

Stop, Think, Write: Create a visual organizer that shows your own knowledge of the concept of "advance organizers".

As with any type of teaching, expository methods work better in some situations than in others. This approach works best when one wants to teach about the relationships between concepts and of course, students must have working knowledge of the concepts in the first place. It is also more effective for students in later elementary grades and beyond.

Figure 8.1

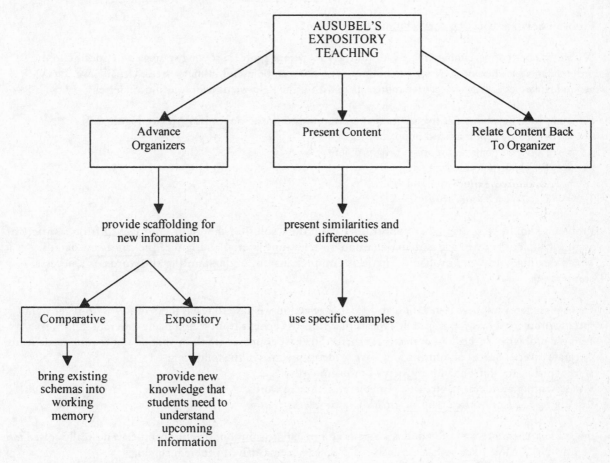

Reaching Every Student: Learning Disabilities and Concept Teaching

A recent approach to teaching conepts that also emphasizes connections with prior knowledge is called **analogical instruction** (Bulgren, Deshler, Schumaker, & Lenz, 2000). This approach has proved helpful for teaching scientific or cultural knowledge in heterogeneous secondary classes that include students who are less academically prepared and students with learning disabilities. The goal of analogical instruction is to identify knowledge that these students already have in memory that can e used as a starting point for learning the new, comples material. Analogies have long been used in problem solving, but until recently, studies of analogies in teaching content have been rare.

PROBLEM SOLVING

Now, more than ever, in our age of rapidly changing information and technological advances, it becomes crucial that educational programs produce students who are capable of solving problems, versus memorizing static information. Students who are taught to be **effective problem solvers** will be better prepared for the world of the future.

Problem: Any situation in which you are trying to reach some goal and must find a means to do so.

Problem Solving: Creating new solutions for problems.

Within the field of psychology there is dispute as to whether problem solving strategies are specific to the problem area or whether there are general strategies that can be useful in many areas. Usually, we start with general strategies and as we become more expert within the field we develop specific strategies.

General problem solving has five stages that correspond to the acronym IDEAL (see Figure 8.2)
- I *Identify* problems and opportunities
- D *Define* goals and represent the problem
- E *Explore* possible strategies
- A *Anticipate* outcomes and Act
- L *Look* back and *Learn*

Problems should be presented as opportunities and their solution should be approached from a variety of angles. Help students to **focus their attention** on relevant material and ignore the irrelevant details. When dealing with word problems linguistic comprehension, **understanding the words**, is a necessary component.

To help students improve **translation and schema selection** we have to teach them to move from general to specific problem solving strategies. It appears that students benefit from seeing many different kinds of example problems worked out correctly for them. The best examples are those that do not require students to integrate several sources of information. Give students practice in the following:
- recognizing and categorizing a variety of problem types
- representing problems in pictures, symbols, graphs or in words
- selecting relevant or irrelevant information in problems

If a student encounters a problem that suggests an immediate solution, they probably haven't really solved a new problem. More likely, what has occurred is called **schema-driven problem solving**.
Schema-Driven Problem Solving: Recognizing a problem as a "disguised" version of an old problem for which one already has a solution.

Exploring Possible Solution Strategies

If you do not have an immediate solution that comes to mind, then you must employ one of two procedures; **algorithms or heuristics.**

Algorithms: Step-by-step procedure for solving a problem; prescription for solutions. Example: 2 X 3 + 5=K would yield a very different answer from 2 X (3+5) =K. You have to know the rules for multiplication.

Heuristics: General strategy used in attempting to solve problems. Several heuristics are listed below.

- **Means-Ends Analysis:** Heuristic in which goal is divided into subgoals and then a means for solving each subgoal is figured out. **Example:** A semester long project could be divided into step-by-step components, each completed by the end of every week, building toward the final goal.
- **Working Backward Strategy:** Heuristic in which one starts with the goal and moves backward to solve the problem. **Example:** Start with the final goal of the semester long project, and working backwards, figure out when each aspect of the project should be completed.
- **Analogical Thinking:** Heuristic in which one limits the search for solutions to situations that are similar to the one at hand. **Example:** The person who invented Velcro found his particular solution in nature, in the burrs that attach themselves to your socks as you walk through the woods.

Another strategy that will aid in the problem solving process is **verbalization.**

Verbalization: Putting your problem solving plan into words and giving reasons for selecting it.

FACTORS THAT HINDER PROBLEM SOLVING

People often fail to solve problems because they seldom consider unconventional uses for materials that have a specific function. This is called **functional fixedness.** Another impediment to solving problems is **response set.**

Functional Fixedness: Inability to use objects or tools in a new way. **Example:** Unable to extract my computer disk from my lap top, I called a friend who said I needed a Mac disk extraction tool to put into the little hole above the disk slot. Stating that I didn't own one of those, he laughed and said it was nothing more than a straightened out paper clip. He was NOT suffering from functional fixedness.

Response Set: Rigidity; tendency to respond in the most familiar way.

Both response set and functional fixedness prevent us from looking at problems divergently, or from many different angles. Opening your mind to divergent thought processes might lead to what Gestaltists call **insight.**

Insight: Sudden realization of a solution. **Example:** A boy lost his airplane in the tree. He jumped up try reach it in the branch but was a bit too short. He shook the tree. It didn't budge. He stared down at the ground and noticed fallen branches lying at his feet. "Aha," he thought. He picked up a branch and used it to knock his shuttlecock out of the tree.

EFFECTIVE PROBLEM SOLVING: WHAT DO THE EXPERTS DO?

You might wonder what it is that experts possess that enables them to be such effective problem solvers. We know that experts possess certain abilities that beginners or novices lack.

- Experts generally possess a great deal of knowledge about the subject area and have many schemas available (domain knowledge).
- Experts can also recognize the patterns needed to solve a problem very quickly
- Experts also have a large store of productions or condition-action schemas so they know what action to take in various conditions
- Understanding the problem and choosing the solution happen almost simultaneously
- Experts' knowledge is elaborated, well-practiced, and organized to make for easy retrieval
- Experts plan out solutions and monitor progress

Expert teachers also possess skills that set them apart from novice teachers. Expert teachers have automatic teaching routines, they work from integrated sets of principles, they look for patterns revealing similarities, they focus on analyzing problems and mentally applying different principles to develop solutions. Expert teachers are expert problem solvers because they can meet the needs of their students by figuring out the best way to clear their confusion and help them to expand upon what they know. Expert teachers also must be able to analyze students' misconceptions and inaccuracies so that students don't develop misleading representations of problems. Sometimes students must be taught to "unlearn" common sense ideas. For people to change basic concepts:

- They must be dissatisfied with the current concept
- They must understand the new concept
- The new concept must be plausible
- The new concept must be seen as useful

Figure 8.2

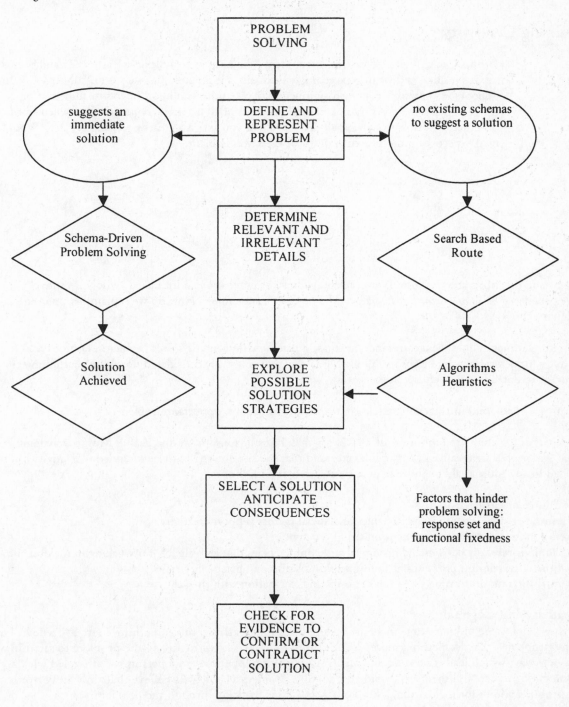

Creativity and Creative Problem Solving

Defining Creativity

> **Stop, Think, Write:** Consider this student. He has severe dyslexia-a learning disability that makes reading and writing exceedingly difficult. He describes himself as an "underdog." In school, he knows if a reading assignment will take others an hour, he has to allow two or three hours. He knows that he has to keep a list of all his most frequently misspelled words in order to be able to write at all. As a teacher, you assign a creative writing project. Would you expect the project he turns in to be creative? Explain.

The person described above is John Irving, celebrated author of what one critic called "wildly inventive" novels such as *The World According to Garp,* and *The Cider House Rules.* How do we explain his amazing creativity?

Howard Gardner defines the creative individual as "a person who regularly solves problems, fashions products, or defines new questions in a domain in a way that is initially considered novel but that ultimately becomes accepted in a particular cultural setting."

Creativity, talent, and intelligence are related; they allow us to solve important problems.

Creativity is the ability to produce work that is original, but still appropriate and useful. Most psychologists agree that people are creative in a particular area and that the "invention" must be intended. Creativity can be applied to any subject, although we frequently associate it with the arts.

The Source of Creativity
Both **intrapersonal** (cognition, personality) and **social factors** support creativity.
Teresa Amabile's three –component model of creativity:
1. **Domain-relevant skills** including talents and competencies that are valuable for working in the domain.
2. **Creativity-relevant processes** including working habits and personality traits.
3. **Intrinsic task motivation** or a deep curiosity and fascination with the task.

Creativity and Cognition
Having a rich store of knowledge in an area is the basis for creativity, but something more is needed. For many problems, that "something more" is the ability to break set-restructuring the problem to see things in a new way, which leads to a sudden insight. Often this happens when a person has struggled with a problem or project, and then sets it aside for a while. Some psychologists believe that time away from the problem allows for incubation, a kind of unconscious working through the problem.

Stop, Think, Write: Think of a problem or project that has presented an obstacle for you. How were you able to solve it? In what way was your solution creative? Did it require some time away from the problem or project for you to see clearly to the solution? When did the flash of insight come to you? Were you sleeping, daydreaming, or perhaps driving to school or work? What implications for the classroom can you draw from this experience?

Stop, Think, Write: How might you, as a teacher, take advantage of a multicultural classroom to nurture creativity among all your students?

Assessing Creativity

Stop, Think, Write: How many uses can you list for a brick?

Divergent thinking: The ability to propose many different ideas or answers.

Convergent thinking: The more common ability to identify only one answer.

E.P. Torrance developed two types of creativity tests-verbal **and** graphic:

Responses to all tasks are scored for:
- **Originality**-determined statistically (to be determined original, answer must be given by fewer than 5 or 10 people out of 100 who take the test.)
- **Fluency**- measured by the number of different responses.
- **Flexibility**- measured by the number of different categories of response.
- Fluency is the best predictor of divergent thinking.

Teachers are not always the best judges of creativity, in fact one report indicated no relationship between teachers' judgments of their students' creative abilities and the actual creativity these students revealed in their adult lives.

Stop, Think, Write: List a few possible indicators of creativity in your students:

Creativity in the Classroom

Teachers are in an excellent position to encourage or discourage creativity through their acceptance or rejection of the unusual and imaginative. In addition to encouraging creativity through everyday interaction with students, teachers can try **brainstorming.**

Brainstorming: Generating ideas without stopping to evaluate them.

The basic tenet of brainstorming is to separate the process of creating ideas from the process of evaluating them because evaluation often inhibits creativity.

Rules for Brainstorming
* Defer judgment.
* Avoid ownership of ideas.
* Feel free to "hitchhike" on other ideas.
* Encourage wild ideas.

The Big C: Revolutionary Innovation

Do you remember the children in Terman's study of giftedness described in Chapter 4? These students all had IQ scores over 140 and grew up to be experts and high-achieving professionals-but they did not innovate. They did not establish a new field or revolutionize an old one but rather mastered well-established domains. Innovators often are rebellious, restless, dissatisfied, courageous, and independent.

Parents and teachers can do much to encourage potential creators and unwittingly can discourage them as well. **Four dangers to avoid:**
* Avoid pushing so hard that a child's intrinsic passion to master a field becomes a craving for extrinsic rewards.
* Avoid pushing so hard that the child later looks back on a missed childhood.
* Avoid freezing the child into a safe, technically perfect way of performing.
* Be aware of the psychological wounds that can follow when a child that performed perfectly becomes the forgotten adult who can continue to perform perfectly-without ever creating something new.

Becoming an Expert Student: Learning Strategies and Study Skills

Key to becoming an expert and accomplishing learning goals are **learning strategies and learning tactics.** Your use of these strategies and tactics reflects your metacognitive knowledge. Teaching these skills to students has become a top priority in education and some important principles for accomplishing these goals are outlined below the following definitions.

Learning Strategies: General plans for approaching learning tasks.

Learning Tactics: Specific techniques for learning, such as using mnemonics or outlining a passage.
* expose students to a number of very *specific strategies and tactics*
* teach *conditional knowledge* about when, where, and why to use various strategies
* *motivate* students to *use the strategies they have learned*
* *direct instruction* to ensure that students have the *appropriate schemas* for making sense of the material

The following **strategies should be taught** to students because all too often we assume that students automatically know how to effectively employ these tactics when they don't.
- how to find the **central idea**
- how to **summarize** the material
- **underlining and highlighting**-key phrases and important topics
- **taking notes**- to focus attention on important ideas
- **visual tools**-graphic organizers and mapping to comprehend relationships
- **READS** - a reading strategy used in later elementary grades: **Review, Examine, Ask, Do it, Summarize.**
- **PQ4R** a method for studying text that involves six steps: **Preview, Question, Read, Reflect, Recite, Review.** This is similar to READS.
- **CAPS** - a literature reading strategy: Who are the *Characters,* What is the *Aim* of the story, What *Problem* happens, How is it *Solved?*
- **KWL**- a stategy to guide reading and general inquiry: What do I *Know* about this subject, What do I *Want* to know, At the end what have I *Learned?*

Application 1: Learning Tactics-What Should You Do?
Read the following statements and decide whether they accurately reflect what the experts know about their usage by writing "True" or "False" before each statement. Check your responses in the answer key.
1. _____ Students never seem to underline or highlight enough material.
2. _____ Limiting how much students underline to three sentences per paragraph improves their learning.
3. _____ Note taking during class helps to encode it into long term memory.
4. _____ Note taking aids learning even when students don't review them before a test.
5. _____ Note taking may distract you from actually listening to and making sense of the lecture.
6. _____ To record key ideas in your own words, you must translate, connect, elaborate, and organize.
7. _____ The use of graphic organizers and mapping is not as effective as underlining or highlighting.
8. _____ The "P" in PQ4R, stands for "Problem solving".
9. _____ The PQ4R method is most appropriate for children before **fifth** grade when they need to establish study skills.
10._____The use of PQ4R forces students to engage in distributed practice.
11. ___ KWL can be used with most grade levels.
12. ___ The "C" in the CAPS model stands for "comprehensive."

Applying Learning Strategies

Assuming students have a repertoire of powerful learning strategies, several conditions must be met in order for them to use them.
- The learning task must be appropriate.
- Students must care about learnin g and understanding.
- The student must believe the effort and investment required to apply the strategies are reasonable, given the likely return.

TEACHING FOR TRANSFER

Transfer: Influence of previously learned material on new material. **Example:** Now that I know how to drive a car with a standard transmission (four on the floor) I will be able to drive my boyfriend's truck which is also standard but has three on the column. **Two kinds of transfer are called low-road and high-road transfer.**

Low-Road Transfer: Spontaneous and automatic transfer of highly practiced skills, with little need for reflective thinking. **Example:** I can move from one computer to another with relative ease because I have experience working with both Macs and IBMs.

High-Road Transfer: Application of abstract knowledge learned in one situation to a different situation. **Example:** In a study I conducted, I trained individuals to improve their performance on a spatial task. At a later date, I gave them a different spatial task and their performances revealed that spatial skills had transferred from one task to another.

Unfortunately, learning does not always transfer because learning occurs in specific situations and students may not always transfer their learning from one situation to another. Greater transfer will occur if students are provided with the opportunities for **overlearning.**

Positive transfer is encouraged when skills are used under conditions similar to those that will exist when the skills are needed later.

Overlearning: Practicing a task past the point of mastery to combat forgetting and improve transfer. **Example:** You have overlearned how to ride a bike so well that you will never forget how and you can probably ride any bike that you encounter (as long as it has two wheels).

> **Stop, Think, Write:** What principles do you anticipate teaching that could be expected to have general transfer?

Diversity and Convergences in Complex Cognitive Processes

This chapter has covered quite a bit of territory, partly because the cognitive perspective has so many implications for instruction. Although they are varied, you can see that most of the cognitive ideas for teaching concepts, creative problem-solving skills, and leanring strategies emphasize the role of the student's prior knowledge and the need for active, mindful learning.

Diversity
Concept learning, problem solving, and strategy-learning processes may be similar for all students, but the prior knowledge, beliefs, and skills they bring to the classroom are bound to vary, based on their experience and culture.

Creativity and Diversity
Even though creativity has been studied for centuries, as Dean Simonton said, "Psychologists still have a long way to go before they come anywhere close to understanding creativity in women and minorities" (2000, p. 156.) The focus of creativity research and writing over the years has been white males. Patterns of creativity in other groups are complex-sometimes matching and sometimes diverging from patterns found in trditional research.

Convergences
As students learn problem solving or try to transfer cognitive tools to new situations, there is a tendency to focus on surface features. For all novices, their challenge is to grasp the abstractions: underllyng principles, structures, strategies or big ideas. It is those larger ideas that lead to understanding and serve as a foundation for future learning (Chen & Mo, 2004).

Journaling Activity Reflect on what you have read in this chapter.

FOUR Ideas that "Square with Me":

THREE Points to Consider Further:

TWO Questions Going Around in My Head

MY NOTES

(Use this space to make additional notes for this chapter)

9

Social Cognitive and Constructivist Views of Learning

Stop, Think, Write: List three things you, as a teacher, intend to model for students. What specifically, will you do to model each thing?

1.

2.

3.

How will you communicate to students the importance of each of these things? Will you simply model the behavior or will you connect your modeling with specific instructions regarding the behavior you hope students will copy? Explain.

SOCIAL COGNITIVE THEORY

In the early 1960's, Albert Bandura demonstrated that people can learn by observing the actions and consequences of others. Bandura's **social learning theory** emphasized observation, modeling, and vicarious reinforcement. Over time, Bandura's explanations of learning included more attention to cognitive factors such as expectations and beliefs in addition to the social influences of moelds. His curent perspective is called **social cognitive theory.**

In social cognitive theory, both internal and external factors are important. Environmental events, personal factors, and behaviors are seen as interacting in the process of learning. The unfolding of events often determine the outcomes of the interaction. Bandura said that whether we demonstrate what we know depends in part on environmental situations and **reciprocal determinism.**

Reciprocal Determinism: the constant interaction of personal factors, behaviors, and the environment in explaining human functioning. An explanation of behavior that emphasizes the mutual effects of the individual and the environment on each other. **Example:** A 13-year-old girl may know all of the answers in science class but may not volunteer any answers because she likes a boy in the class and doesn't want to appear "too smart".

Self-Efficacy

Self Efficacy: Our believes about our personal competence or effectiveness *in a given area*. Banduara (1997) defines self-efficacy as "beliefs in one's capabilities to organize and execute the courses of action required to produce given attainments" (p.3).

Self-Efficacy, Self-Concept, and Self-Esteem

Most people assume self-efficacy is the same as self-concept or self-esteem, but it isn't. **Self-efficacy** is future-oriented, "a context-specific assessment of competence to perform a specific task" (Pajares, 1997, p. 15). **Self-concept** is a more global construct that contains many perceptions about the self, includig self-efficacy. Selfpconcept is developed as a result of external and internal comparisons, using other people or other aspects of the self as frames of reference. Compared to self-esteem, self-efficacy is concerned with judgments of personal capabilities; **self-esteem** is concerned with judgments of self-worth.

Sources of Self-Efficacy

Bandura's Four Sources of Efficacy Expectations:

Mastery Experiences: our own direct experiences. Success raises efficacy, failure lowers efficacy
Arousal: Anxiety lowers efficacy but excitement enhances efficacy
Vicarious Experiences: accomplishments by a model with whom the student identifies, increases self-efficacy
Social Persuasion: Encouraging "pep talks" or specific performance feedback, can help to boost self-efficacy

Our own past experiences are the most powerful determinants of self-efficacy. If we have high self-efficacy in a given area, we will set higher goals, be less afraid of failure, and persist longer when we encounter difficulties. If self-efficacy is low, we may avoid a task altogether or give up easily when problems arise.

Self Efficacy and Motivation

Research indicates that performance in school is improved and self-efficacy is increased when students

- Adopt short-term goals so it is easier to judge progress
- Are taught to use specific learning strategies such as outlining or summarizing that help them focus attention
- Receive rewards based on achievement, not just engagement, because achievement rewards signal increasing competence

Teacher's Sense of Efficacy: a teacher's belief that he or she can reach even difficult students to help them learn.

Self-efficacy theory predics that tachers with a high sense of efficacy work harder and persist longer even when students are difficult to teach, in part because these teachers believe in themselves and in their students. Also, they are less likely to experience burn-out (Fives, Hamman, & Olivarez, 2005).

Self-Regulated Learners

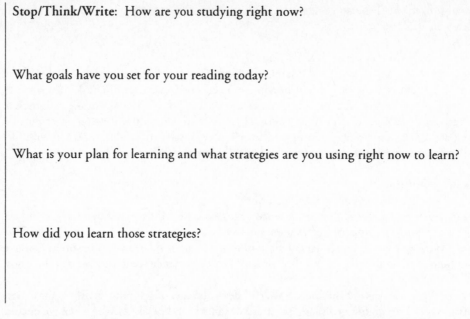

Stop/Think/Write: How are you studying right now?

What goals have you set for your reading today?

What is your plan for learning and what strategies are you using right now to learn?

How did you learn those strategies?

Barry Zimmerman (2002) defines **self-regulation** as the process we use to activate and sustain our thoughts, behaviors, and emotions in order to reach our goals. When the goals involve learning, we talk about self-regulated learning. Self-regulated learners have a combination of academic learning skills and self control that makes learning easier, so they are more motivated, in other words, they have the *skill* and the *will* to learn.

The concept of self-regulated learning integrates much of what is known about effective learning and motivation. Three factors influence skill and will: knowledge, motivation, and self-discipline or volition.

To be self-regulated learners, students need knowledge about themselves, the subject, the task, strategies for learning, and the contexts in which they will apply their learning.

Self regulated learners:
- know themselves. They know their preferred learning styles, what is easy and difficult for them, how to cope with the difficult parts, what their interests and talents are, and how to use their strengths.
- know the subject. They know quite a bit about the subject being studied-and the more they know, the easier it is to learn more.
- know that different learning tasks require different learning strategies.
- can apply the appropriate strategy to the learning task at hand.
- think about the contexts in which they will apply their knowledge-when and where they will use their learning.

Self-regulated learners are motivated to learn (see Chapter 10). They find school interesting because they value learning, not just performing well in the eyes of others. They know why they are studying, so their actions and choices are self-determined and not controlled by others.

Self-regulated learners need volition or self-discipline. Volition is an old-fashioned word for will power. Self-regulated learners know how to protect themselves from distractions and how to cope when they feel anxious, drowsy, or lazy.

Family Influences. Children begin to learn self-regulation in their homes. Parents can teach and support self-regulated learning through modeling, encouragement, facilitation, and rewarding of goal setting. The

Family and Community Partnership Guidelines give some ideas for working with parents to help students become more self-regulating.

Volition: Will power; self-discipline; work styles that portect opportunities to reach goals by applying self-regulated learning.

Self-regulation: Process of activating and sustaining thoughts, behaviors, and emotions in order to reach goals.

Self-regulated learning: A view of lerning as skills and will applied to analyzing learning tasks, setting goals, and planning how to do the task, applying skills and expecially making adjustments about how learning is carried out.

Agency: The capacity to coordinate learning skills, motivation, and emotions to reach your goals.

Teaching Toward Self-Efficacy and Self-Regulated Learning

Most teachers agree that students need to develop skills and attitudes for independent, life-long learning (self-regulated learning and a sense of efficacy for learning). Fortunately, there is a growing body of research that offers guidance about how to design tasks and structure classroom interactions to support stuents' development of and engagement in self-regulated learning. This research indicates that studens develop academcially effective forms of selfregulaed learning (SRL) and a sense of efficacy for learning when teachers:

- involve students in **complex meaningful tasks** that extend over long periods of time.
- allow students to have some **control** over their learning learning processes and products
- establish non-threatening **self-evaluation** processes
- and finally, provide opportunities for students to work **collaboratively.**

STOP/THINK/WRITE

Use the space below to list of some ways that you would feel comfortable involving the families of your students in supporting self-regulated learning.

How can you increase your comfort level to add more methods to your list?

Which of the suggestions listed on the website (in the "Action Options" section) do you believe are most viable?

How will you communicate with parents regarding the importance of self-regulation?

What types of record keeping forms (goal or incentive charts, time-management logs, to-do lists, evening homework appointments, etc) could you share with parents that would be appropriate for your grade level/content area?

CONSTRUCTIVIST'S VIEWS OF LEARNING

Two positions that examine the dynamic interchanges between the learner and the environment are the **constructivist perspective** and **situated learning**. Constructivist approaches are gaining in popularity across all academic subject areas. Definitions may vary but in general, **responsibility is placed within the students for constructing their knowledge.**

Constructivist Approaches: View that emphasizes the active role of the learner in building understanding and making sense of information.
- **Psychological/Individual Constructivism:** focuses on individual knowledge, beliefs, self-concept, or identity. Most interested in meaning as constructed by the individual.
- **Social Constructivism:** focuses on social interactions and the cultural context to explain learning
- Sociological Constructivism (**Constructivists**): concerned with how academic knowledge, common-sense ideas, everyday beliefs, and commonly held understandings about the world are communicated to new members of a sociocultural group.

A question that cuts across all constructivist perspectives is whether knowledge that is constructed can be generalized and transferred to other situations or is it bound to the context in which it was constructed? This question addresses **situated learning.**

Situated Learning: Enculturation or adopting the norms, behaviors, skills, beliefs, language, and attitudes of a particular community. Learning in the real world is not like studying in school. Much of what is learned is specific to the situation in which it was learned. The implications are that students should learn skills and knowledge in meaningful contexts, with **connections to real-life situations in which the knowledge and skills will be useful.**

Central to constructivist approaches are the **following themes:**
- **Complex Learning Environments:** Problems and learning situations that mimic the ill-structured nature of real life. Don't give students stripped down unrealistic problems but try to provide them with authentic tasks and activities similar to what they will encounter in the real world.
- **Social Negotiation:** Aspect of learning process that relies on collaboration with others and respect for different perspectives. Students must be able to talk and listen to each other. This is premised on the intersubjective attitude or commitment to build shared meaning by finding a common ground.
- **Multiple Representations of Content:** Considering various problems using various analogies, examples, and metaphors, consistent with spiral curriculums or revisiting the same subjects at progressive stages of development.
- **Understanding that knowledge is constructed:** Understanding that different assumptions and different experiences lead to different knowledge with an awareness that different influences shape our thinking.
- **Student-Centered Instruction:** Student actively assumes responsibility for his/her learning.

APPLYING CONSTRUCTIVIST PERSPECTIVES

Although **inquiry learning** is an offshoot of the constructivist approach, Dewey conceptualized this approach as early as 1910.

Inquiry Learning: Approach in which the teacher presents a puzzling situation and students solve the problem by gathering data and testing their conclusions. Inquiry teaching allows students to learn process and content at the same time (much as in the above example). **Key components** to this approach are:
- formulate hypotheses to explain the event or solve the problem
- collect data to test the hypotheses
- draw conclusions
- reflect on the original problem and on the thinking processes needed to solve it

Another form of learning in which students employ inquiry methods is called **problem-based learning**. **Problem-Based Learning:** students are confronted with a real problem that has meaning for them; the student's actions matter.

Dialogue and Instructional Conversations

One implication of Vygotsky's theory of cognitive development is that important learning and understanding require interaction and conversation. Students need to grapple with problems in their zone of proximal development, and they need the scaffolding provided by interaction with a teacher or other students. "Scaffolding is a powerful conception of teaching and learning in which teachers and stuents create meaningful connections between teacher's cultural knowledge and the very day experience and knowledge of the student" (McCasline & Hickey, 2001,p.137)

Instuctional conversations-designed to promote learning, tbe teacher's goal is to keep everyone cognitvely engaged in a substantive discussion.

Cognitive Apprencticeships

Over the centuies, apprenticeships have proved to be an effective form of education. A cognitive apprenticeship in school focuses on cognitive objectives such as reading comprehension, writing, or mathematical problem solving. There are many **cognitive apprenticeship models**, but most share **six features:**

- Students **observe an expert** (usually the teacher) model the performance.
- Students get **external support** through coaching or tutoring.
- Students receive **conceptual scaffolding**.
- Students continually **articulate their knowledge**.
- Students **reflect on their progress**, comparing their problem solving to an expert's performance and to their own earlier performances.
- Students are required to **explore new ways** to apply what they are learning.

As they learn, students are challenged to master more complex concepts and skills and to perform them in many different settings.

Even under the best conditions when we have taught students what to learn, how to learn, how to study, and how to apply metacognitive skills, how do we teach them to think? Many programs have been developed for the direct teaching of thinking skills, called **Stand-Alone Thinking Skills Programs.**

Stand-Alone Thinking Skills Programs: Programs that teach thinking skills directly without the need for extensive subject matter knowledge. Students who have had trouble with the standard curriculum may experience success and enhanced self esteem with these programs but a disadvantage is that they may not be able to generalize these skills to specific subject areas.

Teachers can teach good thinking skills by modeling good thinking aloud, providing direct instruction about how to analyze causes, and giving the students practice and interaction in analyzing causes and effects. Many of these components can be found in methods that support critical thinking.

Critical Thinking: Evaluating conclusions by logically and systematically examining the problem, the evidence, and the solution.

Fostering Communities of Learners (FCL) is a system of interacting activites that results in a self-consciously active and reflective learning environment". This is an entire instructional program grounded in constructivist learning theories. This is a complex process of inquiry wth an emphasis on shared philosophy and principles, not procedures and steps.

Diversity and Convergences in Theories of Learning
Diversity
The power and value of diversity is part of the theoretical frameworks of social cognitive and constructivist theories of learning. Social cognitive theory describes the unique reciprocal interactions among personal, environmental, and behavioral factors that shape the individual's learning and motivation. Culture, social context, personal history, ethnicity, language, and racial identity-to name only a few factors-all shape personal characteristics such as knowledge and beliefs, environmental featurs such as resources and challenges, and behavioral actionas and choices.

Convergences
Rather than debating the merits of each approach to learning, consider their contributions to understanding learning and improving teaching. Different views of learning can be used together to create productive learning environments for the diverse students you will teach.

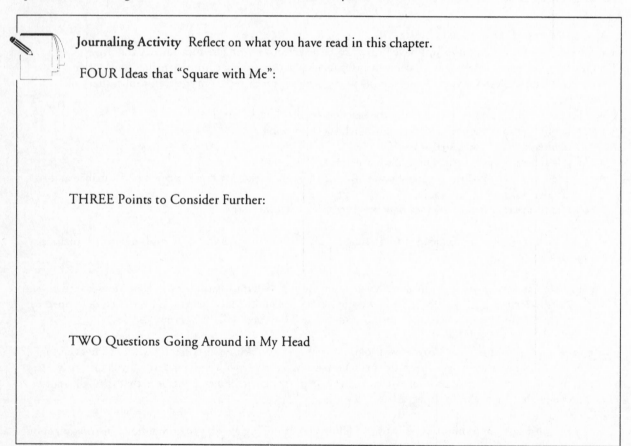

Journaling Activity Reflect on what you have read in this chapter.

FOUR Ideas that "Square with Me":

THREE Points to Consider Further:

TWO Questions Going Around in My Head

MY NOTES

(Use this space to make additional notes for this chapter)

10

Motivation in Learning and Teaching

One of the greatest challenges of your teaching career will be to motivate your students toward self-actualization, achievement, success, and love of learning. What is motivation?

Motivation: an internal state that arouses, directs, and maintains behavior.

Collaborative Activity

In your study group, brainstorm what you, as a teacher, could do to motivate your students:

Stop, Think, Write: Motivation is usually defined as *an internal state that arouses, directs, and maintains behavior.* Psychologists studying motivation have focused on five basic questions. Stop, Think, and Write the answers to the following questions regarding your own motivation to study.

What choices do you make about your behavior related to academic study?

How long does it take you to get started to study for an exam or begin a homework assignment?

What is the intensity or level of your involvement in studying for an exam or completing a class project?

What causes you to persist or to give up?

What are you thinking or feeling while engaged in study?

What is Motivation?

Motivation: is usually defined as an internal state that arouses, directs, and maintains behavior. Psychologists studying motivation have focused on five questions:

1. What choices do people make about their behavior?
2. How long does it take to get started?
3. What is the intensity or level of involvement in the chosen activity?
4. What causes a person to persist or give up?
5. What is the individual thinking and feeling while engaged in this activity?

Intrinsic and Extrinsic Motivation

Intrinsic Motivation: Motivation associated with activities that are their own reward. The source of motivation comes from within ourselves.

Intrinsic motivation is what drives us to do something when we really don't have to do anything (Raffini,1996). It certainly explains what drives us to do what we do in our free time. As educators, we would love to think that all of our students are intrinsically motivated to learn and that the source for the motivation comes from within, but realistically, we have to admit that many of our students would not put forth effort unless they were **extrinsically motivated.**

Extrinsic Motivation: Motivation created by external factors like rewards and punishments. The source of motivation comes from the environment. We are not really interested in the activity for its own sake but for what it will gain us. **Example:** Desiring an "A" motivates you to study. Desiring a paycheck, motivates you to show up to your job on time.

Looking at a behavior, it is very difficult to tell whether the behavior is intrinsically or extrinsically motivated. Once again, the difference between the two lies with whether or not the individual has an **internal or external locus of causality.**

Locus of Causality: The location-internal or external- of the cause of the behavior.

In school, both intrinsic and extrinsic motivation are important. Some subjects are intrinsically motivating to students but to expect that all subjects are equally interesting to all students is a bit unrealistic. To encourage our students to perform, sometimes we must rely on **rewards** and **incentives.**

Rewards: An attractive object or event supplied as a consequence of a behavior. **Example:** If you study real hard, you'll get an "A".

Incentive: An object or event that encourages or discourages a behavior. **Example:** If you arrive late to class without an excuse (at least a really good excuse) you'll be given a detention.

Four General Approaches to Motivation

Behavioral Approaches to Motivation: As you might anticipate, behavioralists look to the external environment for supplying the motivation to perform or not to perform. Incentives hold the promise of something good to be gained or punishments to be avoided, contingent upon behaviors. Rewards serve to maintain behaviors as getting an "A" will reinforce good study habits. To motivate students, we must acknowledge and reward their successes, and help them to see the personal gains of their learning.

Humanistic Approaches to Motivation: This approach to motivation emphasizes personal freedom, choice, self-determination, and striving for personal growth. Humanistic psychologists emphasize the role of needs in determining whether we are motivated to perform. According to the humanists, we are born with the natural tendency or need to strive to achieve to our fullest potentialities. To motivate students we must appeal to their affective domains-their sense of competence, self-esteem, autonomy, and self-actualization.

One of the most renowned humanistic theories was developed by **Maslow** and examines the role of needs in determining motivation. A need is defined as a state of deprivation that motivates a person to take action toward a goal, whether it be physiological, psychological, emotional, or intellectual needs. Maslow has suggested that humans have a **hierarchy of needs** that begins with the most basic needs for survival and culminates with the highest level needs for self-actualization.

Hierarchy of Needs: Maslow's model of seven levels of human needs, from basic physiological requirements to the need for self-actualization.

Self-Actualization: Fulfilling one's potential.

Maslow suggested that humans will sequentially fulfill their needs on each level before moving onto the next level. Maslow called the lower level needs deficiency needs and upper level needs, being needs. With **deficiency needs**, as each is fulfilled, the motivation to fulfill it, decreases. But with being needs, as the individual fulfills each level, the motivation supposedly increases. For instance, as a person's need for intellectual achievement is fulfilled, according to Maslow, the person will be even more motivated toward fulfilling the need for even further intellectual achievement.

Deficiency Needs: Maslow's four lower level needs, which must be satisfied first. Being Needs: Maslow's three higher-level needs, sometimes called growth needs.

*   Physiological Needs: sleep, thirst, hunger
*   Safety Needs freedom from danger, anxiety, and threat to psychological well-being
*   Love Needs acceptance from parents, teachers, peers, and significant others
*   Esteem Needs self-efficacy, competency, belief in one's abilities often validated by others
*   Intellectual Achievement Needs: need to understand and grow intellectually
*   Aesthetic Needs appreciation for culture, literature, music, the arts
*   Needs for Self-Actualization: attempt to realize personal potential, strive to become the best you can be.

Implications of Maslow's theory for the classroom are that before our students will be motivated to fulfill the need for intellectual achievement, their lower level needs must first be met. Students who come to school hurt, sick, distraught over parental divorce, abuse, homelessness, etc., will not be motivated to perform academically.

Cognitive Approaches to Motivation

Cognitivists believe that behavior is determined by our thinking; by goals, expectations, attributions, schemas and the desire to be competent, intellectually functioning individuals. People respond not to external events or physical conditions but rather to their interpretations of these events. In cognitive theories, people are born with intrinsic curiosity and motivation, seeking to problem solve as a form of adaptive behavior. To motivate students, we must stimulate their natural curiosity and support their beliefs about their abilities to succeed.

Application 1: Psychological Theories of Motivation
Read the following activities and for each one determine if it describes motivation from a Behavioral, Humanistic, Cognitive, or Expectancy X Value perspective. Check your responses in the answer key.

1) Becky has organized a study group for her physics class. In addition to wanting to enhance her understanding of physics, Becky wants to increase her social acceptance within her peer group because she is a transfer student and doesn't know anyone. _____

2) John has high expectations that someday he will become a lawyer. From past experience he knows he can present a good argument and he values his ability to engage in undefeatable verbal repartee. To further hone his skills, he decides to join the debating team. _____

3) Jenny is striving for good grades this semester because her father promised her a new car if she could bring all of her "Fs" up to "Cs". _____

4) Sarah wants to experience first hand how plant photosynthesis works and asked her teacher if she could do an experiment to improve her understanding of the process. _____

5) Fred has joined as many extra-curricular clubs as possible because he feels a strong need for affiliation due to the fact that his home-life is fraught with turmoil and abuse. _____

6) Samantha has a difficult time getting up in the morning so she purchased three alarm clocks and placed them all around her room because if she gets one more detention she's grounded.
_____

7) Cali greatly values her job working with marine animals and works hard to advance within the program because she expects to become a marine biologist. _____

8) Gary wants to learn how to operate a computer because he knows he will be able to access lots of valuable information about ecosystems from the internet and greatly improve his understanding.
_____

GOAL ORIENTATION AND MOTIVATION

In order for an individual to achieve, there must be the realistic setting of goals. Goals that are spedific, moderately difficult, and likely to be reached in the near future tend to enhance motivation and persistence (Pintrich & Schunk, 2002; Stipek, 2002)

In classrooms, there are four goal orientations: mastery (learning), performance (looking good), work-avoidance, and social.

Goal Orientations: Patterns of beliefs about goals related to achievement in school.

Mastery Goal: A personal intention to improve abilities and understand, no matter how performance suffers.

Performance Goal: A personal intention to seem competent or perform well in the eyes of others.

Task-involved Learners: Students who focus on mastering the task or solving the problem.

Ego-involved Learner: Students who focus on how well they are performing and how they are judged by others.

Feedback and Goal Acceptance

Two factors that influence effective goal setting in the classroom are *feedback* and goal *acceptance*. With feedback, you need accurate information as to "where you are" and how far you have to go. **Feedback** gives students valuable information about the success or failure of their efforts, whether they have achieved their goals, and how far to increase their goals for the future. Feedback is most effective when it emphasizes progress.

The second factor, **goal acceptance**, addresses the likelihood of students to adopt teacher generated goals or develop their own goals. If students adopt goals, it is likely that they will demonstrate higher motivation toward the task. Students are more likely to adopt goals that are clear, specific, reasonable, moderately challenging, and attainable within a relatively short amount of time.

INTERESTS AND EMOTIONS

Stop, Think, Write: Describe one method, not listed in your textbook, that you, as a teacher, might consider using to build student interest in lesson material.

Emotion plays a large role in determining memory and achievement. Students are more likely to **remember material related to their personal interests** as well as citing lack of interest in a topic as the highest rating as an explanation for failure. Interest was second only to effort as an explanation of success.

Arousal also explains performance and motivation. High arousal appears optimal for simple tasks and low arousal most beneficial for complex tasks. Teachers must work at keeping the level of arousal right for the task at hand so the learning situation is optimal even for students with high anxiety.

Arousal: Physical and psychological reactions causing a person to be alert, attentive, and wide awake.

Anxiety: General uneasiness, a sense of foreboding, a feeling of tension. **Example:** Many of us may experience anxiety before a presentation or an exam. Anxiety can be both a cause and an effect of school failure.

Stop, Think, Write: List one strategy that teachers can use to increase students' motivation for learning before, during, and after instruction.
Before:

During:

After:

SELF-SCHEMAS

Adults tend to use two basic concepts of ability, **entity view of ability** and the **incremental view of ability**.
Entity View of Ability: Belief that ability is a fixed characteristic that cannot be changed. This is the worst case scenario. Students believe failures are (1) due to internal locus (native ability), (2) stable and not subject to change, and (3) uncontrollable. These students generally possess low self-efficacy.

Incremental View of Ability: Belief that ability is a set of skills that can be changed. This is the best case scenario. Students believe successes are (1) due to internal locus (effort), (2) unstable and subject to change, and (3) controllable. Students who subscribe to the incremental view believe that their successes and failures are their own responsibility and that they have the power to influence the outcome. These students generally possess high self-efficacy.

Beliefs About Causes and Control: Attribution Theory

We would all like to understand the causes of our successes so that we can repeat what led to the successes and we want to understand the causes of our failures so that we can avoid them in the future. The study of perceived causes of successes and failures is **attribution theory.** (See Figure 10.1 on page 107 of this guide.)

Attribution Theory: Descriptions of how individuals' explanations, justifications, and excuses influence their motivation and behavior. **Example:** If I think I failed because I didn't study, I will probably be motivated to study in the future.

Weiner is one of the leading educational psychologists responsible for examining how attributions relate to school learning. He suggests that most of the causes to which students attribute their successes or failures can be categorized along three dimensions:
• locus: location of the cause internal or external to the person
• stability: whether the cause stays the same or can change
• responsibility: whether the person can control the cause

Weiner suggests that these dimensions are closely related to personal emotions and motivations.

1. locus (location of the cause internal or external to the person)
2. stability (whether the cause stays the same or can change)
3. controllability whether the perosn can control the cause)

Individuals who believe that they are responsible for their successes and failures have internal locus of control.

Locus of Control: : "Where" people locate responsibility for successes or failures-inside or outside of themselves.

Internal locus of control: These people believe they are responsible for their fate, possess good self-esteem, and like to work in situations in which skill and effort lead to success.

External locus of control: These people feel that other forces are in control of their lives, and prefer to work in situations where luck determines the outcome. Very often these individuals experience low self-esteem.

Legitimate peripheral participation: Genuine involvement in the work of the group, even if your abilities are undeveloped and contributions are small.

Sociocultural Conceptions of Motivation: View that motivation comes from identity through legitimate participation in group activities; engaged participation within a learning community. People engage in activities to maintain their identities and their interpersonal relations within the community.
Example: Brown and Campione developed learning communities from middle school students around research projects in science. Socialization moves from legitimate peripheral participation to central participation in that group.

Stop, Think, Write: Write a statement of internal attribution that you, as a teacher, could make to have a positive effect on student motivation.

Expectancy X Value Theories: Explanations of motivation that emphasize individual's expectations for success combined with their valuing of the goal.

While it is difficult to come up with an actual measure of motivation, this formula looks at motivation as a product of an individual's expectations for success times the value of achieving the goal. To motivate students, we must focus on helping them to set realistic goals and expectations and to value the outcomes of their learning.

Self-Efficacy and Learned Helplessness

Learned Helplessness: The expectation, based on previous experiences with a lack of control, that one's efforts will lead to failure. Students who feel helpless will be unmotivated and reluctant to put forth effort.

What are the connections between all of these factors? Covington and associates suggest that our attributions, beliefs about ability, self-efficacy, and self-worth combine to result in three types of motivational sets:

Beliefs about Self-Worth

- **Mastery Oriented Students:** Students who focus on learning goals because they value achievement and see ability as improvable. They'll take risks, perform best in competitive situations, learn fast, have more self-confidence and energy, are more aroused and not threatened by feedback. They experience persistent, successful learning.
- **Failure-Avoiding Students:** Students who avoid failure by sticking to what they know, by not taking risks, or by claiming not to care about their performance. They lack a strong sense of self-worth and their own competence separate from their performance. They have low self-efficacy. They may eventually become failure-accepting students.
- **Failure-Accepting Students:** Students who believe their failures are due to low ability and there is little they can do about it. They may become depressed, apathetic, and helpless. Teachers may be able to help failure avoiding students from becoming failure accepting students by helping them to find new and more realistic goals. Instead of pitying or excusing these students, teachers need to teach them how to learn and then hold them accountable.

Figure 10.1

ATTRIBUTION AND MOTIVATION

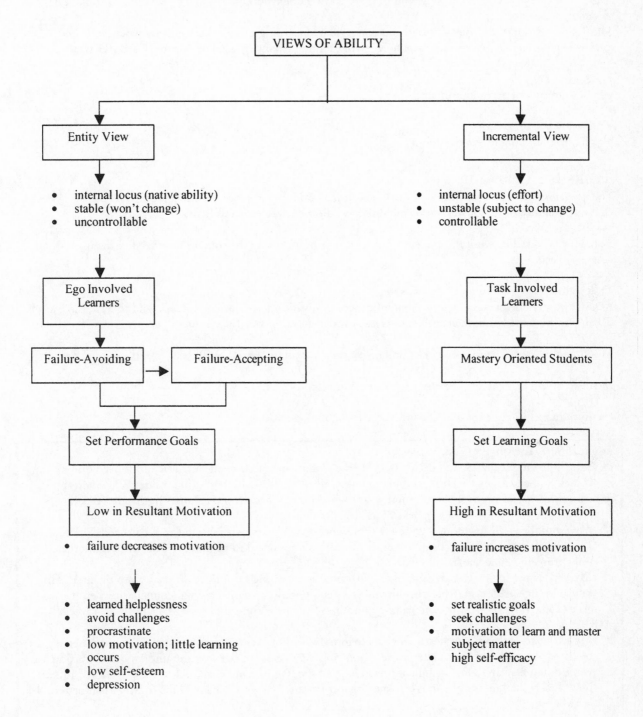

Motivation to Learn in School: ON TARGET

Aside from everything else that we would like to see our students do, most of all we would like to increase student motivation to learn.

The **TARGET** approach to motivation and self-regulated learning examines seven areas where teachers' actions may influence student motivation. We will examine separately each one of the **TARGET** areas:

- Task
- Autonomy
- Recognition of accomplishments
- Grouping practices
- Evaluation procedures
- Time scheduling in the classroom

Tasks for Learning

To understand how an **academic task** can affect students' motivation, we need to analyze the task. Tasks can be interesting or boring for students. And task have different values for students.

Academic Tasks: The work the student must accomplish, including the content covered and the mental operations required.

Task Value

As you know, value of the activity or task influences motivation to perform. Tasks are said to have three kinds of value to students; **attainment value**, interest or **intrinsic value**, or **utility value**.

Attainment value: The importance of doing well on a task; how success on the task meets personal needs.

Intrinsic or interest value: The enjoyment a person gets from a task.

Utility value: The contribution of a task to meeting one's goals.

Application 2: Identifying Task Value
Read the following scenarios and decide whether the activity has attainment, intrinsic, or utility value for the individual. Some tasks may have a combination of attainment, intrinsic, and utility value. When you think about it, these would probably be the most worth while tasks. Check your responses in the answer key.

1) My mom, Louise Mowrer, is a great cook. Her meals are always delicious and well-balanced. She cooks as an expression of love and caring for her family. She is considered to be a wonderful wife and mother. The only problem is that she hates cooking. _____

2) My dad, Phil Mowrer, is a dynamic, well-informed speaker. He exhibits many leadership qualities. He served in high administrative positions within his corporation, chaired church council, so when he was asked to be the President of their campground, in spite of the time and work obligations, he agreed.
_____

3) My backyard is sloped and nearly impossible to mow without rolling the lawn mower. I purchased a gas powered weed whacker as an alternative to mowing. My neighbor borrowed it and ran out of cutting line while doing his yard. He asked me if I had changed the line, (I hadn't) and asked me if I wanted to learn how. I really had no interest in it but knew that if I wanted to weed whack in the future, I had better learn how. _____

4) Cali Popiel was presented with the task of writing a poem in class. After receiving much positive feedback in response to her poetry it was submitted for publication and published in the local newspaper. Recognizing her efforts, her teacher hung the newspaper article in the classroom.
_____

---

5) As an experienced middle-school instructor, Mitch Klett was asked to respond to a classroom situation in the *Instructors' Resource Manual* of this text. He enjoyed responding, as motivation is a topic that interests him and it would also mean a publication for him. _____

6) Theresa Luke does beautiful stained glass artwork. She gives most of it away as gifts for friends and family. When I tell her she should sell it, she says that isn't why she does it. _____

7) John Smith joined the Nature Club at his school. He professed to having little intellectual expertise regarding aspects of nature, but expressed an appreciation for being outdoors surrounded by beauty and tranquillity. _____

8) Becky Jones is very proficient in Algebra, so much so that her friends call her the professor and she is extremely embarrassed about it. The funny thing is that she doesn't really enjoy Algebra but she knows she will need to do well in all of her mathematics courses if she hopes to become an astronaut. _____

9) Paul Waters was a beautiful ice-skater and would gracefully glide across the ice. A very modest man, he didn't want a lot of fuss made over his accomplishments. _____

10) Greg Mowrer didn't want to be president of the senior class because he knew it would be a lot of time and effort that he would rather devote to his lawn service. He was making quite a bit of money to help out with future college expenses but his friends said that he would be of great service to the class if elected, so he agreed. _____

Authentic Task: Tasks that have some connection to real-life problems the students will. face outside of the classroom. A form of authentic learning is called problem-based learning.

Problem-Based Learning: Methods that provide students with realistic problems that don't necessarily have "right" answers. Students meet an ill-structured problem before they receive any instruction. Probing issues with the teacher acting as facilitator, students monitor and organize their own problem solving.

Supporting Autonomy

The second area in the TARGET model is **autonomy.** Self-determination is a key component of intrinsic motivation. Classroom environments that support student autonomy foster greater student interest, sense of competence, self-esteem, creativity, conceptual learning, and preference for challenge. In autonomy oriented classrooms, students are more likely to believe that the work is important. They tend to internalize educational goals as their own. Controlling environments tend to improve performance only on rote recall tasks.

Recognizing Accomplishment

The third TARGET area is **recognition.** Praise needs to be specific, and distributed equally and evenly among the students. At times students may misinterpret praise to mean, "I'm really surprised that someone of your low level ability is doing so well." Be genuine and sincere in your praise without going overboard. Specify the exact behaviors that are being acknowledged versus offering comments such as "super" or "good" or "nice work". This type of praise really offers no information. Students should be recognized for improvement, for tackling difficult tasks, and for creativity to name a few.

Grouping

The fourth area of TARGET is grouping.

Johnson and Johnson (1994) have examined how individuals strive to achieve their goals relative to the ways they relate to one another. They have labeled this interpersonal factor the **goal structure of the task.**

Goal Structure: The way students relate to others who are also working toward a particular goal.

Three types of goal structures are individualistic, competitive, and cooperative.

1. **Cooperative Goal Structures:** arrangement in which students work in mixed-ability groups and are rewarded on the basis of the success of the group. **Example:** When a basketball team wins the NBA championship, every member on the team is rewarded. When teams of students score an average of 10 improvement points on the exam, they will all be rewarded with a field trip. One form of cooperative learning structures is called STAD.

2. **Competitive Goal Structures:** occur when individuals striving to achieve their goals have a bearing on whether or not you will achieve your goals. **Example:** There can be only one winner of a foot-race. If someone else wins, *you* lose. When *you* and your classmates are graded on a curve, only the *top 10%* for example, will receive "A's". Do you see why it is competitive?

3. **Individualistic Goal Structures:** occur when an individual's efforts to achieve his/her goal is not influenced by anyone else's attempt to achieve their goals. **Example:** Every child who reads 20 books this month, will receive a new book from the *I Love to Read Program*. Every students who receives a 90 on the test will get an "A", regardless of how many students get a 90.

Evaluation

The fifth TARGET area is **evaluation.** The type of evaluation you select, whether it is based on individual mastery or competitive grading on a curve, will influence the types of goals students set, be it performance or learning goals. When students feel they are working for grades, and if the amount of good grades to be handed out are limited, students will be less likely to want to assist each other in their attempts to achieve high grades. One way to emphasize learning rather than grades is to use **self-evaluation.** As educators, it must be our aim to help students to value learning over grades. Unfortunately, research indicates that teachers project the importance of doing work as a means to get grades and further project classroom work as "something to be gotten through".

Time

The sixth TARGET area is **time.** Students and teachers alike feel the pressure of too little time for learning and learning tasks, often frantically hoping to complete the designated curriculum for that year. Teachable moments should be indulged without constant concern for the schedule. Constant interruptions of class bells, subject changes, and not enough time for project completion, can defeat the motivation of students when they are not permitted to experience activities to fruition.

Figure 10.2

ENCOURAGING MOTIVATION:
TARGET MODEL

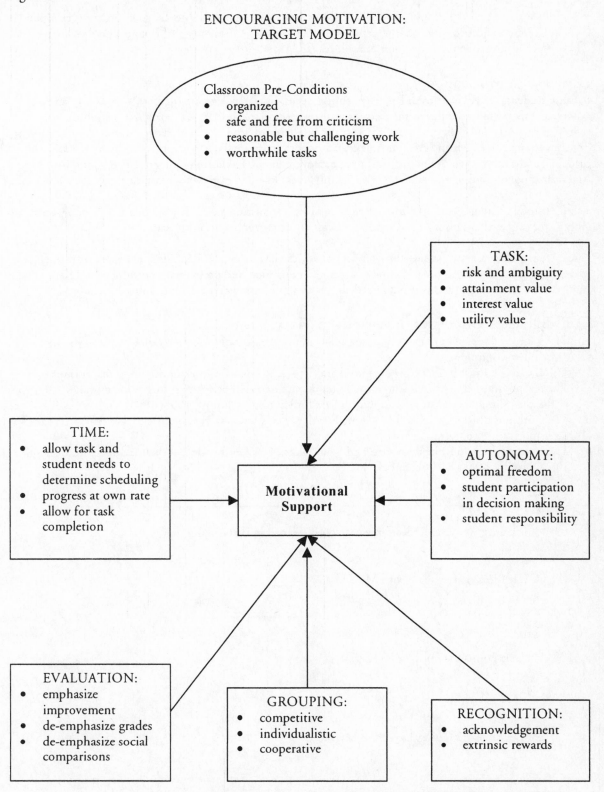

Classroom Pre-Conditions
- organized
- safe and free from criticism
- reasonable but challenging work
- worthwhile tasks

TASK:
- risk and ambiguity
- attainment value
- interest value
- utility value

TIME:
- allow task and student needs to determine scheduling
- progress at own rate
- allow for task completion

Motivational Support

AUTONOMY:
- optimal freedom
- student participation in decision making
- student responsibility

EVALUATION:
- emphasize improvement
- de-emphasize grades
- de-emphasize social comparisons

GROUPING:
- competitive
- individualistic
- cooperative

RECOGNITION:
- acknowledgement
- extrinsic rewards

Diversity and Convergences in Motivation to Learn

1. We have seen that motivation to learn grows from the individual's needs, goals, interest, emotions, beliefs, and attributions in interaction with the tasks set, autonomy and recognition provided, grouping structures, evaluation procedures, and time allowed.

Diversity in Motivation

Because students differ in terms of language, culture, economic privilege, personality, knowledge, and experience, they will also differ in their needs, goals, interests, and beliefs. For example, self-efficacy is a central concept in motivation because it is a strong predictor of academic performance. But there are cultural differences as well. Males and African American students are more likely to be overconfident in their academic abilities, so their predictions of future achievement are less accurate than the predicitons of Asian American students and female students who are much less likely to express overconfidence in their abilities.

Taking this diveristy into account when designing tasks, supporting autonomy, recognizing accomplishments, groups, making evaluations, and managing time can encourage motivation to learn.

Language is a central factor in students' connections with the school. When bilingual students are encouraged to draw on both English and their heritage langauge, motivation and participation can increase. Encouraging students to capitalize on their cultural knowledge can increase motivation and meaning in school.

Convergences: Strategies to Encourage Motivation

Until four basic conditions are met for evey student in every classroom, no motivational strategies will succeed. These conditions are:

1. The classroom must be relatively organized and free from constant interruptions and disruptions.
2. The teacher must be a patient, supportive person who never embarrasses students for mistakes. Everyone in the class should see mistakes as opportunities for learning (Clifford, 1990, 1991).
3. The work must be challenging, but reasonable. If work is too easy or too difficult, students will have litter motivation to learn.
4. The learning tasks must be authentic, and what makes a task authentic is influenced by culture (Bergin, 1999; Brophy & Kher, 1086; Stipek, 1993).

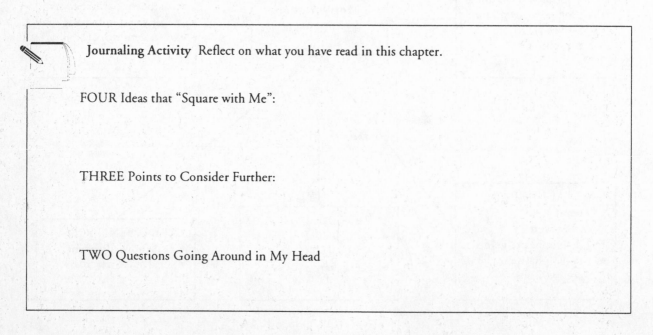

Journaling Activity Reflect on what you have read in this chapter.

FOUR Ideas that "Square with Me":

THREE Points to Consider Further:

TWO Questions Going Around in My Head

MY NOTES

(Use this space to make additional notes for this chapter)

11

Engaged Learning: Cooperation and Community

Social Processes in Learning

When you think about engagement in school, do you think about social and cultural influences on the students' learning? This chapter discusses how pepole learn through ineractions with others and how social interaction, dialgoue, and culture affect learning. Two decages ago, Jerome Bruner, who pioneered the study of indivudal concept learning, said, "I have come increaslingly to recognize that learning in most settings is a communal activity, a sharing of culture: (1986, p. 27).

Our text considers three social influences on students-peers, parents, and teachers.

Peers

Laurence Steinberg and his colleagues have studied the role of parents, pers, and community contexts in school achiebement (Durbin, Darling, Steinberg, & Brown, 1993; Steinberg, 1996, 1998). Based on a three-year study that surveyed 20,000 students in nine high schools in Wisconsin and California, Steiberg concluded that about 40% of these studetns were just going trhought the motions of learning.

Steinberg claims that this lack of investment is due in part to peer pressure. "For a large number of adolescents, peers-not parents-are the chief determinatns of how intensely they are invested in school and how much effort they devote to their education: (1998, p. 331).

Parents and Teachers

Parents and teachers paly a role, too. Adolescents with authoritative parents are more likely to respond to peer pressure to do well in school and less likely to be swayed by peer pressure to use drugs or alocohole, especially when their friends also have authoritative parents (Collins, Maccoby, Steinberg, Hetherington, & Bornstein, 2000).

When children do not have friends or have few friends, parents and teachers can play an imortant role in supporting school achievement.

Collaboration and Cooperation

Even with all the concern about acedemic standards, performance on proficincy tests, and international comparisons of student achievement, schooling has always been about more than academic learning. Of course, academics are the prime directive, "but schools have major responsibilities for other aspects of studens' development as well, such as helping students develop the attitudes, skills, and orientations needed tolead humane lives and act effectively as citizens to stustain democratic institutions" (Battistich, Watson, Solomon, Lewis, & Schaps, 1999).

The majority of studies examining collaboration and cooperation in schools indicate that truly cooperative groups have positive effects on students' empathy, tolerance for differences, feelings of acceptance, friendships, self-confidence, and even school attendance (Solomon, Watson, & Battistich, 2001).

Collaboration, Group Work and Cooperation in Learning

The terms *collaboration*, *group work* and *cooperative learning* are often used as if they mean the same thing.

The distinctions between collaboration and cooperation are not always clear. Ted Panitz (1996) suggests the following differences. **Collaboration** is a philosophy about how to relate to others-how to learn and work. Collaboration is a way of dealing with people that respsects differences, shares authority, and bulds on the knowledge that is distributed amoung other people. **Cooperation**, on the other hand, is a way of working with others to attain a shared goal (Gillies, 2003).

Group work is simply several students working together, they may or may not be cooperating. True cooperative learning requires much more than simply putting students in groups. In cooperative learning, students learn by doing and by teaching each other, however, sometimes one or two members of the group end up doing all of the work for the rest of the group. True cooperative learning requires much, much more.

Cooperative learning: Arrangement in which students work in mixed-ability groups and are rewarded on the basis of the success of the group.

In the early 1990's John Dewey criticized the competitive emphasis of American schools and encouraged educators to downplay the competitive emphasis in favor of structuring schools to be democratic learning communities. Today, cooperative learning is embraced by constructivists for different reasons.

Misuses of Group Learning

Without careful planning and monitoring by the teacher, group interactions can hinder learning and reduce, rather than improve, social relations in classes. Several other disadvantages of group learning are:
- Students value the process or procedures over the learning.
- Rather than challenging and correcting misconceptions, students reinforce misunderstandings.
- Socializing and interpersonal relations may take precedence over learning.
- Students may simply shift dependency from the teacher to the "expert" in the group.
- Status differences may be increased, rather than decreased.

Tasks for Cooperative Learning

Like so many other decisions in teaching, plans for using cooperative groups begin with a goal. What are students suppposed to accomplish? What is the task? Tasks for cooperative groups may be more or less structured. Highly sturctured tasks include work that has right answeres and ill-structured complex tasks have multiple answers and unclear procedures requiring higher-ordered thinking. These ill-structured problems are true group tasks, requiring the resources and skills or all group members.

Highly Structured, review, and Skill-Building Tasks-such as reviewing previously learned material for an exam might be well served by a structured technique such as STAD (Student Teams Achievement Divisions), in which teams of four students compete to determine which team's members can amass the greatest improvement over previous achievement levels (Slavin, 1995).

Ill-Structured, Conceptual, and Problem-Solving Tasks benefit from an open exchange and elaborated discussion. Thus, strategies that encourage extended and productive interactions are appropriate when the goal is to develop higher-order thinking and problem solving. Open-ended techniques such as reciprocal questioning (King, 1994), reciprocal teaching (Palinesar & Brown, 1984; Rosenshine & Meister, 1994), pair-share (Kagan, 1994), or jigsaw should be productive strategies.

Social Skills and Communication Tasks require the assignment of specifice roles and functions within the group to support communication (Cohen, 1994; Kagan, 1994). In these situations, it can be helpful to rotate leadership roles so that minority group students and females have the opportunity to demonstrate and develo leadership skills.

Preparing Students for Cooperative Learning

> **Stop, Think, and Write:** As part of the interview process for an elementary teaching position, you are asked the following: "Do you use group work in your teaching? Why? How would you use it in this school?"

Setting Up Cooperative Groups

The size of the cooperative group is dependent on your learning goals. If the purpose is for group members to review, rehearse information or practice, 4 to 6 students is about the right size. If the goal is to participate in discussions, problem solving, or computer learning, then groups of 2 to 4 students work best. Generally, the groups of students are balanced for ability, gender, and ethnicity. It also makes sense to balance the number of boys and girls. It is the responsibility of the group to ensure that all team members comprehend the material. High-ability students help low-ability students and improve their own performances by teaching others. There is evidence that the more a student provides elaborated, thoughtful explanations to other students in a group, the more the *explainer* learns. Giving good explanations appears to be even more important for learning than receiving explanations.

Giving and Receiving Explanations

In practice, the effects of learning in a group vary, depending on what actually happens in the group and who is in it. Sudents who ask questions, get answers, and attempt explanations are more likely to learn than students whose uestions go unasked or unanswered. Giving good explanations apprear to be even more imprtant for learnig than reveiving explanations (Webb, Farivar, & Mastergeorge, 2002; Webb & Palincsar, 1996).

Assigning Roles

Some teachers assign roles to students to encourage cooperation and full participation. Depending on the purpose of the group and the age of the participants, having assigned roles might help students cooperate and learn. Of course, students may have to be taught how to enact each role effectively, and roles should be rotated so students can participate in different aspects of group learning. Some possible roles include: encourager, gate keeper, coach, question commander, checker, taskmaster, recorder, reflector, quiet captain, materials monitor.

Designs for Cooperation

Reciprocal Questioning: Approach where groups of two or three students ask and answer each other's questions after a lesson or presentation. This process has proved more effective than traditional discussions groups because it encourages deeper thinking about the material. It requires no special materials or testing procedures. After a lesson or presentation by the teacher, students work in pairs or triads to ask and answer questions about the material. The teacher provides question stems, students then are taught how to develop specific questions on the lesson material using the generic question stems. The students create questions, and then take turns asking and answering.

Scripted Cooperation: A method for learning in pairs. Students work together on almost any task, including reading a selection of text, solving math problems, or editing written drafts. Both students take on the same task, then one student presents the information to the other student while the partner comments on the summary, noting omissions or errors. Then the students switch roles and continue taking turns until they finish the assignment.

Reaching Every Student: Using Cooperative Learning Wisely
Cooperative learnig always benefits from careful planning, but sometimes including students with special needs requires extra attention to planning and preparation. When students are learning new or difficult-to-grasp concepts, cooperativfe learning might not be the best choice for students with learning disabilities (Kirk et al., 2006). In fact, research has found that cooperative learning in gerneral is not always effetive for students with learning disabilities (Smith, 2006).

Gifted students also may not benefit from cooperative laerning when groups are mixed in ability. The pace often is too slow, the tasks too simple, and there is too much repetition.

Cooperative learning may be an excellent choice, however, for English language learners (ELL).

In **jigsaw**, each group member is given part of the material to be learned by the whole group and becomes an 'expet" on his or her piece. Students have to teach each other, so everyone's contribution is important, A more recent version Jigsaw II, adds expert groups in which the students who have the same material from each learning group confer to make sure the understand their assigned part and then plan ways to teach the information to their learning group members.

Classroom Community
David and Roger Johnson (1999) describe **three Cs for safe and productive schools:**
- **Cooperative Community**-the idea that at the heart of the community is positive interdependence-individuals working together to achieve mutual goals.
- **Constructive Conflict Resolution**-because conflicts are inevitable and even necessary for learning.
- **Civic Values**-the understandings and beliefs that hold the community together.

Peer Mediation and Negotiation
In every community there are conflicts. David Johnson and his colleagues (1995) provided conflict resolution training to 227 students in 2nd through 5th grade. Students learned **a five-step negotiating strategy:**
1. **Jointly define the conflict.** Separate the person from the problem, avoid win-lose thinking, and get both parties' goals clear.
2. **Exchange positions and interest.** Present a tentative proposal, listen to the other person's proposal; and stay flexible and cooperative.
3. **Reverse perspectives.** See the situation from the other person's point of view and reverse roles and argue for that perspective.
4. **Invent at least three agreements that allow mutual gain.** Brainstorm, focus on goals, think creatively, and make sure everyone has power to invent solutions.
5. **Reach an integrative agreement.** Make sure both sets of goals are met. If all else fails, flip a coin, take turns, or call in a third party-a mediator.

In addition to learning conflict resolution, all students in the study were trained in mediation strategies. Students learned the conflict resolution and mediation strategies and used them successfully, both in school and at home, to handle conflicts in a more productive way.

Civic Values

Civic values is the udnerstandings and beliefs that hold he community together. Values are learned trhough direct teaching, modeling, reading literature, engaging in group discussions, and sharing concerns.

STOP/THINK/WRITE

Consdier this situation, described by Aronson (2000). You are a high-school social studies teacher. Just as you are opening a topic for discussion, Dave, a struggling student, says, "I've decided one thing anyway I don't want to be an American. As soon as I get the chance, I'm leaving." What do you do?

Respect and Protect

One system that has been developed to combat violence in the schools is **Respect and Protect** from the Johnson Institute. The program is **founded on five ideas:**
1. **Everyone is obliged to respect** and protect the rights of others.
2. **Violence is not acceptable.**
3. The program **targets the violence-enabling behaviors** of staff, students, and parents such as denying, rationalizing, justifying or blaming others for violence.
4. There is **a clear definition of what constitutes violence** that distinguishes two kinds of violence-bully/victim violence and violence that arises from normal conflict.
5. The program has both **adult-centered prevention** that improves the school climate and **student-centered interventions** that give students choices and clear consequences.

Community Outside the Classroom: Service Learning

Service learning: An approach to combining academic learning with personal and social development.

Service learning is another approach to combining academic learning with personal and social development for secondary and college students. The Alliance for Service Learning in Education Reform lists several characteristics of service learning. The **activities:**
• **Are organized** and meet actual community needs,
• **Are integrated into the student's curriculum,**
• **Provide time to reflect** and write about the service experience,
• **Enhance both academic learning** and a **sense of caring for others.**

Participation in community service learning can promote political and moral development for adolescents. Student involvement in community service learning can motivate and empower adolescents to critically reflect on their role in society. Some schools now have participation in service learning as a graduation requirement. Studies of service learning have produced mixed results. Some studies have found modest gains on measures of social responsibility, tolerance for others, empathy, attitude toward adults, and self-esteem.

Diversity and Convergence in Social Engagement

Diversity-Understanding and appreciation of diversity is a central consideration in supporting engaged learning. In setting up cooperative groups, for example, be aware that assigning group members by "categories" such as reace or language background may encourage the students to continue to think of one another as members of a cteogry rather than as individuals.

Convergences-What are the convergences about behavioral, emotional, social, and cognitive engagement in schools? The research on school-based youth development and problem prevention programs points to three factors for success: enhancing students' social and emotional competence, connections to others, and contributions to their communities (Greenberg et al.,2003). These three factors parallel the major sections of this chapter-cooperation in classroom groups, creating classroom communities, and connection to communities outside the school.

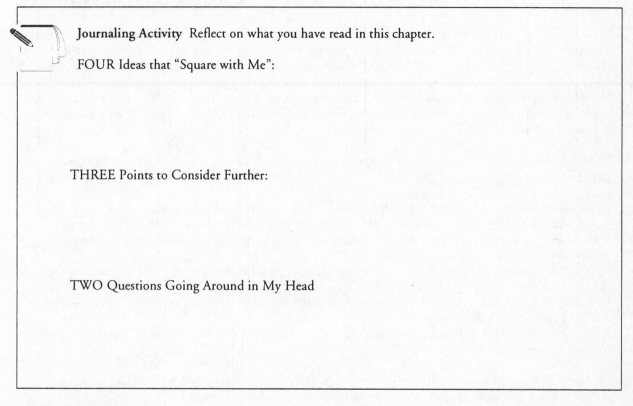

Journaling Activity Reflect on what you have read in this chapter.

FOUR Ideas that "Square with Me":

THREE Points to Consider Further:

TWO Questions Going Around in My Head

MY NOTES

(Use this space to make additional notes for this chapter)

12
Creating Learning Environments

We would like to believe that by establishing a positive learning environment in the classroom from the very beginning of the school year, we will prevent any problems from occurring throughout the year. But problems will arise and appropriate responses by the teacher can stop small problems from exploding into large ones. The *Phi Delta Kappa* gallup poll has consistently published lack of discipline as one of the primary problems facing schools. Every classroom has its own dynamic environment with teachers, students, and the academics in constant interaction. Doyle suggests that **every classroom** is **influenced by six factors** regardless of teacher or student characteristics:

1. **Multidimensionality:** Classrooms are comprised of people, tasks, time pressures, goals, preferences, abilities, and the list goes on and on. All of these dimensions interact to make the classroom a very complex place.
2. **Simultaneity:** Many things are happening at once. The teacher is explaining, students are writing, students are not writing, and the teacher must have 50 eyes to watch all that is transpiring.
3. **Immediacy:** Classroom life is fast paced. Teachers have literally hundreds of exchanges with students throughout the day.
4. **Unpredictability:** Even when you are completely prepared, your students are engaged and responding, you can bet that someone will mow the lawn right outside of your window.
5. **Public:** You will always be observed. Your students will judge how you equitably interact with students, handle situations, and acknowledge their efforts.
6. **Histories:** All the events that transpire combine to form the "classroom history". Your responses to your students will evolve as history develops.

Gaining student cooperation is the key to smoothly operating classroom procedures. Gaining student cooperation can be a challenge that is contingent upon the ages of your students.

> **Stop, Think, Write:** Are there cultural differences in the verbal and nonverbal ways that students show respect, pay attention, and bid for a turn in conversation? How can cultural differences in interaction styles and expectations make classroom management more challenging?
>
>
>
> What plans do you have for meeting this challenge?

The Goals of Classroom Management

Using classroom management solely for the purpose of keeping students docile would be unethical and its true aim is to maintain a positive, productive learning environment.

Classroom Management: Techniques used to maintain a healthy learning environment, relatively free of behavior problems. Effective classroom management results in:

1. More time is allotted for actual learning--examination of time of actual instruction, reveals that much of the school day is spent on other activities. An important goal is to expand **allocated time.**

Allocated Time: Time set aside for learning.

Generally, due to many classroom interruptions, allocated time never equals **engaged time or time on task.** Engaged time or time on task does not insure that actual learning is occurring. Students may be experiencing comprehension difficulty and frustration with absence of productive learning. Successful productive learning is called **academic learning time.**

Engaged Time: Time spent actively learning.

Time on Task: Time spent actively engaged in the learning task at hand.

Academic Learning Time: Time when students are actually succeeding at the learning task.

2. Access to learning: One of the ways that students access the information that is available to them in the classroom is through **participation structures.**

Participation Structures: Rules defining how to participate in different activities.

Some students do not know appropriate rules for when to question, make contributions, for how long they should dominate the floor, etc.. I'll bet you have encountered classmates at the college level who don't know when to quit talking. Teachers must teach students how to verbally participate and convey to them the classroom rules and expectations. Students who don't know how to verbally access information or have been rebuked for inappropriate attempts at participation, may refrain from future attempts and miss out on learning.

3. Management for Self-Management: Students need to gradually assume responsibility for controlling their own behaviors. So the third goal of classroom management is **self-management.** This requires extra effort on the part of the teacher but it is a worthwhile investment for both the student and the teacher in the long run.

Self-Management: Management of your own behavior and acceptance of responsibility for your own actions.

> **Stop, Think, Write:** List three specific techniques you plan to use in your own classroom to make the most of your allocated time for instruction.

CREATING A POSITIVE LEARNING ENVIRONMENT
Procedures
The following classroom management principles were developed from research that compared methods of teachers who had harmonious, high achieving classes with those of teachers whose classes were fraught with problems. The **first step** toward establishing effective management is the **establishment of procedures.**

Procedures: Prescribed steps for an activity. Weinstein et. al. suggests that procedures be established for the following areas:

- *administrative* routines--taking attendance, pledge of allegiance, lunchroom orders
- *student movement--lining* up, entering and leaving the room, hall passes
- *housekeeping*--hanging up coats, stowing galoshes, putting books in a locker or cubby
- *routines for accomplishing* lessons--collecting assignments, handing out materials
- *interactions between teacher* and student-how to get the teacher's help when needed
- *talk among students--such* as giving help or socializing

Rules
Unlike procedures, **rules** are often written down and posted. A few rules that cover specific do's and don'ts of the classroom are much better than an extensive list covering every possible action.

Rules: Statements specifying expected and forbidden behaviors.

Rules differ contingent upon the age of the student. Whatever the age, however, students need to be taught the behaviors that the rule includes and excludes. Different situations call for different rules which may be confusing for elementary students. A good strategy would be to post rules clearly where everyone can see them, leaving no ambiguity. All rules should be explained and discussed to have their full effect. A good way to construct classroom rules is to have both a teacher's and students' Bill of Rights. Rather than posting a list of don'ts, the **Bill of Rights** states the rights of individuals that are to be respected and maintained by all in the classroom. This **teaches democratic procedures as well as responsible decision-making and independence.**

> **Stop, Think, Write:** "Set Them Up For Success". List three classroom rules and three classroom procedures you think will be important for success in your future classroom:
>
> Rules:
> 1.
>
> 2.
>
> 3.
>
> Procedures:
> 1.
>
> 2.
>
> 3

Consequences

As soon as rules and procedures have been selected, you must determine the consequences for infractions. Logical consequences would be restitution for the inappropriate behavior. Weinstein and Mignano (1997) found that **teachers' negative consequences** fell into seven different categories:

- Expressions of disappoiintment.
- Loss of privileges.
- Exclusion from the group.
- Written reflecitons on the problem.
- Detentions-brief meetings after school, during a free period, or at lunch.
- Visits to the principal's office.
- Contact with parents.

PLANNING SPACES FOR LEARNING

Classroom space can be segmented into two areas: **interest areas and personal territories.**

Interest-area arrangements may be a science corner with manipulatives or a reading corner. To plan classroom space, you must first decide the nature of your projects and activities and how you plan to physically group your students.

Personal territories address the physical location of students within the classroom. Interested students generally position themselves near the front of the classroom and the instructor.

Creative Journaling: Sketch a map of a middle-school classroom that would be used by a language arts teacher. Design a space that would allow the teacher and student to:

1. Hold whole-group direct instruction lessons accompanied by overhead transparencies.
2. Hold small-group literature discussions.
3. Carry out whole-group literature discussions.

Figure 12.1

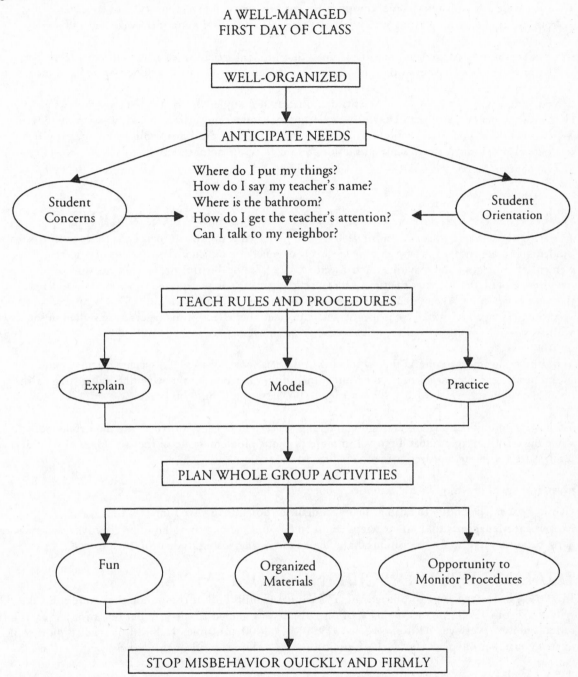

A WELL-MANAGED
FIRST DAY OF CLASS

WELL-ORGANIZED

ANTICIPATE NEEDS

Student Concerns

Where do I put my things?
How do I say my teacher's name?
Where is the bathroom?
How do I get the teacher's attention?
Can I talk to my neighbor?

Student Orientation

TEACH RULES AND PROCEDURES

Explain   Model   Practice

PLAN WHOLE GROUP ACTIVITIES

Fun   Organized Materials   Opportunity to Monitor Procedures

STOP MISBEHAVIOR QUICKLY AND FIRMLY

Getting Started: The First Weeks of School

Effective Elementary Teachers gain students' cooperation within the first critical days and weeks by:

- starting with a **well-organized first day**--name tags, interesting activities and materials, addressing the students' most pressing concerns, and reasonable rules taught with explanation, examples, and practice.
- throughout the first few weeks--**continue teaching rules and procedures**, worked with the class as a whole on **enjoyable activities, misbehavior** was **stopped quickly** and firmly.

Ineffective Elementary Teachers operated their rooms quite differently:
- rules were not workable--vague, complicated, and consequences were not clear or consistent
- procedures for accomplishing routine tasks varied from day-to-day and these were never taught or practiced
- students wandered aimlessly and relied on each other for direction, teachers frequently left the room, became absorbed in paperwork or in helping one student, classrooms were unorganized and inconsistent

Effective managers for secondary students demonstrated many of the same characteristics as effective elementary teachers. Student behavior was closely monitored and infractions dealt with quickly. Teachers closely monitored student progress so that students could not avoid working, yet effective teachers also demonstrated a sense of humor and joked with their students.

MAINTAINING A GOOD LEARNING ENVIRONMENT
As stated previously, an effective way of dealing with problems is to prevent their occurrence in the first place. Students who are engaged in activities are less likely to generate problems. Research informs us that elementary students working with a teacher were on task 97% of the time, while students working on their own were on task only 57% of the time. Of course teachers cannot be expected to work with students all of the time, but keeping students engaged is one way to prevent problems. Kounin (1970) compared effective classroom managers to ineffective managers and concluded that **effective managers were skilled in four areas: withitness, overlapping activities, group focusing, and movement management.**

Withitness: Awareness of everything happening in the classroom. **Example:** A teacher friend of mine positioned a large circular mirror in the front corner of the classroom so that when he was writing on the board, he could still watch what was happening in his classroom behind his back.

Withitness prevents **timing** errors (waiting too long to act) and target errors (blaming the wrong individual while the culprit escapes culpability). When more than one problem occurs at the same time, the withit teacher deals with the more serious problem first.

Overlapping: Supervising several activities at once.

Group Focus: The ability to keep as many students as possible involved in activities.

Movement Management: Ability to keep lessons and groups moving smoothly. The effective teacher avoids abrupt transitions as well as transitions that progress too slowly, losing students in the process.

DEALING WITH DISCIPLINE PROBLEMS
In 2005, Phi Delta Kappa published the 37th annual Gallup Poll of the public's attitude toward public schools. From 1969 until 1999, "lack of discipline" was named as the number one problem facing the schools almost every year (Rose, & Gllup, 1999). In 2000 and since, lack of financial support took over the number oneplace, but lack of discipline was a close second or third every year.

Begin an effective manager does not mean publicly correcting every minor infraction of the rules. The key is to know what is happening and what is important so you can prevent problems. Emmerand colleagues (2006) and Levin and Nolan (2000) suggest seven simple ways to stop misbehavior quickly, moving from lest to most instrusive:
- Make eye contact
- Verbal Hints or "name dropping"
- Ask if student is aware of negative effects of his or her actions
- Remind the students of the procedure or rule
- Ask the student to state the correct rule or procedure and then to follow it
- Offer a choice-stop the behavior or experience a consequence

Special Problems with Secondary Students

Characteristic problems of secondary students and some strategies for fostering compliance include:
1. work completion - teach students to keep a daily planner, enforce consequences for incomplete work
2. students who continually break rules - separate from other students, try to catch them before they break the rules, continue to enforce consequences
3. defiant, hostile students - during an outbreak, try to provide an out for everyone involved by offering the student the opportunity to comply, seek help if the situation escalates and there is noncompliance, conference with parents, counselors or other teachers, maintain records
4. violence or property destruction - send for help and get names of participants and witnesses, report the incidence and implement school policy

THE NEED FOR COMMUNICATION

Communication must be a two-way exchange between the student and the teacher including non-verbal messages. Very often the messages we send are misinterpreted. Often, people will respond to what they *think* was said and not what was intended by the speaker. To send and receive messages accurately practice the **paraphrase rule** in your class.

Paraphrase Rule: Policy whereby listeners must accurately summarize what a speaker has said before being allow to respond.

Another way to foster good teacher student relationships is by **diagnosing who owns the problem,** the student or the teacher. If the student's behavior interferes with your capacity to reach your goals as a teacher, then it is your problem. If the behavior does not directly interfere with your teaching, then it is probably the student's problem. Once you decide who owns the problem, act! If the problem is yours, confront the student and seek a solution. If the problem belongs to the student, try to **counsel the student** by paraphrasing for clarification and **employ empathetic listening.**

Empathetic Listening: Hearing the intent and emotions behind what another says and reflecting them back by paraphrasing.

Avoid jumping in too quickly and permit the student the time to openly express his concerns. Attend to both the verbal and non-verbal messages. Try to differentiate between the intellectual and emotional content of the message. Make inferences regarding what the speaker is feeling. Students learn to trust teachers who will openly listen to them without value judgments.

Application 1: Teacher-Student Owned Problems
Decide whether the following classroom problems are student owned, teacher owned, or shared. Check your responses in the answer key.
1) "Mr. Jones, I don't think I can deliver my oral presentation to the class. I start to stutter from
2) nerves.
3) "Janet, your tardiness is disrupting the class lesson once again and you have missed the explanation regarding how to do your problems."
4) "Girls, the notes you are passing clear across the classroom will have to wait until lunch. It is very distracting to everyone to have to pass your notes and I'm finding it difficult to concentrate."
5) "Mrs. Smith, Bobby is pulling my hair. Ow!"
6) "Francis, I will ask you one more time to sit down and if you refuse to cooperate, I will be forced to ask you to go to the office."
7) "This is a dumb assignment. Why do I have to memorize the periodic table anyway? I'll never use it."

Confrontation and Assertive Discipline

As stated previously, when the student is interfering with your teaching, you must confront the student. This is the time for an "I" message.

"I" Messages: Clear, nonaccusatory statement of how something is affecting you. **Example:** "When you are talking to the person next to you, I can't concentrate on what I'm trying to teach the class."

Canter and Canter (1992) suggest that another direct approach for dealing with teacher owned problems is **assertive discipline.** The Canters suggests that all too often, teachers are either passive (wishy-washy or questioning the student as to why they're misbehaving without informing them of the proper behaviors) or hostile ("You are NOT listening! You straighten up or else!"). Assertive responses indicate that you care about the student and their learning. Assertive responses are calm statements of expectations delivered with confidence and controlled emotions.

Assertive Discipline: Clear, firm, unhostile response style.

If "I" messages and assertive responses fail and a student persists in misbehaving, teacher and student are in a conflict. There are three methods of resolving a conflcit between teacher and student.
1. The teacher imposes a solution.
2. The teacher gives in to the student's demands.
3. "The No-lose method".

The "no-lose mehtods" takes into account the needs of both teacher and student and no one person is expected to give in completely while all participants retain respect for themselves and each others. The no-lose method is a six-step, problem-solving strategy:
1. Define the problem
2. Generate many possible solutions
3. Evalute each solution
4. Make a decision.
5. Determine how to implement the solution.
6. Evaluate the success of the solution

Student Conflicts and Negotiations

Handling conflict is difficult for most of us-for young people it can be even harder.Given the public's concern about violence in schools, it is surpirsing how little we know about conflicts among students (Rose & Gallu, 2001; Johnson, Johnson, Dudley, Ward, & Magnuson, 1995). There is some eveidence that in elementary schools, conflicts most often center on disputes over resources and preferences. Over 20 years ago, a large study of more than 8,000 junior high and senior high stuents and 500 faculty from three major cities concluded that 90% of conflicts among students are resolved in destructive ways or never resolved at all (DeCecco & Richards, 1974).

One form of conflict in schools involves the kind of teasing and harassment described in the text as bullying. Bullying has been shown to lead to school violence. One answer is prevention. Students need guidance in resolving conflicts. Different strategies are useful, depending on whether the goal, the relaitonship or both are important to those experiencing conflict. It can help to reverse roles and see the situation through the eyes of the other.

No matter what the stiuation, the cooperation of fmailies can help to create a positive learnig environment in the classroom and school. A combination of recognition for appropriate behavior, hints about what is unacceptable, discussion about how behavior affects others, and student involvement in discipline decisions encourages student responsibility, but these approaches are difficult when students are aggressive.

Diversity and Convergences in Learning Environments

Diversity: Culturally Responsive Management

African American males are disciplined more often and more harshly in American schools. Cultural differences in behavioral expression can be the basis for misunderstandings in classroom management. The effective teacher considers cultural differences and takes them into account when managing the classroom and student behavior

Culturally Relevant Management: Taking cultural meanings and styles into account when developing management plans and responding to students.

Warm Demanders: Effective teachers with African American students who show both high expectations and great caring for their students.

Convergences

Integrating Ideas

In a study conducted in Australia, Ramon Lewis (2001) found that recognizing and rewarding appropriate student behaviors, talking with students about how their behavior affects others, involving students in class discipline decisions and providing nondirective hints and descriptions about unacceptable behaviors were associated with students taking greater responsibility for their learning.

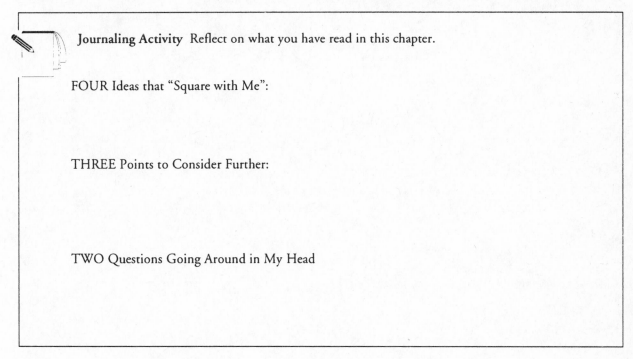

Journaling Activity Reflect on what you have read in this chapter.

FOUR Ideas that "Square with Me":

THREE Points to Consider Further:

TWO Questions Going Around in My Head

MY NOTES

(Use this space to make additional notes for this chapter)

13
Teaching for Learning

THE FIRST STEP: PLANNING

The seed of classroom instruction and learning is teacher planning. This is an area of great interest to educational researchers. Their findings reveal:

- Planning influences what students will *learn--planning* transforms time and materials into activities, assignments, and tasks for students
- Teachers must plan on several levels and all levels must be coordinated with one another--by the term, year, month, week, day
- Plans reduce uncertainty in teaching--yet they should be flexible and not rigid scripts
- To plan creatively and flexibly, teachers need wide-ranging knowledge about:
  - students--their interests and abilities
  - subjects being taught
  - alternative ways to teach and assess understanding
  - working with groups
  - expectations and limitations of school and community
  - how to apply and adapt materials and texts
  - how to combine all of the above into meaningful activities
  - There is no one model for effective planning--it is a creative problem-solving process

Stop, Think, Write: List some alternatives to seatwork.

Objectives for Learning

Before you begin your classroom instruction you must determine the goals of teaching. What changes in your students would you like to take place? Written down, this takes the form of **instructional objectives.**

Instructional Objectives: Clear statement of what students are intended to learn through instruction.
Example: The students will be able to explain the democratic form of governance.

There are different types of objectives for different learning goals. **Behavioral Objectives** use words like list, *define, add, or calculate,* but **cognitive objectives** use terms like *comprehend, recognize,* create, and apply.

Behavioral Objectives: Instructional objectives stated in terms of observable behaviors. **Example:** Students will be able to list capitals for every US state.

Cognitive Objectives Instructional objectives stated in terms of higher level thinking operations. **Example:** Within mathematics, the students will be able to apply estimation procedures to arrive at close approximations of the actual results.

Several experts in the field have outlined their notions of educational objectives and what should be included therein. These are outlined below.

Mager: Objectives should be so **specific** that they clearly state what students will be doing when demonstrating their achievement and how you will know they are doing it. These objectives are thought of as **behavioral** and there are three components:
1. describes what the student must do
2. lists the conditions under which the behavior will occur
3. gives the criteria for acceptable performance

Gronlund: Objectives should be stated first in **general** terms followed by a few specific sample behaviors. This is generally thought to be a **cognitive** approach. The rationale behind this widely used approach is that teachers could never list all of the behaviors that might be listed in problem-solving for example, so it's better to state a few general objectives and clarify them with specific examples.

When the material to be learned is loosely structured, providing students with the objectives may give them the necessary framework for understanding why the material is important and what are the ultimate goals of achievement. In this case, knowing objectives appears to improve achievement but when the activities are structured and organized, knowing objectives appears to have little effect on achievement.

> **Stop, Think, Write:** Think about your assignments for one of your classes. What kind of thinking is involved in doing the assignments?

Flexible and Creative Planning-Using Taxonomies
Many years ago, a group of experts lead by Benjamin Bloom examined educational objectives and divided them into three domains: affective, cognitive, and psychomotor. These objectives comprised a **taxonomy**.

Taxonomy: Classification system. **Example: Bloom's taxonomy** for the **cognitive domain** can be seen on the next page.

Cognitive Domain: In Bloom's taxonomy, memory and reasoning objectives.

Bloom's Taxonomy for the Cognitive Domain

Objectives	Description of Process	Examples of Processes
1. Knowledge (remembering)	remembering, recognizing without necessarily understanding, using or changing it	How many ounces in a pound......................... What is the possessive rule............................. Define algorithm.........................
2. Comprehension (understanding)	understanding the material without necessarily relating it to anything else	Why convert unlike fractions.......................... Define a mammal.. Explain photosynthesis................................
3. Application (applying)	using a general concept to solve a particular problem	Using volume, figure amount of sandbox sand... ...... Construct a geometric figure that...................... Conjugate these verbs ....

4. Analysis (analyzing)	Breaking something down into its parts	Analyze the properties of H20........................ The Roman empire fell because................. Causal factors of gang violence are......................
5. Synthesis (creating)	creating something new by combing different ideas	Combine household items for your art project... Reggae is a blend of .... Biology plus philosophy equal Piaget's theory.......
6. Evaluation (evaluating)	judging the value of materials or methods as they might be	Are basals or whole language better.................... How can we cheaply reduce pollution......... Which form of classroom management...........

The objectives shown above in the parentheses reflect revisions forthcoming in the taxonomy called **Bloom 2001**. They are descriptive of cognitive processes which in turn act on four separate kinds of knowledge-factual, conceptual, procedural, and metacognitive. See your text for further clarification of the relationships between the cognitive processes and the four kinds of knowledge.

Educators have commonly thought that these objectives are hierarchical, each skill building on the preceding ones, but this is not always so. Knowledge and comprehension are often thought of as *lower level* objectives and the other objectives fall into the *higher level* category. These objectives are useful in planning assessments. Knowledge-level objectives, for example can be measured by true-false, short answer, or multiple choice tests. For measuring synthesis however, reports, projects, and portfolios may be more appropriate.

Collaborative Activity
Brainstorm with members of your study group assignments that promote higher levels of thinking. Refer to the information in your text on the cognitive domain and Bloom's taxonomy to assist you with your discussion.

Application One: Assessment Statements for Bloom's Cognitive Objectives
Read the following examples that might be used to assess student performance. Determine which objective of Bloom's Cognitive taxonomy is being addressed. Check your responses in the answer key.

1) Compare and contrast enrichment versus acceleration in terms of readiness, academic benefits, and social and emotional adjustment for precocious youth.
2) Explain what is meant by the melting pot philosophy.
3) What is the associative rule of multiplication?
4) Solve the geometric proofs by utilizing the appropriate theorems.
5) Read the following passage and diagram the sentences found there.
6) Generate a theory of adolescent purchasing practices from observations of mall behaviors, questionnaires, and personal interviews.

Affective Domain: Emotional objectives. **Example:** Listed below are basic objectives from the emotional domain.

1. Receiving: Being aware of or attending to something in the environment.
2. Responding: Showing some new behavior as a result of experience.
3. Valuing: Showing some definite involvement or commitment.
4. Organization: Integrating a new value into one's general set of values, giving it some ranking among one's general priorities.
5. Characterization by value: Acting consistently with the new value.

These objectives are very general and if you were to write affective objectives you would have to specifically state what your students are doing when (for example), *responding:* The subject is self-defense and the students will repeat the demonstrated movement of a spinning back-kick.

Psychomotor Domain: Physical ability objectives. **Example:** The students will demonstrate proficiency in writing the circular letters from the alphabet, in cursive.

These taxonomies range from the simplest perceptions and reflex actions to skilled creative movements. To assess student performance, you would ask him or her to demonstrate the skill and then using a rating scale, assess levels of proficiency.

Application Two: Identifying Domains of Objectives
Choose the domain that best describes each statement below--Affective, Cognitive, or Psychomotor.
_____ 1. Climb the ropes and touch the gymnasium ceiling in 4 out of 5 attempts
_____ 2. Compare the gross national product of Mexico to that of the US
_____ 3. Determine the volume of a pool with a 15 foot diameter and 4 foot height
_____ 4. Select poetic literary works that you find emotionally moving and explain why
_____ 5. Using your knowledge of the periodic table, perform an experiment using NaCl and H_2O and write the principle that you discover
_____ 6. Devise a routine set to music on the uneven parallel bars in gymnastics class
_____ 7. Demonstrate an understanding of number estimation
_____ 8. Show that students can work cooperatively on a community improvement project

---

Stop, Think, Write: You are preparing to teach an eighth-grade literature unit emphasizing the history and experiences of Asian Americans. Write one learning objective you will use for this unit.

Planning from a Constructivist Perspective

Traditionally, the sole responsibility for planning has been the teachers', but that is changing with the **constructivist approach.** Here, the students and the teacher work together to plan activities, content, and approaches that will ultimately achieve the teacher's global goals.

Perrone suggests that the students and teachers try to identify ideas, themes, and issues that will provide understanding of the subject matter. Perrone suggests the use of a **topic map** as a way of thinking about how the theme can generate learning and understanding and as a guide, help students and teachers to identify activities, materials, projects and performances that will support the development of the students' understanding and abilities. The focus is not so much on students' products as on the *process* of learning and thinking behind the products.

Today, themes and integration across subject areas, guide the planning and designing of units. Themes are appropriate at both the elementary and secondary level and may require teachers to plan together across curriculum areas.

Constructivist Approach: View that emphasizes the active role of the learner in building understanding and making sense of information. With the constructivist approach, assessment differs from the traditional paper-and-pencil approach and may include such *authentic assessments as* portfolios, exhibitions, demonstrations, and performances (see Chapter 15 of your text or this guide).

Characteristics of Effective Teachers
Although research in this area is incomplete, evidence suggests that three characteristics of effective teachers are knowledge, clarity, and warmth.

1. **Knowledge:** Teacher's knowledge of facts and concepts is not directly related to student learning, however, teachers who know more may make clearer presentations and recognize student difficulties more readily. Therefore, it is believed that knowledge is necessary but not sufficient for effective teaching because being more knowledgeable helps teachers be clearer and more organized.

2. **Clarity and Organization** : Teachers who provide clear presentations and explanations tend to have students who learn more and who rate their teachers more positively. For greater clarity:
- try to anticipate students' problems with the material
- have definitions ready for new terms and prepare examples for concepts; think of analogies
- organize the lesson in a logical sequence and include checkpoints to ensure comprehension
- plan a clear introduction to the lesson; what the students will learn and how they'll approach it
- during the lesson, make clear connections between facts using **explanatory links**
- stick with your plan, use familiar words, don't digress, and signal transitions to new topics

Explanatory Links: Words such as *because, therefore, consequentially,* used to connect facts and concepts. Explanatory links tie ideas together and make them easier to learn. **Example:** Because the sun lines up with satellite dishes during the month of March, we experience disturbance to our television picture.

3. **Warmth and Enthusiasm:** Research has found that ratings of teacher enthusiasm for their subject are correlated with student achievement gains. Warmth, friendliness, and understanding are the teacher traits most strongly related to student attitudes.

EXPLANATION AND DIRECT INSTRUCTION
Direct Instruction
In the 1970s and 1980s, thee was an explosion of reseach that focused on effective teaching. The results of all this work identifed a model of teaching that was related to improved student learning. Barak Rosenshine calls this approach **direct instruction** (1979) or **explicit teaching** (1986). Tom Good (1983a) uses the term **active teaching** for a similar approach.

Direct Instruction/Explicit Teaching: Instruction for mastery of basic skills. This approach, was tested by research and found to be effective for whole groups because the emphasis is on the instruction of basic skills and those types of skills that are assessed by standardized tests. Group averages improve, but the achievement of individuals may not and when the objectives are in the cognitive domain (writing creatively, solving complex problems, etc.) then this approach may not be suitable. Another term for direct instruction is **active teaching.**

Active Teaching: Teaching characterized by high levels of teacher explanation, demonstration, and interaction with students.

Rosenshine's Six Teaching Functions

Rosenshine summarizes six teaching functions of direct instruction:

- **Review and check the previous day's work**: reteach if necessary
- **Present new material**: teach in small steps providing examples and non-examples
- **Provide guided practice**: question students, give practice problems
- **Give feedback and correctives**: examine student answers and reteach if necessary
- **Provide independent practice**: provide opportunities for students to apply new learning on their own and in groups working toward a goal of 95% success rate. Skills should be overlearned and automatic.
- **Review weekly and monthly**: include review items as homework to consolidate learning.

Critics of direct instruction suggest that it is limited to lower level objectives, is based nontraditional teaching methods, discourages independent work, and ignores innovative models. The student is seen as a passive vessel waiting to be filled up with knowledge rather than an active constructor of knowledge.

Proponents, however, suggest that when implemented properly with plenty of guided and independent practice and feedback, students will learn actively.

Seatwork and Homework

One classroom technique that is overused is **seatwork**. One study found that American elementary students spend 51% of mathematics time in school working alone, while Japanese students spend 26% and Taiwanese students spend only 9%.

Seatwork should follow a lesson, provide students with supervised practice, and not become the primary mode of instruction. Whereas research has indicated that there exists a strong positive correlation between the amount of homework assigned and student grades, all too often, too much busywork is assigned that does not meet objectives nor effectively contribute to learning.

Seatwork: Independent classroom work.

To benefit from Seatwork and or homework, students must stay involved, be held accountable for completing work correctly, be offered feedback and guidance and in the case of **homework,** the assignments must be meaningful extensions of class lessons, not just busywork. Students should see the *connection* between the Seatwork or homework and the lesson. Tell them why they are doing the work. Hold them accountable for their work giving them the opportunity to correct the errors or revise the work, counting the results toward the class grade.

The debate continues regarding the effects of homework (Cooper & Valentine, 2001a, 2001b; Corno, 2000). See *Point/Counterpoint* in Chapter 12 of your text.

Q and A/ Questions and Recitation

Recitation Format of teacher questioning, student response, and teacher feedback. A typical recitation pattern consists of the following:

- *structure:* setting the framework
- *solicitation:* asking questions
- *reaction:* praising, correcting, and expanding

Regarding solicitation or asking **questions**, educators ask both **high-and low-level questions** and research indicates that both are effective. Simple questions that allow for a high percentage of correct responses, are better for younger and lower-ability students. Harder questions at both higher and lower levels, with more critical feedback, are better for high-ability students. Questions should also be both **divergent and convergent**.

Convergent Questions: Questions that have a single correct answer. **Example:** In what year did Columbus discover America?

Divergent Questions: Questions that have no single correct answer. **Example:** In what ways can we work toward eliminating air pollution?

Discussions: Conversations in which the teacher does not have the dominant role; students pose and answer their own questions. There are many **advantages** to group discussions:

- students are directly involved and have the chance to participate
- students learn to express themselves clearly, to justify opinions, to tolerate different views
- provides students with the opportunity to ask for clarification, examine their own thinking, follow personal interests, and assume responsibility for taking leadership roles
- students are helped to evaluate ideas and synthesize personal viewpoints
- discussions are useful when students are trying to understand difficult concepts

Disadvantages to **group discussions** are:

- unpredictable and may digress into exchanges of ignorance
- some members of the group may have difficulty participating
- teachers must ensure group members possess background knowledge on which to base the discussion
- large groups may be unwieldy and some people may dominate the conversation

TEACHER EXPECTATIONS
Two Kinds of Expectation Effects

Rosenthal and Jacobsen (1968) conducted a study in that captured the attention of the national media in a way that few studies by psychologists have since then. In this study,which told teachers that several of their students would make significant intellectual gains that year, and sure enough, they did. The researchers suggested that this was due to **self-fulfilling prophecy.**

Self-fulfilling Prophecy: A groundless expectation that comes true simply because it was expected. Because of its similarity to the story of from Greek Mythology of King Pygmalion's trnasformed statue, this has come to be known as the **Pygmalion Effect.**

Pygmalion Effect: Exceptional progress by a student as a result of high teacher expectations for that student.

Actually, two kinds of expectation effects can occur in classrooms. The first, self-fulfilling prophecy described above, the teacher's beliefs about the students' abilites have no basis infact, but student behavior comes to match the initialy inaccurate expectaiont. The second kind of expectaion effect occurs when teachers are fairly accurate in their initial reading of studnets' abilities and respond to students appropriately. This is called a **sustaining expectation effect.**

Sustaining expectation effect: Student performance maintained at a certain level because techers don't recognize improvements. **Example:** A student has a rough start in the beginning of the year due to family problems and the teacher forms the opinion that this student lacks academic ability and motivation. In spite of increased effort on behalf of the student, the teacher continues to maintain his belief about the performance level of the student, making it more difficult for the student to achieve.

There are many other sources of teacher expectation such as gender, IQ scores, medical or psychological reports, knowledge of ethnic background, physical characteristics, names, previous achievement, and socioeconomic class.

Do Teachers' Expectations Really Affect Students' Achievement?
Students who are expected to achieve:
- tend to be asked more and harder questions
- to be given more chances and a longer time to respond
- tend to be interrupted less than other students
- teachers give them cues and prompts
- teachers are more encouraging in general
- they smile at these students more often and show greater warmth through non-verbals
- teachers demand better performance
- teachers give more praise for good answers

Students who are not expected to achieve:
- teachers ask easier and fewer questions
- teachers allow less wait time for answers
- teachers are less likely to give prompts
- teachers are more likelyh to resond with sympatheetic acceptance or praise inadequate responses
- receive less praise than high-achieving students for the same correct answer

STUDENT-CENTERED TEACHING: EXAMPLES in READING, MATH and SCIENCE

Neither high expectations nor the appropriate use of any teaching format can ensure that students understand. To help students reach this goal, Eleanor Duckworth believes that teachers must pay very close attentionto understanding their students' undertstandings (Meek, 1991).

Learning and Teaching Reading and Writing
For years the debate has raged as to whether students should be taught to read and write through code-based (**phonics**) approaches or through meaning- based (**whole language**) approaches that focus on the meaning of the text. Advocates of whole language believe that reading is a natural process much like mastering your own language. They feel that words should not be presented out of text and broken into little abstract pieces. Teaching and learning are seen as reciprocal and collaborative and teachers and students make decisions together about the curriculum.

Whole Language Perspective: A philosophical approach to teaching and learning that stresses learning through authentic, real-life tasks. This approach emphasizes using language to learn, integrating learning across skills and subjects, and respecting the language abilities of student and teacher.

Advocates of whole language also insist that the curriculum should be integrated combining spelling, listening, reading and writing across all subject areas, even math and science. There are many advantages to whole language however, advocates of code-based approaches have shown that skill in recognizing sounds and words supports reading. The more fluent and automatic you are in identifying words, the more effective you will be in getting meaning from context. The best approach probably makes sensible use of both phonics and whole language.

The goal of **reciprocal teaching** is to help students understand and think deeply about what they read (Palincsar, 2986; Palincsar & Brown, 1984, 1989). To accomplish this goal, students in small reading gropus lean four strategies:
- **Summarizing** the content of a passage
- **Asking** a question about the central point
- **Clarifying** the difficult parts of the material
- **Predicting** what will come next

These are strategies that skilled readers apply almost automatically, but poor readers seldom do- or they don't know how.

Reciprocal Teaching: A method, based on modeling, to teach reading comprehension strategies.

Learning and Teaching Mathematics

Because of the way mathematics has been taught in the past, there is a great need for constructivist approaches. Many students feel that mathematics doesn't make sense and most of it is a lot of memorization. Teaching and learning in a constructivist classroom is requires that:
- the thinking processes of the students are the focus of attention;
- one topic is covered in-depth rather than attempting to "cover" many topics
- assessment is ongoing and mutually shared by teacher and students

Learning Science: Many eductors note that the key to understanding science is for students to directly examine their own theories and confront the shortcomings (Hewson, Beeth, & Thorley, 1998). For **conceptual change** to take place, students must go through six stages:
1. initial discomfort with their own ideas and beliefs
2. attempts to explain away inconsistencies between their theories and evidence presented to them
3. attempts to adjust measurements or observations to fit personal theories
4. doubt
5. vacillation
6. conceptual change

Learning and Teaching Science

Conceptual change teaching in science: A method tht helps students understand (rather than memorize) concepts inscience by using and challenging the students' current ideas.

The goal of conceptual change teaching in schience is to help students pass through these six stages of learning. The **two central features** of **conceptual change teaching** are:
- Teachers are committed to teahcing for student understanding rather than "covering the curriculum"
- Students are encouraged to make sense of science using their current ideas-they are challendged to describe, predict, explain, justify, debate, and defend the adequacy of their understanding. Dialogue is key. Only when intuitive ideas prove inadequate can new learning take hold (Anderson & Roth, 1989)

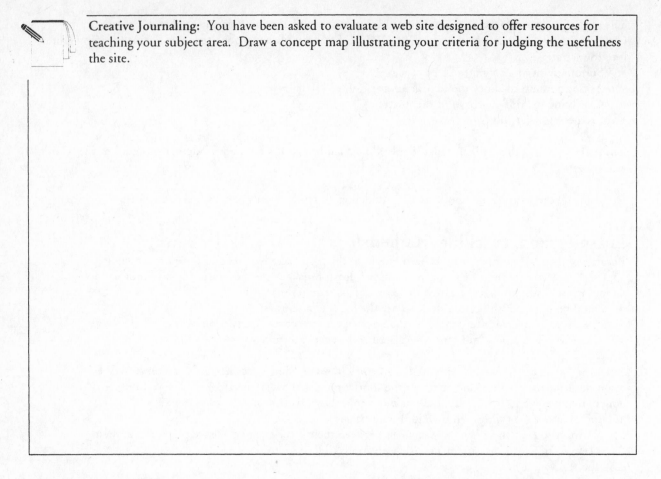

Creative Journaling: You have been asked to evaluate a web site designed to offer resources for teaching your subject area. Draw a concept map illustrating your criteria for judging the usefulness the site.

Reaching Every Student: EFFECTIVE TEACHING IN INCLUSIVE CLASSROOMS

Despite debates about preferred methods of instruction, different goals require different methods. What methods of instruction will you use in an inclusive classroom and how will you meet the needs of your individual students? Effective teachers of mainstreamed students do the following:

- Use time efficiently, have smooth management routines to avoid behavioral problems
- Ask questions at the right level of difficulty
- Give supportive positive feedback, helping them to figure out answers if they're on the right track
- Avoid segregation of mainstreamed students
- Integrate special services (speech therapy, remedial reading, etc.) into the class setting
- Make sure your language and behavior with mainstreamed students is a good model for everyone
- Teach about differences among people as part of the curriculum
- Have students work together in cooperative groups
- Keep schedules and activity patterns of all students in the class as similar as possible

Whereas it is strongly recommended that wherever possible, provide services for disabled students within their own classroom, resource rooms may also be employed.

More and more, special education and regular education teachers are combining forces to meet the needs of disabled students in a new approach called cooperative teaching. Both teachers exchange roles to make the best use of expertise, materials, and time, benefiting the regular as well as the disabled students.

Technology and Exceptional Students

Computers are seen as an educational boon for both disabled and non-disabled students. Some of the ways that computers have been found to benefit disabled students are listed below:

1. They can provide step-by-step tutoring, and repeat information as often as necessary
2. They are engaging and interactive, increasing motivation
3. They use images, sounds, and gamelike features
4. Programs are being developed to help hearing people use sign language
5. Hearing impaired benefit from visual programs
6. Programs will "speak" words for students with reading difficulties
7. For the writing disabled, word processors produce perfect penmanship
8. For gifted students, computers can be an enriching resource for sharing information and projects

With these tremendous advances in technology have come new barriers, however. Many computers have graphic interfaces, requiring precise movements of the mouse. These maneuvers are difficult for students with motor problems or visual impairments. Researchers are working on ways for users to access information nonvisually. One current trend is **universal design.**

Universal design: Considering the needs of all users as new tools, or learning programs, or websites

Check with the resource teachers in your district to find out what is available in your school.

Diversity and Convergences

Diversity: Differentiated Instruction

The basic idea of **differentiated instruction** is that teachers must take into account not only what they are teaching but also who they are teaching. In differentiated classrooms, students work at different paces, sometimes exercising varied learning options, and they are assessed using indicators that fit their interests and needs (George, 2005). Without differentiated instruction, students in many classes and schools are grouped by ability, and all the problems of tracking follow them (see Chapter 4).

Convergences

In spite of the criticisms and debates, there is no one best way to teach. Different goals and student needs require different teaching methods. Every student may require direct, explicit teaching for some learning goals some of the time, but every student also needs to experience more open, constructivist, student-centered teaching as well.

Journaling Activity Reflect on what you have read in this chapter.

FOUR Ideas that "Square with Me":

THREE Points to Consider Further:

TWO Questions Going Around in My Head

MY NOTES

(Use this space to make additional notes for this chapter)

14
Standardized Testing

Stop, Think, Write: List two concerns about standardized testing that are frequently expressed by families of students.

How would you, as a teacher, respond to each of these concerns?

EVALUATION, MEASUREMENT, and ASSESSMENT

Teaching involves making many kinds of judgments-decisions based on values: "Should we use a different text this year?" "Is this film appropriate for my students?" "Will Jacob do better if he repeats the first grade?"

Measurement is quantiative-the description of an event or characteristic using numbers. Meaurment tells how much, how often, or how well by providing scores, ranks or ratings.

Increasingly, measurement specialsits are suing the term assessment to desribe the process of gathering information about students' learning. Assessment is broader than testing and measurement because it includes all kinds of ways to sample and observe students's skills, knowledge, and abilities. **Assessment** can be any one of many prodeucres used to gather information about student performance (Linn & Miller, 2005).

Example: Assessments can be formal, informal observations, development of portfolios, or the creation of artifacts.

Measurements mean nothing without a reference point against which to compare. Your weight on the scale means nothing without comparing it to height/weight charts for someone your age and body build, or you could compare it to yesterday's weight, or to the weight you would like to attain (or lose). So measurements mean nothing without comparing these to something else and in education we commonly make **two kinds of comparisons;** norm-referenced and **criterion-referenced.**

Norm-Referenced Tests

Norm-Referenced Testing: Testing in which scores are compared with the average performance of others.
Example: Juanita scored in the top 5% of her swimming class. Jamie's reading score is average for his honors class but superior to national scores for someone his age.

In norm-referenced testing, we can find a student's relative standing by comparing her or his performance to the average performance of a **norm group.**

Norm Group: A group whose average score serves as a standard for evaluating any student's score on a test. **Example:** When you take a college entrance exam, your score is compared to other students across the nation who are also hoping to enter college. Regardless of the actual scores, the top students will have the best chance to pick the colleges of their choice.

There are **three types of norm groups** in education: **class, district, or national.** Listed below are some *advantages* to norm-referenced tests.
- Norm-referenced tests are good for covering a wide range of general objectives.
- Norm-referenced tests are useful for measuring the overall achievement of students who have come to understand complex material by different routes.
- Norm-referenced tests are useful for selecting the top candidates when only a few can be admitted to the program.

Norm-referenced measurements also have their *limitations.*
- Knowing students' percentiles or ranks does not tell us what they know or can do. Knowing that Juanita is the top swimmer in her class does not tell us how well she can swim.
- Norm-referenced tests are not appropriate for measuring affective and psychomotor objectives.
- Norm-referenced tests foster competition and comparison of scores and may be damaging to the self-esteem of low achievers.

Criterion-Referenced Tests

The second type of comparison of test scores is called **criterion-referenced testing.**

Criterion-Referenced Testing: Testing in which scores are compared to a set performance standard. Criterion referenced tests measure the mastery of very specific objectives. **Example:** We don't care that Juanita is the top swimmer in her class (norm-referenced). We want to know whether she has mastered the criterion of being able to swim 10 laps and tread water for fifteen minutes. Jamie may have to meet the criterion of getting 90 out of 100 reading questions correct if he wants to maintain his "A" in reading.

Some of the **advantages of criterion-referenced testing** are listed below.
- Teachers know exactly what a student can and cannot do by how well they have mastered the objectives.
- When teaching basic skills, it is more important to know that a child has mastered the basics versus knowing where that child stands relative to other students.
- Some standards for performance must be set at 100%, eg. driving ability, how to operate a skill-saw, knowledge of the alphabet.

Criterion-referenced tests also have their **limitations.**
- Many subjects cannot be broken down into a specific set of objectives.
- Standards may be arbitrary; is one point difference that important in setting standards?
- It may important to know how others are doing nationally if your criteria are too low and the performances that you are measuring as "As" might only be "Cs" nationally.

Application One: Criterion or Norm-Referenced?
Read the following evaluation situations and determine whether it is criterion or norm-referenced. Check your responses in the answer key.

1. Peggy's reading comprehension score far exceeds the national average for her age group. _____
2. Jack got 9 out of 10 throws in the basketball hoop. _____
3. George can jump 15 feet in the long jump. _____
4. Ms. Duplessey's morning French class has a higher average achievement score than the afternoon class. _____
5. Rebecca's painting won the blue ribbon at the county fair. _____
6. Franklin can type 45 words per minute. _____
7. Our baseball team won the league championship. _____
8. Tim got 560 verbal and 600 math on his SATs _____
9. Jerome got a 90 on his chemistry test. _____
10. Hamako can recite every line of the Gettysburg Address with no errors. _____

WHAT DO TEST SCORES MEAN?

Everyday, more than one million **standardized tests** are administered in schools throughout this country. Most are norm-referenced.

Standardized Tests: Tests given, usually nationwide, under uniform conditions and scored according to uniform procedures.

All students all over the country are supposedly tested according to the same conditions. But before your students are administered the test, the test will be piloted on a **norming sample**.

Norming Sample: Large sample of students serving as a comparison group for scoring standardized tests.

Whether your students have scores from standardized tests or classroom made tests, there are a **variety of ways** that their **scores can be represented**. The first of these is called a **frequency distribution**.

Frequency Distribution: Record showing how many scores fall into set groups.

The information from a frequency distribution can also be represented pictorially or in the form of a **histogram**.

Histogram: Bar graph of a frequency distribution.

When we want to describe the typical or average scores of our students, we may talk about measures of **central tendency**.

Central Tendency: Typical score for a group of scores. There are three measures of central tendency; the **mean, median, and mode**.

Mean: Arithmetical average **Example:** You add all of the scores together and divide by the number of scores. The formula for finding the mean is as follows:

$\quad$ =the sum of
N-˙the number of scores
X=a student's score

Therefore, to find the mean (written as $\overline{X}$) use this formula: $\overline{x}=\dfrac{\Sigma x}{N}$

Median: Middle score in a group of ranked scores. **Example:** In the following ranked array of scores, the median is the middle score or "75".   (70, 72, 72, 73, 75, 77, 79, 81, 81)

Mode: Most frequently occurring score. **Example:** In the following array, the mode is "81". (75, 75, 78, 79, 80, 81, 81, 81, 81, 82, 82, 83, 84, 86)

Sometimes, more than one score occurs with the same frequency as another score and both scores occur more than any other score. This signifies a **bimodal distribution.**

Bimodal Distribution: Frequency distribution with two modes. Example: In the following distribution, the two modes are "83" and "88". (79, 80, 82, 83, 83, 83, 84, 86, 88, 88, 88) Both 83 and 88 occur three times.

The **measure of central tendency** gives us just that; **a central measure**, an average measure, a middle measure, a typical measure. It gives us the **best representation of that distribution of scores.** If we want to know the typical performance of the students in our classes, we look to the measure of central tendency. But it doesn't tell us how the scores range or spread out from the mean. **For example;** the mean of the following distribution of scores (78, 82, 82, 82, 82, 84) is 82. But the mean of the following distribution of scores (40, 78, 90, 92, 94, 96) is also 82 and look at how different the scores are in each distribution. If we were to draw conclusions based only on the means, we really wouldn't have the whole picture. That is why it is also important that we examine the **standard deviation.**

Standard Deviation: Measure of how widely the scores vary from the mean. Scores that spread out further from the mean have greater **variability.**

Variability: Degree of difference or deviation from the mean. **Example:** The means from the two previous distributions are 82. The second distribution has scores which spread out further from the mean so we say that it has greater variability.

The Standard Deviation

The formula for calculating the standard deviation follows:

1. Calculate the mean of your scores (written as $\overline{X}$)

2. Subtract the mean from each score to find how far each score deviates from the mean.($x-\overline{x}$)

3. Square each difference to get rid of the negative signs. $\left(x-\overline{x}\right)^{2}$

4. Add all of the squared differences. $\Sigma\left(x-\overline{x}\right)^{2}$

5. Divide this total by the number of scores. $\dfrac{\Sigma\left(x-\overline{x}\right)^{2}}{N}$

6. Find the square root and you will have the standard deviation. $\sqrt{\dfrac{\Sigma\left(x-\overline{x}\right)^{2}}{N}}$

Knowing the mean and the standard deviation of a set of scores can tell us quite a bit of information. If the mean of a set of history test scores is 70 and the standard deviation is 4, and if you got a 78, then you know that you scored two standard deviations above the mean or in the 97.5% for your class. Refer to the normal distribution curve in your text to figure out the percentiles. But if the mean of a set of math test scores is 70 and the standard deviation is 8, and if you got a 78 on your math test, then in math you scored only one

standard deviation above the mean, placing you at the 84% within your class. Your performance in math is good but you are even stronger in history relative to your classmates (assuming the performance levels in both classes are equivalent). Standard deviations are very useful for helping us to understand test scores. Knowing the standard deviation tells us much more than just knowing the **range of scores.**
Range: Distance between the highest and the lowest score in a group.

Standard deviations are particularly helpful when the distribution of scores conforms to the normal distribution or the bell-shaped curve.

Normal Distribution: The most commonly occurring distribution, in which scores are distributed evenly around the mean. See your text for an example of a normal distribution. The normal distribution has **certain properties:**
- the mean, median, and mode are all the same score
- 68% of the scores are located within ± 1 standard deviation from the mean
- approximately 16% of the scores fall beyond one standard deviation on both ends of the distribution comprising the remaining 32% of the scores

Types of Scores
One kind of score reported from standardized tests is called a **percentile rank score.**

Percentile Rank: Percentage of those in the norming sample who scored at or below an individual's score. **Example:** If the mean from the norming sample is 500 (as it is with the SAT college entrance exam) and you got a score of 500, then you would be at the 50th percentile.

Another type of score tells us whether our students are performing at levels equivalent with other students their own age or **grade-equivalent.**

Grade-Equivalent Score: Measure of grade level based on comparison with norming samples from each grade. **Example:** If all of the sixth graders take a reading test and the average score is 44, and you score a 44, then you are reading at a sixth grade level.

Often, we would like to make **comparisons between scores** achieved by students in different districts and on different tests and maybe even in different subject areas. But how are we to do this when tests and test conditions were not identical across test situations? It would be like comparing apples to oranges. Therefore, we have to transform or standardize our test scores by putting them in a **common scale. Example:** An analogy I give to my students deals with adding unlike fractions. If we want to add 1/4 to 1/3 then we have to put them in a common scale or give them a common denominator. In this case we would turn them both into twelfths and 1/4 would become 3/12 and 1/3 would become 4/12 and then we could add them resulting in 7/12. Standard scores do essentially the same thing with test scores. **Common standard scores are z scores and T scores.**

Standard Scores: Scores based on the standard deviation.

z Score: Standard score indicating the number of standard deviations a person's score is either above or below the mean. **Example:** If the mean on the test is 70 and the standard deviation is 4, and you scored a 78, then you are two standard deviations above the mean and you would have a z score of two. If on another test, you also scored a 78, and the mean on that test was 70 but the standard deviation was 16, then you scored one-half of a standard deviation above the mean and your z score would be .5. If the mean was 70, and the standard deviation was 8 and you got a 62, well then you scored one standard deviation below the mean giving you a z score of -1. z scores can be positive (if you score above the mean) and negative (if you score below the mean) and they can also be decimals. The formula for a z score follows.

$$z = \frac{x - \bar{x}}{SD}$$

1. Take each student's score and from it, subtract the mean for that set of scores.
2. Divide the difference obtained in step 1 by the standard deviation for that group of scores.
3. Remember that z scores can be positive, negative, or decimals.

Figure 14.1

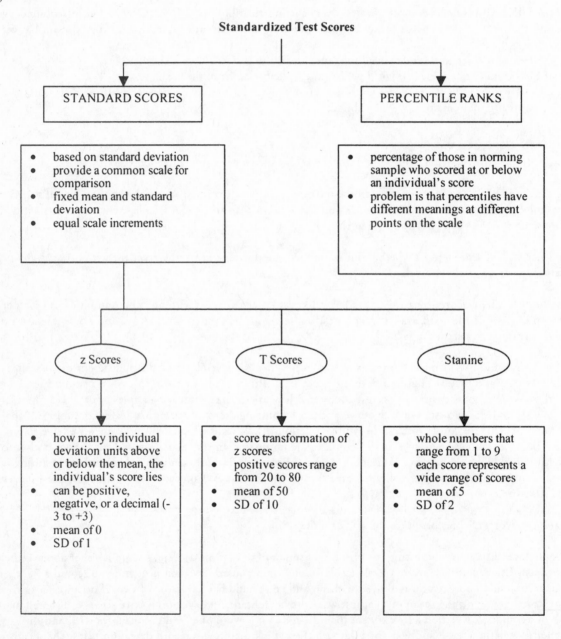

Standardized Test Scores

STANDARD SCORES

- based on standard deviation
- provide a common scale for comparison
- fixed mean and standard deviation
- equal scale increments

PERCENTILE RANKS

- percentage of those in norming sample who scored at or below an individual's score
- problem is that percentiles have different meanings at different points on the scale

z Scores

- how many individual deviation units above or below the mean, the individual's score lies
- can be positive, negative, or a decimal (-3 to +3)
- mean of 0
- SD of 1

T Scores

- score transformation of z scores
- positive scores range from 20 to 80
- mean of 50
- SD of 10

Stanine

- whole numbers that range from 1 to 9
- each score represents a wide range of scores
- mean of 5
- SD of 2

Since it is often inconvenient to use decimals and/or negative numbers, we can perform one more score transformation called **T scores**.

T Scores: Standard score with a mean on 50 and a standard deviation of 10. A T score of 50 means an individual got an average score. Multiplying the z score by 10 gets rid of the decimal and adding 50 to it, makes it a positive number. The formula for transforming z scores into T scores is written below.

$$T = 10(z) + 50$$

One other widely used standard score method is called **stanine scores**. Developed and most widely used by the military, stanines comes from the name, standard nine.

Stanine Scores: Whole number scores from 1 to 9, each representing a wide range of raw scores. The mean is 5 and the standard deviation is 2.
(See Figure 14.1 above)

Application 2: Calculating Standard Scores
Take the following students' scores from their exams and using the means and standard deviations from each test, calculate the z score and T score for each student.

Student	Math mean=80 SD=5	History mean=50 SD=10	English mean=34 SD=8
Todd	X=85	X=55	X=50
Stephanie	X=90	X=40	X=30
Carlos	X=80	X=60	X=42
Terri	X=70	X=65	X=3 8
Todd	z=	z=	z=
Stephanie	z=	z=	z=
Carlos	z=	z=	z=
Terri	z=	z=	z=
Todd	T=	T=	T=
Stephanie	T=	T=	T=
Carlos	T=	T=	T=
Terri	T=	T=	T=

Stop, Think, Write: List two key points you would want to be sure to include when you, as a teacher, discuss standardized test scores with your students. Describe what you would say to make these points clear to your students.

Interpreting Test Scores

One of the most **difficult challenges** that educators face is **understanding exactly what is meant by our students' scores.** We must remember that test scores do not tell the whole story and that a **score is just one sample of behavior.** We must also consider the quality of our tests for assessing achievement and therefore we must **consider two other factors** regarding our tests; **reliability and validity.**

Reliability: Consistency of test results. **Example:** If you were to take a test one day and then, assuming you forgot no information nor checked answers with anyone, if you took it again, we would expect that your performance would be relatively consistent.

There are **three types of reliability:**

1. **Test-Retest Reliability**--When you give the exact same test at two separate times and obtain consistent results.
2. **Alternate Forms Reliability**--Different but equivalent forms of a test that cover the same content area, eg. your ACT, SAT college boards. You get a different form each time you take it.
3. **Split-Half Reliability**--This yields a measure of internal consistency because you compare half of the test items with the other half (odd versus even numbered items).

Standard Error of Measurement: Hypothetical estimate of variation in scores if testing were repeated. A reliable test has a small standard error of measurement.

When interpreting test scores, teachers also must take into consideration this **margin of error.** Teachers should never formulate opinions about student ability by the exact score a student obtains. Many test companies will report students scores within a band of likely scores called **confidence intervals.**

Confidence Intervals: Range of scores within which an individual's particular score is likely to fall.

The next factor that must be considered once we have established that our test is reliable is whether or not the test measures what it is supposed to measure and nothing else. This is called **validity.**

Validity: Degree to which a test measures what it is intended to measure. **Example:** We know that when we use a thermometer, it will measure temperature and nothing else. It is a valid instrument. There are three types of validity related evidence that we may try to gather with the first having the greatest impact for the classroom teacher.

1. **Content-Related Validity Evidence**--This is where we must ask ourselves if our test items reflect the content that was addressed in class and in the texts.
2. **Criterion-Related Validity Evidence**--This is an indicator of how well we can predict performance on a criterion on the basis of a prior measure. There is good criterion validity between the PSAT and the SAT.
3. **Construct-Related Validity Evidence**--This addresses some psychological construct or characteristic such as IQ or motivation. This evidence is gathered over years to determine patterns within the construct being measured.

Content validity is an important issue when interpreting the scores from teacher made tests. I know of a teacher who would deduct points from students' science tests when they had inaccurate dates at the top of their papers. Given this situation, you have to question what their science scores mean. It is not a valid representation of science achievement.

Absence of Bias
We know that IQ tests are biased in favor of students from middle-class socioeconomic status but research on test bias reveals that most standardized school tests predict school achievement equally well across all groups of students. Whereas, standardized aptitude and achievement tests are not biased against minorities in predicting school performance other factors may put minority students at a disadvantage.
* language of the test and tester is often different from the language of the students
* questions are often more geared to the dominant culture
* answers that support middle-class values are often awarded more points
* being verbal and talking a lot is rewarded on individually administered tests
* different groups have had different opportunities to learn the material tested 258

Concern about **cultural bias** has lead some psychologists to develop **culture-fair** or **culture-free** tests.

Culture-Fair/Culture Free Test: A test without cultural bias. **Example:** Many of these tests rely more on performance than on verbal content. Unfortunately, the performances of students from lower-socioeconomic backgrounds and minority groups are no better on these tests than on the standard Wechsler and Binet Intelligence Scales.

Courses designed to prepare students for college entrance exams yield positive results when students practiced on a parallel form of the test for brief periods, when they familiarized themselves with the procedures of standardized tests, and when they received instruction in general metacognitive skills discussed in previous chapters.

TYPES OF STANDARDIZED TESTS
Achievement Tests
The most common standardized tests administered to students are **achievement tests.**

Achievement Tests: Standardized tests measuring how much students have learned in a given content area.

These tests can be given to groups or to individuals and in any subject area. As teachers you will encounter a wide variety of norm-referenced achievement tests. To aid teachers with information from the test results, test publishers will usually provide teachers with individual profiles for each student showing scores on subtests. These scores may be presented in a variety of ways such as raw scores, stanine scores, grade equivalent scores, national percentile scores, scale scores, and the range in which the student's score is likely to fall. If a student is experiencing difficulty within subject areas or is evidencing learning disabilities, then professionals (school psychologists, counselors) may rely on the use of **diagnostic tests.**

Diagnostic Tests: Individually administered tests to identify special learning problems. Elementary school teachers are more likely than secondary school teachers to receive information from diagnostic tests. Diagnostic tests may be used to:
* assess the ability to hear differences among sounds
* remember spoken words or sentences
* recall a sequence of symbols
* separate figures from their background
* express relationships
* coordinate eye and hand movements
* describe objects orally and blend sounds to form words
* recognize details in a picture
* coordinate movements and other abilities needed to learn, remember, and communicate learning

Both aptitude and achievement tests measure developed abilities. Achievement tests may assess abilities developed over a short amount of time such as a week long unit on spelling or they measure abilities developed over time such as an IQ test. **Aptitude tests** serve yet another purpose.

Aptitude Tests

Aptitude Tests: Tests meant to predict future performance. **Example:** The Scholastic Aptitude Test (SAT) is meant to predict how well students will do in college.

ISSUES IN STANDARDIZED TESTING
Accountability and High-Stakes Testing

STOP/THINK/WRITE
How has standardized testing affected your life so far? What opportunithes have been opened or closed to you based on test scores? Was the process fair?

Our country currently faces a state of test escalation due to such factors as accountability, minimum competency, and inter-national competition. Because of the emphasis placed on test scores, many refer to this as high-stakes testing. Many are suggesting the establishment of a national exam while others suggest that we should decrease the use of standardized tests in schools because the consequences may lead to "**teaching to the test**" or decision making that may adversely affect minority students.

High-Stakes Testing: Standardized tests whose results have powerful influences when used by school administrators, other officials, or employers to make decisions.

Accountable: Making teachers and schools responsible for student learning, usually by monitoring learning with high-stakes tests.

High-stakes testing is a complex and controversial practice. To be valuble, testing programs must have anumber of characterisitics:
• Match the content standards of district
• Be part of the larger assessment plan
• Text complex thinking
• Provide alternate assessment strategies for students with identifiable disabilities
• Provide opportunities for retesting
• Include all students
• Provide appropriate remediation
• Make sure all students tested have adequate opportunities to learn
• Take into account the student's language
• Use test results for children, not against them (Haladyna, 2002)

Standardized achievement tests must be chosen so that the items on the test actually measure knowledge gained in the classroom.

Reaching Every Student: Helping Students with Disabilities Prepare for High-Stakes Tests

Test preparation programs can help students improve their scores significantly. Test preparation for students with disabilities needs to occur earlier for students with disabilities. The strategies taught should be closely aligned with the specific types of problems that the students willencounter on the test and should be embedded in good content instruction. The best way to help students deal with test anxiety is to better equip students with the academic skills they will need to succeed (Carter et al., 2005).

NEW DIRECTIONS IN STANDARDIZED TESTING

Standardized tests continue to be controversial. In response to dissatisfaction with traditional forms of assessment, new approaches have emerged to deal with some of the most common testing problems. The goal of **alternative assessment** is to create standardized tests that assess complex, important, real-life outcomes. This appraoch is also called direct assessment, performance assessment, or alternative assessment. These terms refer to procedures that are alternatives to traditional multiple-choice standardized tests, because these directly assess student performance on real-life tasks (Hambleton, 1996; Popham, 2002).

Authentic Assessment

Authentic Assessment: Measurement of important abilities using procedures that simulate the application of these abilities to real-life problems.

Newer tests will feature more **constructed-response** formats. This means that students will create responses (essays, problem solutions, graphsy, diagrams), rather than simply selecting the one correct answer. This will allow tests to measure higher-level and divergent thinking.

Constructed-response format: Assessment procedures that require the student to create an answer, instead of selecting an answer from a set of choices.

Diversity and Convergences in Standardized Testing

In the 1970s, the National Assessment of Educational Progress (NAEP) began to test a national sample of students at ages, 9, 13, and 17. One of the provisions of the No Child Left Behind Act is that all states must give the NAEP tests in reading and mathematics every other year in grades 4 and 8 (Linn, Baker, & Betebenner, 2002).

Diversity In those early years of NAEP testing, there was a gap between the scores of White and Black students at all three age levels. For the next two decades, the "acheivement gap" as it was called narrowed. But after 1988, the gap began to widen again, caused perhaps by increases in child poverty and a greater emphasis on low-level skills in high-poverty schools (McClure, 2005).

With high-stakes testing have come concerns about another kind of diversity-students with disabilities. IDIEA (Individauls with Disabilities Improvement Edcuation Act) mandates that studnets with diabilities must be included in general testing, but with accommodations or appropriate modifications, if needed (Spinelli, 2002).

Convergences Three years after the No Child Left Behind Act was instituted, almost 75% of the states and districts in a recent survey reported that the scores were rising on the tests used for NCBL assessment. It appears, on the surface at least, that the achievement gaps are closing, but cautions are advised and further study is needed

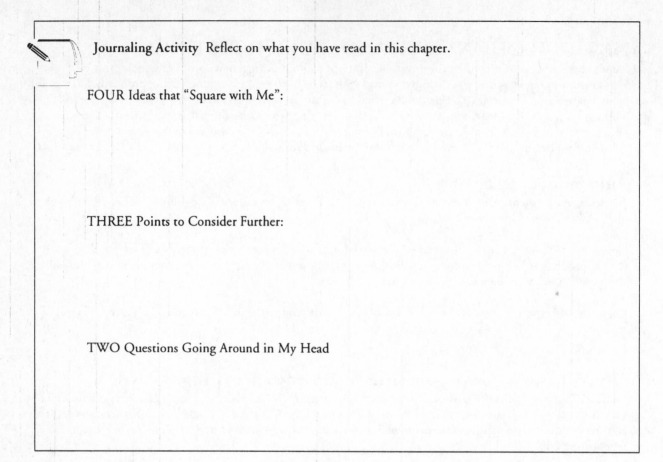

Journaling Activity Reflect on what you have read in this chapter.

FOUR Ideas that "Square with Me":

THREE Points to Consider Further:

TWO Questions Going Around in My Head

MY NOTES

(Use this space to make additional notes for this chapter)

15

Classroom Assessment and Grading

FORMATIVE and SUMMATIVE ASSESSMENT

Even though you may not have much of a voice in determining your district's or school's grading policy, you will ultimately decide how that policy is used and what measures you will use to assess your students' achievement. **Two functions of assessment** are **formative and summative**.

Formative Assessment: Ungraded testing used before or during instruction to aid in planning and diagnosis. **Example:** You may give your students a pretest in science to determine if review is required. You may also give your students a formative test in the form of a diagnostic test to monitor the learning process; to see if are they comprehending the material or if there are any trouble spots.

Pretest: Formative test for assessing students' knowledge, readiness, and abilities. **Example:** Mrs. Jones, (the teacher your fifth grade students had last year), did not complete all of the fourth grade math curriculum and by giving a pretest you discover that you have to back up and teach fractions before you can begin teaching fifth grade mathematics.

Diagnostic Test: Formative test to determine students' areas of weakness, not to be confused with the standardized diagnostic test of learning disabilities. **Example:** You give your third graders a diagnostic reading test and discover that some of your "fastest" readers are not comprehending what they have read and together you work out strategies that will help them to slow down and become more reflective about their reading.

Pretests and diagnostic tests are not graded so these make good practice tests for students who suffer from test anxiety. Another type of formative assessment that frequently checks student performance is called **Curriculum-Based Assessment (CBA).**

Curriculum-Based Assessment (CBA): Evaluation method using frequent tests of specific skills and knowledge. CBA is a variety of approaches for observing student performance and making decisions about appropriate instruction. This method has been used primarily with students with learning problems but is effective for all students because instruction is adapted to meet the pace and needs of students as determined by the assessment probes.

Summative Assessment: Testing that follows instruction and assesses achievement. It provides a *summary* of accomplishments and levels of achievement. **Example:** At the end of the biology unit, Jim Reynolds gives his class a summative exam to see if they have learned a sufficient amount of material to warrant moving on to the next unit.

The only **difference between summative and formative assessment** is **how the results are used.** The same test can be used for summative or formative assessment, the purpose determines the type of assessment.

Planning for Testing

Before designing your tests, it is a good idea to use a **behavior-content matrix**.. This is a test specification plan that will help you to generate items to match your learning objectives. More important objectives should have more items. Your test plan will increase the validity of your test by ensuring that you ask a reasonable number of questions to cover each topic. Dempster (1991) suggests that for testing to yield the most benefits:

* testing should occur frequently to encourage retention of material
* teach material, give students a test soon after, then retest on the material later
* cumulative questions are the key to effective learning and retention and increase the application of previously learned skills

Unfortunately, school curriculums are so full that there is little time for frequent testing. Dempster (1993) suggests that we teach fewer topics in greater depth to allow for more practice, review, testing, and feedback.

Objective Testing

Types of commonly used forms of classroom and standardized tests are called **objective tests**. As the name implies, these tests are objective and will be scored without bias as the answers are not open to interpretation. Gronlund suggests that the guiding principle in determining which types of test questions to use should be those items that best assess how accurately students have met the learning objectives.

Objective Tests: Multiple-choice, matching, true-false, short-answer, and fill-in tests; scoring these tests requires no interpretation as in essay exams.

Multiple choice questions are useful for asking factual questions but can also test higher level objectives as well. Items will assess more than recognition and recall if the student is required to apply or analyze concepts, but these items are much more difficult to write. Multiple choice questions are comprised of a stem and alternatives (the choices which include the correct response, and **distractors**). The difficult part of writing a multiple choice question is coming up with distractors that aren't obviously incorrect.

Distractors Wrong answers offered as choices in a multiple-choice item.. Stem The question part of the multiple choice question.

Whenever possible, **phrase the stem in positive terms** (unless you capitalize, italicize, underline or bold the word NOT), make it clear and simple, presenting only a single problem, and include as much wording as possible in the stem so that it doesn't have to be repeated in the alternatives.
Alternatives should fit the grammatical form of the stem, so that no answers are obviously wrong. Avoid the use of words such as *always, never, all,* or only because test-wise students detect these as obvious distractors, and don't have two alternatives that mean the same thing since this signals to students that both must be wrong. Avoid using the exact wording from the text as students will recognize the answers without knowing what they mean. Avoid overuse of *all of the above* and *none of the above* as these may be helpful to students who are guessing. Don't include any obvious patterns such as letter position or length because this may bias your test in favor of students who are test-wise.
To determine the quality of the objective tests that you give, conduct an item analysis to target test items that need to be modified or eliminated. The **difficulty index (p)** tells us the percentage of people who gave the right response to the item. For norm-referenced tests, items with difficulty indices of around .50 are best. These items will most likely differentiate among individuals with differing levels of achievement. The **discrimination index (d)** tells us how each item *discriminates* between individuals who performed well on the test overall and those who did not. In other words, good items are answered correctly by those students who do well on the entire test but are missed by those students who perform poorly on the entire test.

Stop, Think, Write: Write a multiple-choice, true/false or fill-in-the blank test question that would test students' achievement of the following objective: After completing the unit, you will be able to list, in order, the steps involved in brushing your teeth.

Essay Testing

Essay exams are appropriate for assessing the written responses of students, for administering a test when you have more time for scoring than for test construction, and for assessing the types of objectives found in the higher levels of Bloom's taxonomy. By requiring students to generate answers, we can be sure that they have met some learning objectives. Essay tests take much more time answer than objective tests and therefore should be limited to the assessment of complex learning outcomes. Because they require more time, it may be best to break up your testing over several days. If you have an extensive amount of material to cover, objective tests may be a better route or you could combine essay with objective. The more items you include on a test, the lower the standard error of measurement and the more accurate the assessment. Whatever the choice, students need ample time to respond and time pressures may cause anxiety and lower performance in some students.

A major problem with essay exams is the evaluation of student responses. Starch and Elliot (1912) discovered that when 200 English teachers evaluated responses to the same essay questions, their scores ranged from 64 to 98. Several qualities of essays may influence scoring; (1) neatly written, verbose, jargon-filled essays with few construction or grammatical errors were given the best grades, and (2) teachers may reward quantity versus quality. The following year, Starch and Elliot found similar results for history and geometry papers demonstrating that subjectivity occurs across subject areas. Gronlund (2003)suggests several strategies for effective grading of essay exams:

- construct a model answer and then you can assign points to its various parts
- give points for the organization of the answer and internal consistency
- then assign grades and sort the papers into piles by grade
- finally, skim the papers in each pile to ensure consistency
- when grading tests with several essay questions, grade all responses to one question before moving on to the next and after you finish scoring question number one, shuffle the papers so no student has all of their questions scored first, last, or in the middle.
- asking students to put their names on the backs of their exams to ensure anonymity
- a final check would be to have another teacher familiar with your goals grade your exams without knowing what grades you have assigned. This is especially helpful if you are a novice teacher.

Application One: Characteristics of Objective and Subjective Tests
The following statements are characteristic of either objective tests or essay tests. Reflect on each statement to determine which form of test applies. Check your responses in the answer key.

1. When you have an extensive amount of content area to cover, this test can sample much more.
   _____

2. Best for assessing ability to organize, integrate, and express ideas. _____
3. When your time for test construction is shorter than your time for scoring. _____
4. Characterized by quick, reliable, unbiased scoring procedures. _____
5. Most commonly used form of test by test experts and classroom practitioners. _____

---

6. Good for measuring outcomes at the knowledge, comprehension, and application levels of learning. _____

7. Easy to score, tough to prepare. _____
8. Encourages students to remember, interpret, and use the ideas of others. _____
9. Quality of the test is determined by the scorer. _____
10. More reliable when your number of students is small. _____

ALTERNATIVES TO TRADITIONAL ASSESSMENT

Some of the same criticisms of standardized tests (recall of facts versus problem solving, control of the curriculum, etc.) are also aimed at classroom tests. Some suggest that viable alternatives to traditional testing are **authentic tests.**

Authentic Tests: Assessment procedures that test skills and abilities as they would be applied in real-life situations.

Wiggins (1989) suggests that if our instructional goals are for students to think critically and do research then we should have them think critically and do research and then assess their performances. Authentic assessment requires students to perform, accept criticism and feedback, and then to improve the performance. (See Figure 15.1)

Authentic Classroom Assessments

Offshoots of authentic assessment are several new approaches with the goals of *performance in context.* Within this framework, students are required to engage in problem-solving activities. Knowledge of facts are still required but they are applied in a procedural context to solve a real-life problem. Two new approaches are **portfolios** and **exhibitions.**

Portfolio: A collection of the student's work in an area, showing growth, self-reflection, and achievement. **Example:** written work, artistic pieces, graphs, diagrams, photographs, videotapes, lab reports, computer programs or anything that represents the subject being taught and assessed.

Components of portfolio assessment include work in progress, revisions, student self-analyses, and reflections on what the student has learned. Teach students how to create and use portfolios.

Exhibitions: A performance test or demonstration of learning that is public and usually takes an extended time to prepare. **Example:** Our graduate students have the option of presenting their theses research in the form of a poster presentation. Their research is evaluated by a committee, as is their poster, their presentation, and their ability to orally convey the idea behind their research and how professionally they address questions.

With exhibitions, communication and understanding is essential as are extensive amounts of time dedicated to preparation. Many suggest that "exhibitions of mastery" replace tests for graduation or course completion requirements.

EVALUATING PORTFOLIOS AND PERFORMANCE

Students' performances are NOT assessed relative to each other but are compared to set standards, in other words, they are criterion and not norm-referenced. Checklists, rating scales, and scoring rubrics are useful for assessing performances.

Scoring Rubrics: rules that are used to determine the quality of a student performance. **Example:** Student faces audience, stands straight, makes eye contact, etc.

Students should be involved in the development of scales and scoring rubrics so they know in advance what is expected, and are challenged to perform to standards of quality. When they're given practice in designing and applying score rubrics, their work and performances improve. Performance assessment requires careful judgment by teachers and clear feedback to students as to what needs improvement.

As discussed in the previous chapter, of particular concern with these assessment methods is reliability, validity, and generalizability. As seen previously, ratings of portfolios and essays are not consistent across raters. The more expert the evaluator, however, the more reliable the scores. Regarding validity, some research suggests that students who are rated as master writers on portfolios are judged less capable on traditional methods but as to which method is more accurate, only further research will tell. Equity or fairness in grading is a concern, as with evaluation of essays, but having a network of support from teachers, peers, families, and others will help to round portfolios and exhibitions into shape with an extensive amount of feedback versus one teacher's evaluation.

Informal Assessments are ungraded (formative) assessments that gather information from multiple sources to help teachers mae decisions (Banks, 2005). There are many kinds of informal assessments-keeping notes and observations about student performance, rathing scales, and checklists. Every time teachers ask questions or watch students perform skills, the teachers are conducting informal assessments.

Figure 15.1

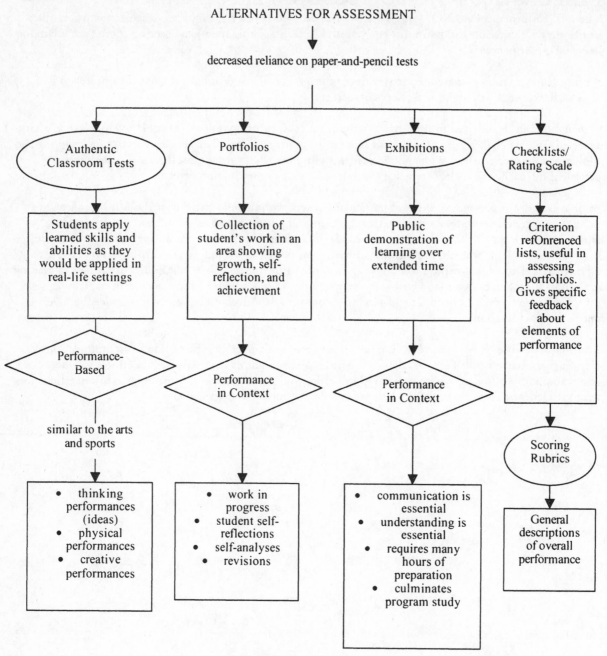

ALTERNATIVES FOR ASSESSMENT

decreased reliance on paper-and-pencil tests

Authentic Classroom Tests

Students apply learned skills and abilities as they would be applied in real-life settings

Performance-Based

similar to the arts and sports

- thinking performances (ideas)
- physical performances
- creative performances

Portfolios

Collection of student's work in an area showing growth, self-reflection, and achievement

Performance in Context

- work in progress
- student self-reflections
- self-analyses
- revisions

Exhibitions

Public demonstration of learning over extended time

Performance in Context

- communication is essential
- understanding is essential
- requires many hours of preparation
- culminates program study

Checklists/ Rating Scale

Criterion refOnrenced lists, useful in assessing portfolios. Gives specific feedback about elements of performance

Scoring Rubrics

General descriptions of overall performance

Involving Students in Assessments

One way to connect teaching and assessment while developing students' sense of efficacy for learning is to involve the students in the assessment process. Students can keep track of their own progress and assess their improvement.

Effects of Grading on Students

Research suggests that high standards, competitive class atmosphere, and low grades increases absenteeism and dropout rates, especially with disadvantaged students. Are we then to lower our standards and not give "Fs" when warranted? Failure has been shown to have both negative and positive consequences as some studies reveal that a 100% failure rate and a 100% success rate are both bad for learning to cope with failure, an important lesson in life. Sometimes failure is necessary for students to understand the relationship between hard work and success. Once again, remember how it was when you learned to ride your bike. Educators must replace easy success with challenge yet ensure that tasks are "do-able", but help students to learn from their mistakes when they fail. Failing a grade level, however, can be devastating and results from research suggest that it is best to promote students and provide summer remediation and continued help.

Students often need help in determining why their mistakes are wrong. Teacher feedback plays an important role in correcting faulty strategies so that students don't make the same mistakes again. Written comments are effective but they should be kept brief for younger students and should recognize good work and improvements as well as corrective feedback.

Retention in Grade   Research shows that retained students are more likely to be male, members of minority groups, and living in poverty (Beebe-Frankenberger, Bocian, MacMillan, & Gresham, 2004). Most research finds that grade retention is associated with poor long-term outcomes such as dropping out of school, higher arrest rates, fewer job opportunities, lower self-esteem (Grissom & Shepard, 1989; Jimerosn, Anderson, & Whipple, 2002).

Effects of Feedback   The results of several studies of feedback fit well with the notion of "successful" or constructive failure. These studis have consluded that it is more helpful to tell students *why* they are wrong so they can learn more appropriate strategies (Bangert-Drowns, Kulik, Kulik & Morgan, 1991).

Grades and Motivation

If grades are based on memorization, student study time will be spent on just that. If you test only at the knowledge level of Bloom's taxonomy you are motivating students to get the grade rather than engage in any sort of meaningful learning. If the grade reflects meaningful learning, working for a grade and working to learn become the same thing.

Low grades, however, do not motivate students. Rather than failing students, give them incompletes and the opportunity to revise and improve their work. Maintain high standards and provide needed help and they will see the relationship between effort and success.

GRADING AND REPORTING: NUTS AND BOLTS
Criterions-Referenced versus Norm-Referenced Grading

To determine final grades, decisions must be made as to what the grades reflect. Should students' performances be weighed against standards of mastery as in **criterion-referenced grading** or should these reflect what that student knows in comparison to classmates as with **norm-referenced grading**. We will explore each of these separately?

Criterion-Referenced Grading: Assessment of each student's mastery of course objectives. Here the grade represents a list of accomplishments.

Criterion-referenced grading has the advantage of spelling out the criteria in advance so that every student can achieve an "A" if he or she meets the criteria. Student performance can be compared to clearly defined instructional goals. Some school districts use reporting systems where report cards list objectives along with judgments about the student's attainment of each.

Norm-Referenced Grading: Assessment of students' achievement in relation to one another. Here, the ability of students within the class will play a large role in determining individual grades. One form of norm-reference grading is called grading on the curve. There is good evidence that this type of grading damages the relationshiops among students and between eachers and students (Krumboltz & Yeh, 1996).

PREPARING REPORT CARDS
The Point System and Percentage Grading

One popular system for combining grades from many assignments is a **point system**. Each test or assignment is given a certain number of total points, depending on its importantce. Points are then awarded on the test or paper based on specific criteria. If tests of comparable importance are worth the same number of points, are equally difficult, and cover a simialr amount of material, this system can be fair and practical. But in most schools, these points still must be converted into some form of final grade. So the teacher has to decide the standards for assigning grades.

Another system for assigning grades is consistent with criterion-referenced grading in that grades are determined by percentage of mastery. It is called **percentage grading**.

Percentage Grading: System of converting class performances to percentage scores and assigning grades based on predetermined cut-off points. Two examples of the most typical percentages and cut-off scores follow.

90-100%=A; 80-89%=B; 70-79%=C; 60-69%=D; below 60%=F
94-100%=A; 85-93%=B; 76-83%=C; 70-75%=D; below 70%=F

As you can see, criterion-referenced percentage grading can be as arbitrary as norm-referenced grading in the assignment of grades. Furthermore, it suggests that we place a high premium on test construction to assume that if a student scores an 88 on the test, then that student has mastered 88% of the subject matter. Also, is one point difference so significant as to place one student at the B level and another student gets an A? No grading system is without its flaws, which is why alternative methods for grading continue to be employed.

The Contract System and Grading Rubrics

Contract System: System in which each student works for a particular grade according to agreed-upon standards. The contract lists what must be done at each grade level to receive that grade.

The **contract system** helps to reduce student anxiety about grades, however, the emphasis may be placed on accomplishing the tasks in a quantity, rather than a quality, mode. Teachers must be very specific about the standards that will distinguish acceptable from unacceptable work. If clearly developed rubrics specify what performances are expected for each assignment, then this may circumvent the problem of some students turning in inadequate additional work just to receive the next higher grade. A good way to prevent this is by including a **revise option**.

Revise Option: In a contract system, the chance to revise and improve work. This system helps to ensure quality control.

Stop, Think, Write: Create a rubric for scoring a person's performance at washing a car.

Grading on Effort and Improvement

A theme that can be applied regardless of which grading system you utilize is grading on **improvement** and **effort.** We should all consider whether grades should be based upon the final level of performance and learning or on an average of performances throughout. Another consideration addresses the high achieving students who have little room for improvement based upon their initial high levels of achievement. A good improvement grading method for both low and high achievers would be to assign grades based upon their **individual learning expectation (ILE).**

Individual Learning Expectation (ILE): Personal average score. **Example:** Remember this term from cooperative learning. Points are given for improvement over your own personal average or for perfect performance. Teachers can use this when figuring a final grade or giving other classroom rewards. Another options is to recognize good student effort through oral or written comments, notes to parents, or other recognitions (see Chapter 13 for more information on ILE).

Cautions: Being Fair

The attributions ta teacher makes about the causes of student success or failures can affect the grades that students receive.

Halo Effect: The tendency for a general impression of a person to influence our perception of any aspect of that person. Example: Stephanie is popular, well-groomed, personable and helpful. Even though her performance is essentially equivalent to Poindexter's, who is pompous, argumentative, and superior, you give her a higher grade.

In order to ensure fairness of grading in your classroom;
- explain your grading policies early on to your students
- set reasonable standards
- base your grades on as much objective evidence as possible
- be sure students understand test directions
- correct, return, and discuss test questions as soon as possible
- as a rule, do not change a grade unless a clerical or calculation error
- guard against bias in grading
- keep pupils informed of their standing in the class
- give students the benefit of the doubt--no measurement techniques are without error

Stop, Think, Write: You are using a contract system in one of your classes. One of the requirements for an A is "to write a book report." However, some students are reporting on books that you think they read last year, and some are handing in short, superficial reports. How can you structure the contract system so that the students will do higher quality work?

Application Two: Tests of Tests

To test your knowledge of tests, see if you can match the correct type of test with its corresponding definition. Select the word from the left column that best matches the phrase on the right. Put the number of the matching word in the blank in front of the letters next to the large letters in the matrix below. If your answers are correct, all numbers across, down, and diagonally will total the same number. Check your responses in the answer key.

1. Authentic Tests   _____a. A collection of the student's work in an area, showing growth, self-reflection, and achievement

2. Portfolio   _____b. A general description of different levels of performance, equivalent to different scores or grades

3. Exhibition   _____c. System in which each student works for a particular grade according to agreed-upon standards

4. Contract System   _____d. Norm-referenced grading that compares students' performance to an average level

5. Dual Marking System _____e. System of assigning two grades, one reflecting achievement, the other effort, attitude, and actual ability

6. Percentage Grading   _____f. A performance test or demonstration of learning that is public and usually takes an extended time to prepare

7. Grading on the Curve _____g. System of converting class performances to percentage scores and assigning grades based on predetermined cutoff points

8. Objective Testing   _____h. Assessment procedures that test skills and abilities as they would be applied in real-life situations

9. Scoring Rubric   _____ i. Tests that will be scored without bias as the answers are not open to interpretation

A	B	C
D	E	F
G	H	I

What is the correct number _____?

BEYOND GRADING: COMMUNICATION

As educators, you will be the key figure in many of your students' lives. Elementary teachers in particular spend as much time with their students as the students' own parents. This will provide you with the opportunity to get to know your students as individuals with concerns, needs, and expectations. As educators, you will be expected to hold conferences with the parents of your students and the focus of many of these conferences may be the grades they have earned.

The Buckley Amendment (also called the Family Educational Rights and Privacy Act of 1974 and the Educational Amendments Act of 1974) guarantees the right of access of test results and any student records, to the student and parents of the student. If the records contain information that is thought to be incorrect, parents have the right to challenge the entries and have the information removed, if they win the challenge. This places a premium on accurate, valid, reliable tests and records. Scores and grades should be based upon firm, solid evidence. Comments and anecdotes should be accurate and unbiased.

Your parent/teacher interactions must be conducted as professionally as possible. You should assume a leadership role, but remain willing to listen and work toward the resolution of the problem. Maintain a friendly atmosphere and when dealing with parents who are angry and upset, try to hear the concerns of the participants rather than focus on the emotional tone of their words. Remember that both you and the parents have something in common, interest in the welfare of their child and promoting intellectual growth and self-actualization of that student. Listed below are some guidelines for a successful parent/teacher conference.

- plan ahead: formulate your goals for the conference
- begin with a positive statement about the student
- listen actively, empathize with the parents, accept their feelings
- establish a working partnership to assist the student
- plan follow-up contacts
- end with a positive statement about the student

Diversity and Convergences in Classroom Assessment

Classroom assessment should, first and foremost, support student learning. But stereotypes and biases can interfere with assessment.

Diversity Several studies have found that teachers may hold lower expectations for ethnic minority students and these biases can influence teaching and assessment (Banks, 2005).

Convergences Quality teching and quality assessment share the same basic principles and these principles hold for all students including being aware of and responding to student differences.

An important federal law, the Buckley Amendment, may affect you as a teacher. Also called the Family Educational Rights and Privacy Act of 1974 and the Educational Amendments Act of 1974, this law states that all educational agencies must make test results and any other informaion in students' records avaialbe to the students and/or their parents.

Journaling Activity Reflect on what you have read in this chapter.

FOUR Ideas that "Square with Me":

THREE Points to Consider Further:

TWO Questions Going Around in My Head

MY NOTES

(Use this space to make additional notes for this chapter)

CHAPTER 1 PRACTICE TESTS

Essay Question

1. You tell a friend you are taking a class in educational psychology and she responds, "Why educational psychology? All you really need to teach is common sense, right?" How will you respond?

Multiple Choice Questions

1. On January 8, 2002, President George W. Bush signed into law the
   a. Elementary and Seondary Education Act
   b. Adequate Yearly Progress Mandates
   c. No Child Left Behind Act (NCLB)
   d. IDEA-Individual Disability Education Act

2. Which of the following is NOT a requirement of NCLB?
   a. Standardized achievement tests for students grades 3 through 8
   b. Schools must report Adequate Yearly Progress toward proficiency in subjects tested
   c. All students much reach proficiency by the end of the 2013-2014 school year
   d. Students failing to reach proficiency shall be provided a free or reduced school lunch

3. Current thinking regarding acceleration of bright students (skipping grades) suggests
   a. that these students will probably become social misfits
   b. that bright students are more susceptible to "academic burn-out" and should not be pressured to advance
   c. that this choice depends on many specific individual characteristics
   d. that parents are the best judges as to whether this will be beneficial for their child

4. The purpose of this type of study is to describe events in a particular class or several classes
   a. experimentation
   b. case study
   c. correlational studies
   d. descriptive study

5. Which of the following is the best example of experimentation?
   a. the teacher observes playground behaviors to determine whether first-grade boys or girls engage in more rough and tumble play
   b. the teacher surveys students' parents regarding their children's' sports related experiences
   c. the teacher uses a whole language approach with one reading group and basals with the other to determine which approach is more effective
   d. the teacher records the social interactions of one student for a month to explore why the child is a social outcast

6. Which of the following is NOT characteristic of correlations?
   a. can indicate cause-and-effect relationships
   b. allow you to predict events
   c. signify that a relationship exists between two variables
   d. is determined by a numerical value that ranges from .00 to $\pm$ 1.00

7. Which of the following studies best characterizes descriptive research?
   a. Three groups of hyperactive children receive different methods of behavior modification to determine which method has the most calming effect
   b. b. Researchers train boys and girls on a series of spatial tasks to determine if training can eliminate gender differences
   c. Researchers examine the classrooms of novice teachers to discover common problem areas for the beginning teachers
   d. Administrators reduce teachers' pay and give them large classes to see if they will continue to teach

8. A well established relationship between two or more factors
   a. theory
   b. longitudinal relationship
   c. rule
   d. principle

9. Good beginning teachers
   a. develop the habit of questioning and analyzing accepted practices
   b. learn to look behind the effective techniques identified in research to ask "why"
   c. develop a repertoire of effective principles and practices so that some activities become automatic
   d. all of the above

10. Beginning teachers everywhere share many concerns including:
    a. discipline
    b. motivating students
    c. accommodating differences among students
    d. evaluating student work
    e. dealing with parents
    f. all of the above

CHAPTER 2 PRACTICE TESTS

Essay Questions

1. With respect to acceleration of cognitive development, defend the Piagetian position that cognitive acceleration may possibly have deleterious (harmful) effects.

2. A group of deaf children were found in a European orphanage. Remarkably, these children had created their own language for communication that no one had ever heard before. Explain why the Piagetian constructivist position can explain this phenomenon better than the Vygotskyian position.

Multiple Choice Questions

1. Central to the development of language and literacy in the early years
   a. are the student's home experiences
   b. b. is exposure to educational programs such as "Sesame Street"
   c. c. is the onset of spoken language by the child
   d. is the number of older siblings in the family

2. Which of the following is NOT one of the criteria for Piaget's stages
   a. The sequence of the stages does not vary
   b. The end point of a previous stage is the staring point for the next
   c. Stages are determined by the age of the child
   d. We know what stage represents the child's thinking by observing how they solve problems

3. Theories proposed by Lev Vygotsky grant greater emphasis for cognitive development on
   a. changes in rates of growth in brain weight and skull size
   b. the child's culture
   c. genetically inherited abilities that manifest as IQ of the child
   d. how early the child acquires speech

4. Teachers can help students develop their capacities for formal thinking by
   a. using direct instruction to provide them with as much factual information as possible
   b. putting students in situations that challenge their thinking and reveal their shortcomings
   c. teaching them the rules for abstract reasoning and problem solving
   d. encouraging them to attend to their physical environment

5. A criticism of Piaget's theory of development is
   a. that Piaget underestimated the cognitive abilities of younger children
   b. that culture may play a greater part in determining cognitive differences among the children of the world
   c. that there are inconsistencies within a stage in terms of what a child can do
   d. all of the above

6. Vygotsky suggested that private speech
   a. should be discouraged among school-age children
   b. increases with task difficulty
   c. occurs among those children who will later move their lips while reading silently
   d. none of the above

7. Adults who provide information and support necessary for the child to grow intellectually are using
   a. cognitive self-instruction
   b. imitative learning
   c. scaffolding
   d. collaborative learning

8. The area where a child cannot solve a problem alone, but can be successful under adult guidance or in collaboration with a more advanced peer is called
   a. the point of transition
   b. the ladder of learning
   c. zone of proximal development
   d. assisted learning

9. The basics of word order and sentence structure is called
   a. semantics
   b. grammar
   c. phonology
   d. syntax

10. Realizing that there is a logical stability to the physical world while also understanding that elements can be changed or transformed and can still conserve many of their original characteristics is thinking that is characteristic of which stage?
   a. sensorimotor
   b. preoperational
   c. concrete operational
   d. formal operational

CHAPTER 3 PRACTICE TESTS

Essay Questions

1. Debate the two positions regarding the relative influence of parents upon their children and the impact of that influence in determining the type of people the children will become as adults. Do you agree with Harris (1998) who asserts that peers exert the more critical influence?

2. As a means for addressing issues of morality, Kohlberg utilized moral dilemmas, giving students opportunities to clarify their values through interactive discourse and debate. Generate a moral dilemma, dealing with issues of cheating appropriate at the high school level. Remember, this should be a dilemma for high school students, one that is not easily resolved. This dilemma is meant to promote discussion and debate by your students toward better understanding of their own morality. Check the answer key for a sample dilemma.

Multiple Choice

1.   Research supports the notion that academic self-concept influences course selection. Students avoid courses based on "illusions of incompetence." Which group of students gradually lower their perceptions of their own abilities, particularly in math and science?
   a. elementary school girls
   b. 9th to 12th grade girls
   c. elementary school boys
   d. Chinese-American boys

2.   With respect to the role that friendships play in the development of the child, adults who were rejected by peers as children
   a. are more capable of maintaining intimate relationships
   b. tend to have more problems like dropping out of school or committing crimes
   c. appear better able to cope with failure
   d. have difficulties forming close bonds with their own children

3. Regarding divorce, when parents have joint custody
   a. they may attend parent-teacher conferences on an alternating basis
   b. they are entitled to information *only while their child is residing with them*
   c. a court must determine their legal rights regarding educational decisions about the child
   d. both are entitled to receive information and attend parent-teacher conferences

4. When students have chaotic and unpredictable home lives, they need
   a. teachers who set clear limits, are consistent, and enforce rules firmly but not punitively
   b. warm, firm structure in school
   c. teachers who respect students and show genuine concern
   d. all of the above

5. If as a teacher you suspect that one of your students is a victim of child abuse
    a. you should contact the child's parents
    b. call the police
    c. report your suspicions to your principal, school psychologist, or social worker
    d. all of the above

6. Research indicates that giving adolescents accurate info about sex
    a. results in fewer unwanted pregnancies
    b. actually encourages them to experiment
    c. makes girls appear sex-crazed if they're prepared for intercourse
    d. has been the cause of a great number of civil lawsuits instigated by parents

7. According to Erikson and Marcia, a healthy delay in an adolescents commitment to personal and occupational choices is called
    a. undifferentiated perspective taking
    b. moratorium
    c. identity foreclosure
    d. generativity

8. A cognitive structure that is a belief about who you are, is called
    a. self-concept
    b. self-esteem
    c. self-efficacy
    d. collective self-esteem

9. It is sometimes difficult for ethnic-minority students to establish a clear identity because
    a. they are members of both a majority culture and a subculture
    b. they often hear and accept messages that de-value their group
    c. values, learning styles, and communication patterns of the students' subculture may be inconsistent with the expectations of the school and the larger community
    d. all of the above

10. Research on moral reasoning suggests that one difference in male-female reasoning is
    a. men feel more guilty when they are being inconsiderate
    b. men feel more guilty when they are untrustworthy
    c. men feel more guilty when they show violent behaviors
    d. men feel more guilty when they lack empathy toward others

CHAPTER 4 PRACTICE TESTS

Essay Questions

1. Discuss the arguments for and against full inclusion of exceptional students.
2. Summarize some strategies for enhancing creativity among your students.

Multiple Choice Questions

1. The best predictor of divergent thinking is (are)
   a. student IQ
   b. fluency scores
   c. flexibility scores
   d. originality scores

2. Which of the following is the single best predictor of academic giftedness?
   a. group achievement tests
   b. reading achievement scores
   c. midterm GPAs
   d. individual IQ tests

3. Which of the following is NOT something you should do if you suspect that a student in your class is having absence seizures?
   a. consult the school psychologist or nurse
   b. question the student to insure that they are understanding
   c. repeat yourself periodically
   d. try to gently rouse the child

4. Research indicates that hearing impaired children who learn manual approaches relative to those who learn only oral approaches
   a. perform better in academic subjects
   b. are more socially mature
   c. use sign language, finger spelling, or both
   d. all of the above

5. Students classified as having low vision
   a. can be helped with corrective lenses
   b. can read with the aid of a magnifying glass or large-print books
   c. must use hearing and touch as the primary learning channels
   d. rely solely on variable speed tape recorders

6. The ages at which most children can pronounce all English sounds in normal conversation are
   a. between the ages of 3 to 4
   b. between the ages of 4 to 6
   c. between the ages of 5 to 7
   d. between the ages of 6 to 8

7. When whole classes are formed based on ability, the process is called:
   a. between-class ability grouping or tracking
   b. performance placement
   c. within-class ability grouping
   d. flexible grouping

8. Within an IEP, the "rights of the parents and students" means that
   a. students may be assigned surrogate parents to participate in planning when the parents are unavailable
   b. confidentiality of school records must be maintained
   c. testing practices must not discriminate against students from different cultural backgrounds
   d. all of the above

9. Spasticity (a characteristic of cerebral palsy) is best defined as a.
   a. general lack of coordination and balance
   b. loss of bladder control
   c. overly tight or tense muscles
   d. brief loss of contact

10. Highly related to standardized IQ scores are measures of
    a. creativity
    b. scholastic achievement
    c. reflective/impulsive tempo
    d. midlife adjustment disorders

CHAPTER 5 PRACTICE TESTS

Essay Questions

1. Your text states "that even students who speak the same language as their teachers may still have trouble communicating, and thus learning school subjects, if their knowledge of pragmatics does not fit the school situation."Explain what is meant by this statement and what teachers can do about it.

2. Provide arguments as to whether multicultural education should emphasize similarities or differences.

Multiple Choice Questions

1. According to our text book, about how many children live in poverty?
   a. 2 million
   b. 13 million
   c. 500, 000
   d. 5 million

2. Many students and teachers assume that low SES students are not very bright because
   a. they may wear old clothes
   b. they may speak ungrammatically
   c. they may be less familiar with books and school activities
   d. all of the above

3. _____ is the term used to refer to "groups that are characterized in terms of a common nationality, culture or language."
   a. Gender
   b. Minority group
   c. Race
   d. Ethnicity

4. Having a masculine or androgynous gender role identity versus a feminine gender role identity is associated with
   a. higher self-esteem
   b. tendencies toward aggressive behaviors
   c. competitive characteristics
   d. higher levels of achievement in school

5. Studies conducted by Gamoran found that the achievement differences between low-track and high-track students
   a. were no greater than the differences between high and low achieving students in the same classroom
   b. not large enough to warrant tracking
   c. were greater than the differences between high school drop-outs and graduates
   d. were greater for females than for males

6. Males' superior spatial performance in navigating, mental rotation, and trajectory prediction is thought to result from
   a. evolution favoring these skills in males
   b. male participation in athletics
   c. males' more active play styles
   d. all of the above

7. Identifying the particular learning styles of a given ethnic group
   a. can help to provide the basis for grouping together similar individuals
   b. can become just one more basis for stereotyping
   c. is helpful because every individual in a group shares the same learning style
   d. it helps teachers to prejudge how a student will learn best

8. According to Suzuki, when Asian Americans are stereotyped as hardworking and passive
   a. they are channeled in disproportionate numbers into scientific/technical fields
   b. they may lack the ability to assert themselves verbally
   c. they may become overly conforming
   d. all of the above

9. When Hawaiian children's rules for responding allow that they "chime in" with contributions to a story despite it being considered an interruption in school, this is viewed as a difference in
   a. learning styles
   b. resistance culture
   c. participation structures
   d. second-language acquisition

10. Recent research has revealed that higher control parenting
    a. leads to lower academic achievement for inner-city children
    b. leads to defiance and adoption of resistance cultures
    c. is effective for behavioral but not for academic objectives.
    d. is linked to better grades for Asian and African American students.

CHAPTER 6 PRACTICE TESTS

Essay Questions

1. An issue that should be considered regarding the application of principles of behavior modification, is its effect on the individual subject to the strategy. Is it ethical to modify others' behaviors?

2. A hot topic regarding the use of positive reinforcers is the effectiveness of the reward. According to Kohn (point/counterpoint), rewarding students for learning actually makes them less interested in the material. Discuss the pros and cons of providing extrinsic rewards for learning.

Multiple Choice Questions

1. To encourage persistence of response, which of the following schedules of reinforcement is most appropriate?
   a. variable interval
   b. continuous schedules
   c.   fixed interval
   d. fixed ratio

2. When a more preferred activity serves as a reinforcer for a less preferred activity, this is called
   a. Premack principle
   b. positive practice
   c. shaping
   d. task analysis

3. Mr. Thompson told Stephanie that since she was quietly working on her project all through the class period, then she could be the first one to leave the hot classroom at recess. This is an example of
   a. presentation punishment
   b. positive reinforcement
   c. removal punishment
   d. negative reinforcement

4. Jimmy is afraid of heights. In PE class, the boys are learning how to climb the ropes. Recently, prior to PE Jimmy develops stomach cramps and has to go to the nurse's office. This is an example of
   a. observational learning
   b. operant conditioning
   c. classical conditioning
   d. contiguity learning

5. Which of the following statements is descriptive of token reinforcement systems?
   a. They are easy to implement and can be established within a short amount of time
   b. They should be used to reinforce high achieving students
   c. They may be too complicated to implement with slow learners
   d. When a token economy is first established, tokens should be given out continuously

6. When attempting to eliminate mildly disruptive behaviors in the classroom, the first recommended approach is to utilize
   a. soft and private reprimands
   b. praise and ignore techniques
   c. social isolation
   d. response cost

7. Which of the following is an example of the use of "response cost"?
   a. Joachim throws spit wads and is forced to continue past the point of interest
   b. Brandy is asked to leave the room
   c. The unruly students have lost their fifth chance and consequently, their recess
   d. Jackson was just given another red mark next to his name

8. When Pavlov's dog salivated when Pavlov entered the room, the dogs salivation is considered to be
   a. a neutral response
   b. an unconditioned response
   c. an unconditioned stimulus
   d. a conditioned response

9. Which of the following is NOT a strategy used to decrease behaviors?
    a. satiation
    b. positive practice
    c. reprimands
    d. response cost

10. Mastery usually means a score of _____ on a test or other assignment.
    a. 80 to 90%
    b. 75%
    c. 100%
    d. none of the above

CHAPTER 7 PRACTICE TESTS

Essay Questions
1. Discuss the advantages and disadvantages of rote memorization. Reflect upon your experiences as a student and think about the situations in which rote memorization was an effective learning strategy.
2. How does perception influence learning and why is it, that when all students in a classroom are presented with the same material and then are later asked to recall what they have learned, they don't all represent the material in the same way?

Multiple Choice
1. Mechanisms for seeing, hearing, tasting, smelling, and seeing are called
    a. the sensory register
    b. the sensory memory
    c. sensory information store
    d. none of the above

2. A problem solving process that makes use of logic, cues, and other knowledge to construct an answer is called
    a. retrieval
    b. spreading of activation
    c. reconstruction
    d. retention

3. Executive control processes describing peoples awareness of their cognitive machinery and how it works are called
    a. metacognitive skills
    b. organizational skills
    c. declarative skills
    d. mnemonics

4. The keyword method does not work well if
    a. it is difficult to identify a keyword for a particular item
    b. keywords may be more easily forgotten than vocabulary learned in other ways
    c. younger students have difficulty forming their own images
    d. all of the above

5. The best single method for helping students to learn is to
   a. organize the material for them
   b. make it meaningful
   c. provide them with mnemonics
   d. reinforce their learning with incentives and rewards

6. Which of the following is NOT one of the characteristics of *experts* functioning within an area?
   a. They function at the cognitive stage
   b. Their functioning has become proceduralized
   c. They possess extensive prerequisite knowledge
   d. They function at the autonomous stage

7. I can remember how content, safe, and warm I felt as a child driving home with my family after an evening of night-time ice-skating. This is an example of
   a. episodic memory
   b. procedural memory
   c. short term memory
   d. a story grammar

8. The long term semantic memory is the memory for
   a. syntax
   b. procedures
   c. meaning
   d. rules

9. The more deeply you process information, relative to its name, physical appearance, and function, *you will* have an easier time recalling information about it from long term memory. This notion is consistent with
   a. situated learning theories
   b. levels of processing theory
   c. associationistic theories
   d. behaviorist theories

10. When you are studying to prepare for an exam, you hope to solidify all of the information in
    a. the sensory register
    b. working memory
    c. short term memory
    d. long-term memory

CHAPTER 8 PRACTICE TESTS

Essay Questions
1. Explain Ausubel's use of an "advance organizer."
2. Why is it sometimes necessary to help students "unlearn" common sense ideas?

Multiple Choice
1. A prototype for the concept of liquids might be
   a. mercury
   b. glass
   c. milk
   d. water

2. Exemplars are best defined as
   a. the best representation of a concept or category
   b. a specific example or memory of a given category
   c. a category with a "fuzzy" boundary
   d. abstract concepts

3. An introductory statement broad enough to encompass all the information that will follow:
   a. negative transfer
   b. overgeneralization
   c. advance organizer
   d. specific transfer

4. Discovery learning is often called
   a. Rule-eg method
   b. deductive reasoning
   c. Eg-rule method
   d. expository learning

5. Your interpretation of a word problem is called
   a. a translation
   b. a linguistic schema
   c. a relational proposition
   d. a search-based route

6. When the problem is divided into a number of intermediate goals or subgoals, and then a means of solving each intermediate subgoal is figured out:
   a. backward-reaching transfer
   b. means-end analysis
   c. overlearning
   d. situated learning

7. Which of the following best illustrates the notion of functional fixedness?
   a. a man who can't find his hammer uses a rock to hammer a nail back into a floor board
   b. a woman who can't find the cork for a half finished bottle of wine, pours the wine into ajar.
   c. a woman who has her Xmas tree wrapped in a plastic tarp doesn't know how she will get it to the curb because she has no wheelbarrow and doesn't think to drag it out in the plastic.
   d. a woman can't find her turkey pins so she straightens out some paperclips to use instead.

8. A step-by-step procedure for solving a problem is called a(n)
   a. analogy
   b. heuristic
   c. means-ends analysis
   d. algorithm

9. Which of the following is not characteristic of "expert" problem solving?
   a. experts use pattern recognition to represent a problem quickly
   b. experts have a large store of condition-action schemata
   c. experts have misconceptions or intuitive notions about a subject
   d. experts have a fund of declarative, procedural, and conditional knowledge

10. Characteristic of Ausubel's expository teaching approach is (are)
    a. meaningful rather than rote reception learning
    b. materials presented in a carefully organized, sequenced, and finished form
    c. deductive reasoning from the rule or principle to example
    d. all of the above

CHAPTER 9 PRACTICE TESTS

Essay Questions
1. Discuss misuses of group learning and problems associated with cooperative learning structures?

Multiple Choice:
1. Bandura's social learning theory emphasized:
    a. observation
    b. modeling
    c. vicarious reinforcement
    d. all of the above

2. Reciprocal Determinism is a term that explains
    a. the learner's contribution to meaning and learning through individual activity
    b. how behavioral, cognitive, and environmental factors operate as interacting determinants of each other
    c. learning as inherently social and embedded within a particular cultural setting.
    d. a commitment to build shared meaning by finding common ground and exchanging interpretations

3. In observational learning, observers are less likely to imitate the model
    a. if the model is a fictional character
    b. if the model is punished for an inappropriate behavior
    c. if the model is a same-age peer
    d. if the model is a high status individual

4. Which of the following is not one of the forms of reinforcement proposed by Bandura to encourage observational learning?
    a. direct reinforcement
    b. self reinforcement
    c. vicarious reinforcement
    d. negative reinforcement

5. The field of constructivism that suggests that we live in a relativistic world that can only be understood from individually unique perspectives is called
    a. social constructivism
    b. psychological constructivism
    c. individual constructivism
    d. radical constructivism

6. A spiral curriculum is a method of teaching that emphasizes
    a. integration of a topic across all subject areas
    b. reading circles based upon ability grouping
    c. introduction of the fundamental structure of all subjects in the early years, revisiting them in more complex forms over time
    d. all of the above

7. A relationship where a less experienced learner acquires knowledge and skills under the guidance of an expert
   a. Cooperative Pairs
   b. Cognitive Apprenticeship
   c. Social Cognitive Conversation
   d. None of the above

8. A form of learning in which students employ inquiry methods is called:
   a. Problem-based Learning
   b. Authentic Learning
   c. Learning for Inquiry Purposes
   d. Cooperative Learning

9. Aspects of learning that rely on collaboration with others and respect for different perspectives describes one element of
   a. Theories of Moral Development
   b. Reciprocal Determinism
   c. Constructivist Approach
   d. Stand Alone Thinking Programs
   e. None of the above

10. Social influences, achievement outcomes, self-influences- all three forces are:
    a. Behavioral learning theories
    b. Cooperative learning structures
    c. Higher level reasoning approaches
    d. Observational learning
    e. Reciprocal influneces

CHAPTER 10 PRACTICE TESTS

Essay Questions

1. Think about preschool children and their high levels of natural curiosity and need to explore and master their environments. We don't have to promise rewards to children to get them to e.g., take apart a clock, or drag all of the pots and pans out of the kitchen cabinets. What do you think happens to their natural motivation to learn, once they enter elementary school? Why, as time goes on, do we have to rely on extrinsic means to get them to perform? What are your thoughts on this issue?

2. Summarize and discuss the research by Thorkildsen, Nolen, & Founier (1994), and Nicholls, Nelson, & Gleaves (1995) which examined students' beliefs about motivation and fairness.

Multiple Choice

1. The theory that explains how events can influence students' intrinsic motivation by affecting their sense of self-determination, control, and feelings of competence, is called
    a. cognitive evaluation theory
    b. sociocultural theory
    c. attribution theory
    d. self-promotion theory

2. Interest is second only to effort as a reason for success, according to students. Teachers must be cautious when using interests to enhance learning so as not to make use of
    a. fantasy
    b. seductive details
    c. classroom experts
    d. student hobbies

3. The theory that examines the perceived causes of individuals' successes or failures is called
    a. attribution theory
    b.   need for achievement theory
    c.   performance goal theory
    d. the entity theory of motivation

4. Research shows that when teachers respond to students' mistakes with pity, praise for a "good try", or unsolicited help, students are more likely to
    a. show appreciation for their teachers and try harder
    b. model these empathetic behaviors with one another
    c. attribute the causes of their failures to lack of ability
    d. cheat

5. Young children before the ages of 11 or 12 tend to believe that ability
    a. is largely what you're born with
    b. won't change no matter how hard you try
    c. is related to effort and trying hard makes you smart
    d. means that someone who succeeds without working at all must really be smart

6. Anxiety in the classroom
    a. is a general uneasiness, a sense of foreboding, a feeling of tension
    b. is both a cause and an effect of school failure
    c. both a trait and a state
    d. all of the above

7. When students are required to engage in activities that have some connection to the real-life problems and situations that students will face outside of the classroom this is aptly named
    a. false learning
    b. inert knowledge
    c. authentic tasks
    d. problem based learning

8. Jeremy joined the soccer team because he truly loves soccer even though he spends most of his time on the bench. Soccer has what kind of value for Jeremy?
    a. attainment
    b. interest
    c. utility
    d. authentic

9.Classroom environments that support student autonomy are associated with
    a. creativity
    b. self-esteem
    c. preference for challenge
    d. all of the above

10. A study of low-achieving first grade students found that in order to finish a task, students
    a. made up answers
    b. filled in the page with patterns
    c. copied from other students
    d. all of the above

CHAPTER 11 PRACTICE TESTS

Essay Question

1. Discuss misuses of group learning and problems associated with cooperative learning structures?

Multiple Choice Questions

1. In setting up cooperative learning structures, teachers should consider:
    a. Assigning the role of leader to a shy, yet bright student.
    b. Allowing students to observe until they feel comfortable with the group
    c. Assigning an adult to each cooperative group to promote interaction.
    d. Size, purpose and a balance of ability, gender, and ethnicity of members.

2. This process has proved more effective than traditional discussions groups because it encourages deeper thinking about the material:
    a. Reciprocal questioning where students learn to summarize the content of a passage, ask questions about central points, clarify material and predict what will come nest.
    b. Cognitive apprenticeships where young people work with knowledgeable guides.
    c. STAD-Student Teams-Achievement Divisions
    d. Social skills training.

3. Face to face interaction, positive interdependence and individual accountability describe which type of learning?
    a. Teacher directed learning
    b. Cooperative learning
    c. Inquiry learning
    d. Authentic learning

4. _____ is a way of dealing with people that respects differences, shares authority, and builds on the knowledge that is distributed among people.
   a. Collaboration.
   b. Cooperation.
   c. Group work.
   d. All of the above.

5. For a large number of adolescents, _____ determines how intensely they are interested in school:
   a. Ethnic background
   b. Parent support
   c. Size of graduating class
   d. Peers

6. According to our text, elementary school children tend to select friends:
   a. based on hair and eye color
   b. who have been members of shared cooperative learning groups
   c. who share their orientation toward school
   d. all of the above

7. In a study discussed in our text, students who choose well rounded peer groups tended to characterize their parents as:
   a. authoritative
   b. autocratic
   c. permissive
   d. univolved

8. _____ is working with others to attain a shared goal.
   a. Collaboration
   b. Cooperation
   c. Group Work
   d. Creative brainstorming

9. Which of the following elements define true cooperative learning groups?
   a. Face-to-face interaction
   b. Positive interdependence
   c. Individual accountability
   d. Group Processing
   e. All of the above

10. This design for cooperative learning requires no special materials or testing procedures and can be used with a wide range of ages:
   a. Student Teams Achievement Divisions
   b. Reciprocal questioning
   c. Jeopardy review game
   d. Flashcard Pair Review

Chapter 12 Practice Tests

Essay Questions

1. Suppose you are a secondary teacher and a very large, senior boy is openly defying you in front of the class. You have repeatedly told him to take his seat but he towers over you, smirking, and mimicking your words. How do you handle the situation?

2. A current classroom management approach that is hotly debated among educators, is the assertive discipline approach by Canter and Canter. Provide arguments both pro and con for the utilization of this approach in the classroom.

Multiple Choice

1. Knowledge and expertise in classroom management are marks of
   a. Burn out in teaching
   b. Stress and exhaustion
   c. Novice ability
   d. Expertise in teaching

2. Ms. Brown was busy writing the class assignment on the board with her back turned toward the classroom. A spit wad hit the board by Ms. Brown. She had been watching the reflection of the class in her classroom door and said , "Jimmy, we need to talk after class. Please come remove the spit wad from the chalkboard." Ms. Brown can be said to possess
   a. an uptight attitude
   b. skill at overlapping
   c. withitness
   d. movement management

3. Sometime students miss out on classroom learning because they are too intimidated or don't know how to go about asking questions. They have been laughed at before and they always seem to say the wrong thing. An area of classroom management that should be addressed with these students is
   a. interactions between teacher and student
   b. personal space
   c. student movement
   d. administrative routines

4. Class rules are designed to inform the class
   a. how materials are to be distributed in the classroom
   b. how grades will be determined
   c. the way activities are accomplished in the classroom
   d. the expected and forbidden actions in the class

5. You might consider posting making and posting signs that list the rules for different activities because
   a. different activities may require different rule and this can be confusing
   b. it provides clear and consistent cues about participation structures
   c. they serve as reminders for the rules that have been previously explained and discussed
   d. all of the above

6. An effective way to ensure that your *entire classroom* becomes an "action zone" is to
   a. move around the room whenever possible
   b. establish eye contact with students seated far away
   c. vary the seating arrangement
   d. all of the above

7. Which of the following teacher response styles is characterized by the following statement? "You are disrupting the learning process of the entire class."
   a. hostile
   b. passive
   c. assertive
   d. unresponsive

8. Mr. Castagne was helping one of the students with his pottery when Jennifer was emptying pieces from the kiln. Tomas threw a ball of clay at Jennifer but missed Jennifer and broke one of the pieces that had just come out of the kiln. Mr. Castagne looked up and said, "Jennifer, you need to be more careful. Your clumsiness broke someone's project." Kounin would call this mistake a(n)
   a. target error
   b. timing error
   c. awareness error
   d. allocated error

9. The paraphrase rule encourages accurate communication because
   a. if students aren't paying attention, they have a second chance to hear the information
   b. many students will drop their negative attitudes when required to repeat what they first said
   c. many respond to what they think was said or meant, not necessarily to the speaker's intended message
   d. the teacher's tone of voice and facial expression may inhibit students from expressing what they really think.

10. An essential goal of classroom management is to expand the sheer number of minutes available for learning. This is called:
   a. academic learning time
   b. engaged time
   c. time on task
   d. seat to seat time

CHAPTER 13 PRACTICE TESTS

Essay Questions
1. Educators debate the best practices for reaching students who are to be considered "at-risk" or in jeopardy of academic failure. What are some of the teaching practices that are shown by research to be effective and why are these methods criticized by other educators and psychologists?

2. Discuss ways that teacher planning can influence how and what the students learn in the classroom?

Multiple Choice
1. Regarding instructional planning, which of the following is most important?
   a. teachers should "overplan" and fill every minute so there is no "dead-air" in instruction
   b. teachers should stick to their plans no matter what, because they guide instruction
   c. unit planning with a specific goal in mind
   d. that teachers select a model of planning, stay with it, and refine it over time

2. Which of the following statements reflects the *organization level* of the affective domain?
   a. I think I'll attend the Ultimate Kick-Boxing Tournament when it comes to town
   b. I think I might like to attend the introductory Tai Kenpo class to see if I like it
   c. I'm enrolling in Tai Kenpo and arranging my schedule so that I can attend class every Monday
   d. I'm going to enter the kick-boxing tournament now that I have my black belt

3. According to your text, an appropriate instructional method for communicating a large amount of material to many students in a short amount of time is
   a. lecture
   b. recitation
   c. questioning
   d. seatwork

4. A key component to effective seatwork within the classroom is
   a. careful monitoring to ensure that students are not copying each others' work
   b. having students work independently so that you can spend the majority of your time with the one or two students who require extra help
   c. ensuring that students know what to do if they need help
   d. requiring that students spend no more than 10 minutes on task or they will lose interest

5. In which of the following situations would lecture be more appropriate than the constructivist approach?
   a. fostering a complete understanding of the theory of relativity
   b. learning which primary colors combine to create secondary colors
   c. learning the average amount of chocolate chips in a bag of store-bought cookies
   d. understanding the relative position of plants, crickets, and snakes within the food chain

6. Which of the following is one of the shortcomings of direct instruction?
   a. a direct instruction lesson cannot be a resource that students use to construct understanding
   b. direct instruction cannot ensure that students understand
   c. direct instruction cannot help students perceive connections among ideas
   d. direct instruction prevents teachers from addressing misconceptions

7. Group discussions are most appropriate when
   a. students are attempting to evaluate ideas and synthesize personal viewpoint
   b. students are discussing common sense issues with little chance of misconceptions
   c. when teachers wish to pose questions and probe for information
   d. when some members have difficulty participating and need encouragement

8. One of the reasons that so many students have difficulty understanding mathematics is that
   a. abstract reasoning is required before students are developmentally ready
   b. people believe mathematics to be mostly the memorization of formulas
   c. students are left to construct their own mathematical concepts
   d. algorithms often confuse the correct selection of problem solving approaches

9. The best way to evaluate a student's performance in the psychomotor domain is to
   a. grade on effort and perseverance since this domain addresses inherited abilities
   b. observe and rate the student's proficiency in producing a product or performing a skill
   c. select a panel of unbiased judges as in professional competitions
   d. allow the students to rate their own performances

10. Which of the following is consistent with the constructivist approach
    a. teachers and students together make decisions about content, activities, and approaches
    b. teacher has overarching goals that guide planning
    c. the focus is on students' process of learning and thinking
    d. all of the above

CHAPTER 14 PRACTICE TEST

Essay Questions
1. A large portion of a student's educational experience is devoted to standardized testing. Many suggest that standardized testing should be eliminated altogether. Discuss the pros and cons of standardized testing.

Multiple Choice
1. Scores which are based on the standard deviation of a distribution of scores is (are) called
    a. T Scores
    b. z Scores
    c. Standard Scores
    d. all of the above

2. Norm-referenced tests are most appropriate for
    a. measuring affective and psychomotor objectives
    b. informing students about what students can do and what they know
    c. measuring mastery of basic skills
    d. assessing the range of abilities in a large group

3. Extreme scores in a distribution cause mean inflation or deflation. To yield an accurate representation of typical test scores a better measure would be the
    a. median
    b. mode
    c. range
    d. standard deviation

4. The kind of reliability evidence that is obtained by having individuals take two different test forms that assess the same content or subject matter is called
    a. split-half reliability
    b. alternate forms reliability
    c. test-retest reliability
    d. internal consistency

5. Which of the following is true regarding grade equivalent scores? They are obtained from:
    a. multi-age norming sample
    b. different forms of tests are used at different grade levels
    c. a seventh grader with a grade equivalent score of 10 should probably be promoted to a higher grade level
    d. grade equivalent score units mean the same thing at every grade level

6. When the score bands overlap when interpreting student performance on an achievement test, this indicates that
    a. the scores are within the average range compared to the national norming sample
    b. achievement levels in these two areas are very different
    c. achievement levels in these two areas are very similar
    d. we can be 95% confident that the scores actually fall within this range

7. Which of the following is true regarding a normal distribution?
   a. the mean, median and mode are all the same score
   b. the majority of scores lie within one standard deviation above and below the mean
   c. plotted scores form a bell-shaped curve
   d. all of the above

8. On an IQ test with a mean of 100 and a standard deviation of 15, Selma obtained a score of 114 and Andy got a score of 105. What conclusions can be drawn about their performances?
   a. Selma is much smarter than Andy
   b. Selma and Andy's performances are essentially identical because they are both within one standard deviation above the mean
   c. Andy scored higher than approximately 61% of the students who took the test and Selma scored higher than approximately 83% of the students who took the test
   d. Both Andy and Selma possess average intelligence

9. The hypothetical estimate of variation in scores if testing were repeated is called
   a. the standard deviation
   b. the true score
   c. the standard error of measurement
   d. the range

10. Research on test bias (Sattler, 1992) shows that most standardized tests
   a. have items that are difficult for minorities to answer correctly
   b. predict school achievement equally well across all groups of students
   c. have well-established procedural fairness
   d. are biased against minorities in predicting school performance

CHAPTER 15 PRACTICE TEST

Essay Questions
1. Explain the paradox of "Successful Failure".

2. Many educators incorrectly employ methods of norm-referenced grading. I know of instances where educators, upon seeing the low distribution of students' scores, will impose a curve shifting all grades upwards to the temporary satisfaction of students who are more concerned with maintaining a high grade point average than learning the material. Discuss some of the other disadvantages associated with norm-referenced grading systems.

Multiple Choice

1. Starch and Elliot's research involving essays revealed that
   a. essays are actually incapable of measuring Bloom's *synthesis* objectives
   b. teachers are very subjective in their evaluations
   c. subjectivity was confined to specific subject areas
   d. students whose essays were verbose received the highest grade

2. Which of the following is NOT related to increased absenteeism and dropout rates?
   a. high standards
   b. competitive class atmosphere
   c. large percentage of lower grades
   d. authoritarian teachers

3. The primary difference between summative and formative assessments is
   a. the purpose for which they are administered
   b. formative assessments are graded and summative assessments are not
   c. formative assessments must be administered by licensed practitioners
   d. the time of year in which they are administered

4. The current thinking regarding retention or holding a child back a grade is
   a. if they appear socially and emotionally mature, it may be advantageous
   b. the opportunity to cover the same material again is beneficial
   c. promote at all costs and provide summer remediation
   d. that it decreases the likelihood that they will later drop out of school

5. Teachers don't always give the type of feedback that informs students why their answers are incorrect. In a study by Bloom and Bourdon, only _____ percent of the teachers noticed a consistent type of error in a student's arithmetic computation and informed the student.
   a. 4
   b. 8
   c. 16
   d. 32

6. With a point system of grading, if you convert each score to a percentage, average the percentages, rank the percentages and then look for natural gaps to assign grades you are using
   a. norm-referenced grading
   b. criterion-referenced grading
   c. authentic assessment
   d. dual marking systems

7. To provide assessment of student performance and the teaching methods used, (when the student is one who possesses learning problems) we would probably use
   a. portfolio assessment
   b. curriculum based assessment
   c. authentic tests
   d. prescriptive assessment

8. The Buckley Amendment
   a. provides legal guidelines for conducting parent/teacher conferences
   b. establishes guidelines for financial assistance for students diagnosed with learning disabilities
   c. ensures that minority groups are administered culture-fair tests
   d. permits parents to review or challenge material in their child's school records

9. Which of the following is NOT an example of criterion-referenced grading?
   a. portfolios
   b. percentage grading
   c. grading on the curve
   d. exhibitions

10. Sometimes, teachers form a general impression about a student and that impression may positively or negatively influence the teacher when assigning the student a grade. This effect is called
   a. self-fulfilling prophecy
   b. dual marking effect
   c. halo effect
   d. error of measurement

CHAPTER 1 ANSWER KEY

Essay Question:
1. Professional learners (teachers) know effective strategies for learning: good organizational skills, memory techniques, process information at deep levels of understanding versus rote memorization, possess good study strategies, and are motivated to be able to apply their learning and seek to improve. Amateur learners (students) must be given time to develop the finer aspects of "how" to learn, in addition to learning "what" or the subject matter. It is suggested that teachers be good guides and learning coaches so that students learn to become expert learners too.

Multiple Choice:
1. c   2. d   3. c   4. d   5. c   6. a   7. c   8. d   9.d 10.f

CHAPTER 2 ANSWER KEY

Application One: Brain Terminology
1.e 2.a 3.c 4.f 5.d 6.b 7.b 8.a 9.h 10.i

Application Two; Matching Key Terms and Definitions
a. 2   b. 9   c. 4   d. 7   e. 5   f. 3   g. 6 h. 1   i. 8 The correct number is 15.

Essay Questions
1. Research by David Elkind (1991) suggests that the pressure on parents and preschool teachers to create "superkids" who can read, write, and speak a second language, can be harmful to children. Elkind believes that preschool children who are pushed to achieve and are not given the opportunities for non-structured informal play are missing a very important aspect of their cognitive development, are showing symptomatic stress, and becoming dependent on adults for guidance. Early focus on "right" and "wrong" answers can lead to competition and self-esteem. It can also cause "academic burn-out".

2. Piaget's theory posits that children, as biological organisms, must engage in adaptation within the environment in order to survive. Construction of a language system for communication is one such attempt at becoming intellectually proficient within one's environment. Vygotsky's theory places greater emphasis on the adults within the child's culture as providing the linguistic tools necessary for cognitive development. The children from the orphanage defy this notion that language must be "transmitted" from the environment, adults and or able peers, and therefore addresses the notion that developing individuals **will** actively construct the means for communication even when incapable of hearing the culture's system of verbal communication.

Multiple Choice
1. a   2. c   3. b   4. b 5. d   6. b   7. c   8. c   9. d   10. c

CHAPTER 3 ANSWER KEY

Application 1: Characteristics of Students Who Cheat

1. false	2. true	3. true	4. false	5. false	6. true
7. true	8. true	9. true	10. false	11. true	

Essay Questions

1. Harris posits that based on certain findings, peer group influences are greater than parental influences:(1) parenting styles are not predictive of children's personalities, (2) children turn out different even when parents treat them the same way, (3) the personality of adoptive parents and children are unrelated, (4) caretaker and location have no impact on child's personality, and (5) parental behavior only influences the child when the child is with the parent. She further that states that the peer relationship is essential for human survival and more predictive of behavior. Conversely, Kagan, Williams and other psychologists suggest that in spite of the influences of peers, much research supports the notion that parents exert great influence on how children turn out in both cognitive abilities and behavior.

2. A moral dilemma for high school students regarding cheating: Frank's science instructor grades on a curve with the highest 10% of the scores getting an "A" and the lowest 10% getting an "F". Frank's best friend Jack somehow obtained a copy of the science final exam and told Frank that other students also have a copy of the exam. Jack said that Frank would be stupid if he didn't look at the exam, especially since he was trying to get into an Ivy league college and his science grade would probably go down if he didn't get an "A". Considering that Frank's instructor grades on the curve, the students who had obtained copies of the exam would definitely get "A's" driving the curve higher for everyone else, decreasing their chances at getting a good grade. Should Frank report his classmates and friends? Should Frank look at the exam? What would you do in Frank's situation?

Multiple Choice
1. b 2. b 3. d 4. d 5. c 6. a 7. b 8. a 9. d 10. c

CHAPTER 4 ANSWER KEY

Application 1: IQ Myths and Facts

1. false	2. true	3. false	4. true	5. false
6. false	7. false	8. false	9. false	10. true

79

Essay Question

1. In support of *full* inclusion, all children need to learn with and from other children. Exceptional children need to be in an environment that is as normal as possible; the "real world" with all of its real world experiences. Disabled students should not be denied the opportunity to participate in society for how else will they learn how to function in society and to become self-sufficient? Many say that special education has failed to help disabled students but the opponents of *full* inclusion suggest that these disabled students spend a portion of their time in regular classrooms. Therefore, the regular classrooms are also partially to blame. Opponents suggest that *full* inclusion places a tremendous burden on regular educators who have little preparation, support, and resources.

Multiple Choice
1. b 2. d 3. d 4. d 5. a 6. d 7. a 8. d 9. c 10. b

CHAPTER 5 ANSWER KEY

Application 1: Understanding Differences

1. consistent
2. inconsistent-mothers from the Republic of China attribute school failure to lack of effort more often than the Caucasian-American mothers.
3. inconsistent-studies done in the 1950's and in 1990, show that when black children were asked to pick the more attractive or smarter doll, they usually chose the white doll over the black doll.
4. inconsistent-78% of non-Hispanics believed Hispanics preferred to live off of welfare.
5. inconsistent-only 4% of the scientists, engineers, and mathematicians are African American or Hispanic American.
6. consistent 7. consistent 8. inconsistent-most stories are about boys and girls prefer to read about girls.
9. inconsistent-guidance counselors would only protest if it were a boy in this same situation. 10. inconsistent- white middle-class parents value ladylike behavior for their daughters.

Application 2: Creating Culturally Compatible Classrooms

1. Mexican Americans, Asian Americans 2. Mexican Americans
3. African Americans, Native Americans, Asian Americans 4. African Americans
5. Native Americans
6. Hispanic Americans, African Americans, Asian Americans 7. Asian Americans
8. Asian Americans 9. African Americans
Culture and Community
10. African Americans 11. Hispanic Americans

Essay Questions

1. Even when students speak the same language as the teacher, as with the Hawaiian and Native American children, cultural differences may prevail in how these children interact with others in a scholastic setting. There are many unwritten rules for participation. If a child's interaction style conflicts with and is perceived by a teacher as something negative, that child will be less inclined to participate in the future. Teachers need to make rules for communication clear and explicit. Use cues to signal students when changes occur. Explain and demonstrate appropriate behavior. Be consistent in responding to students.
2. Many suggest that one of the chief aims of education is to foster commonality and to help students learn a public identity. To emphasize differences is to maintain divisions among groups of people when we are in a crisis state of racial bigotry. We should emphasize the commonalities that we share and collectively work together toward the same goals. Others suggest that knowledge of other societies and customs gives students choices that may be more meaningful to them than those offered to them by society. We are not in jeopardy of dividing an already divided country but instead should be learning HOW to value diversity and teach all students to affirm their feelings of worth.

Multiple Choice Questions

1. b 2. d 3. d 4. a 5. c 6. d 7. b 8. d 9. c 10. d

CHAPTER 6 ANSWER KEY

Application 1: Modifying Behaviors

1. Trish's arguing is being positively reinforced because she is getting what she wants, a later bedtime. 2 Moira's strategies are being negatively reinforced because when she hits on the right combination, the crying stops.

3. Jimmy's obnoxious behaviors are being positively reinforced byy all the attention he is receiving.

4. Carrie's and her friend's cheating is being positively reinforced by the good grades they receive because their instructor has not updated his exams.

5. Mr. Barkley's students were experiencing presentation punishment over the threat of the "scotchies" and therefore decreased their good behavior to avoid punishment.

6. The nurse is negatively reinforcing Pablo's visits to her office because his visits allow him to escape an aversive situation; oral reports.

7. Shirley is positively reinforcing her student's improved performances on their exams.

8. Tim was positively reinforcing the students by allowing them to engage in the fun activity of throwing spitballs with no fear of repercussion.

9. Principal Gonzales positively reinforced the students who performed well with a class trip.

10. The student teacher positively reinforced the students learning by making it fun and by rewarding them with pumpkins.

Application Three: Modifying Aggression

Two responses are correct; (1) The teacher is trying to decrease their fighting through presentation punishment, the scary vice principal. (2) She is trying to increase their "playing nice behaviors" and says that once they demonstrate these positive behaviors, then she will make the aversive situation (the scary vice principal) go away. This is negative reinforcement.

Application 2: Matching Key Terms and Definitions, Operant Conditioning

a. 2   b. 9   c. 4   d. 7   e. 5   f 3   g. 6   h.   1   1.   8   The number is 15.

Essay Questions

1. We might object to principles of behavior modification from the premise that it is pure manipulation and what right does one individual in control have to manipulate other's behaviors. We could argue that every time we compliment another individual, we are in essence using positive reinforcement and increasing their behavior. Teachers need to be able to establish organization and control but what is too much control and when are behavioral principles abused? As indicated in your text, improvements in conduct won't necessarily ensure academic learning but in some situations, reinforcing academic skills may lead to improvements in conduct. Whenever behavioral principles are to be used, emphasis should be paced on academic learning because academic improvements generalize to other situations more successfully than do changes in classroom conduct.

2. Some psychologists fear that by rewarding students for learning, then learning is not perceived as valuable in and of itself. It may be perceived that learning is something that is so aversive that students must be "paid off" in order to learn. Once the rewards end, it is argued that the motivation to perform may decline. Others suggest that everyone appreciates acknowledgement and praise for a job well done. Rewards can bolster the confidence of students who lack ability or interest in the task initially. Certainly, as students learn with the aid of rewards, they will not forget the material once the rewards have stopped. Furthermore, some students may not learn without the rewards. My daughter is a good student who works hard to get "A's" and has told me that she would work for the learning anyhow but that it is nice to get rewards and that it also provides additional incentive.

Multiple Choice

1. a   2. a   3. d   4. c   5. d   6. b   7. c   8. d   9. c   10. a

CHAPTER 7 ANSWER KEY

Application 1: Behavioral and Cognitive Approaches
1. cognitive 2. behavioral 3. cognitive 4. behavioral 5. cognitive 6. behavioral 7. behavioral 8. cognitive 9. cognitive 10. behavioral

Application 2: Fill in the blanks
1. serial position effect 2. chunking
3. episodic memory 4. procedural
5. an acronym
6. maintenance rehearsal 7. part learning
8. propositional network 9. scripts
10. automaticity

Essay Questions

1. Those who argue against rote memorization suggest that it opens the door for memorization of terms and definitions with little comprehension of the meaning. Without understanding, there would be little application of learning beyond the academic setting. Therefore, learning that can't be applied would become useless and obsolete.

2. What people learn is never an exact replica of what they have read or been told. All people perceive based on what we already know and then we interpret what we have perceived based on what we already know. Perceptions are not pure but rather the meaning we give to the sensory data. Individual differences will also account for student differences in perception and learning.

Multiple Choice
1. d   2. c   3. c   4. d   5. b   6. a   7. a   8. c   9. b   10. d

CHAPTER 8 ANSWER KEY

Application 1: Learning Tactics-What Should You Do?
1. False   2. False   3. True   4. True   5. True   6. True
7. False   8. False   9. False   10. True   11. True   12. False

Essay Questions:

1. Ausubel's strategy always begins with an advance organizer. This is an introductory statement broad enough to encompass all the information that will follow. The organizers can serve three purposes. They direct your attention to what is important in the coming materials, they highlight relationships among ideas that will be presented, and they remind you of relevant information you already have.

2. Many novices or beginners approach subject areas with misunderstandings because up to the point where formal instruction begins, most of their knowledge has been constructed through perception and intuition. Many of their ideas about the physical world are wrong. For example, many young children believe that the sun follows them wherever they go, because they see the sun wherever they go. Teachers must first find out what children believe and what they think they know and then begin to clear up misconceptions and help them to formulate schemas based on accurate information and concepts.

Multiple Choice
1. d   2. b   3. c   4. c   5. a   6. b   7. c   8. d   9. c   10. d

CHAPTER 9 ANSWER KEY

Essay Question:
1. Without careful planning and monitoring by the teacher, group interactions can hinder learning and reduce rather than improve social relations in classes. If one student plays the dominant role, or some students fail to contribute, then interactions can be unproductive and unreflective. Although the high ability students generally benefit from playing the role of instructor, sometimes they resent being cast in the role of the person who has all of the information. Sometimes, socializing takes precedence over learning the material and dialectical reflections may usurp completion of projects. Also, students may reinforce each other's misunderstandings. Lastly, some may become convinced that they can't learn without the support of the group.

Multiple Choice
1.d 2.b 3.b 4.d 5.d 6.c 7. b 8.a 9. c 10. d

CHAPTER 10 ANSWER KEY

Application 1: Psychological Theories of Motivation
1. Cognitive & Humanistic 2. Expectancy X Value
3. Behavioral 4. Cognitive 5. Humanistic 6. Behavioral
7. Expectancy X Value 8. Cognitive

Application 2: Identifying Task Value
1. attainment value 2. attainment and intrinsic value 3. utility value   4. attainment value
5. attainment, intrinsic, and utility value   6. intrinsic value   7. intrinsic value
8.   utility value   9. intrinsic value   10.   attainment and utility value

Essay Questions

1 When children enter school, the direction of their natural learning and motivation changes drastically. Whereas prior to formal schooling, their learning was spontaneous, unstructured, and not segmented by subject area, now they are told what to learn, when to learn, how to learn and it is all teacher directed and subject specific. It is no longer spontaneous and natural, but now it is contrived, competitive, and very structured. Extrinsic rewards and punishments are used to motivate and from your chapter readings, you should know that students experience decreased intrinsic motivation when someone else imposes tasks and activities upon them rather then allowing them to assume responsibility for their own learning. But playing the devil's advocate, if it were left up to students to devise their own curriculum, would English, Math, and History be part of it? What do you think?

2. Thorkildsen et. al., interviewed 93 students grades 2 through 5. The interviewers described four approaches to motivation--encouraging focus on the task (thought to be fair by 98% of the students), praising excellent performance (only 30% believed public praise is fair), giving rewards for excellent performance (seen as fair by 50% of the students), and giving rewards for high effort (seen as fair by 85% of the students). Students from this study held different beliefs on motivation and surprisingly many emphasized task focus and effort over reward and praise. The Nicholls et. al., study interviewed 128 African-American students on their opinions regarding collaborative learning versus traditional instruction. Older students were more likely than younger students to see collaborative inquiry as fairer and more motivating. The older the students, the more strongly they agreed that schools should foster motivation and understanding, not just memory for tasks.

Multiple Choice
1. c 2.b 3.a 4.c 5.c 6.d 7.c 8.b 9.d 10.d

CHAPTER 11 ANSWER KEY

Essay Question
1. Without careful planning and monitoring by the teacher, group interactions can hinder learning and reduce rather than improve social relations in classes. If one student plays the dominant role, or some students fail to contribute, then interactions can be unproductive and unreflective. Although the high ability students generally benefit from playing the role of instructor, sometimes they resent being cast in the role of the person who has all of the information. Sometimes, socializing takes precedence over learning the material and dialectical reflections may usurp completion of projects. Also, students may reinforce each other's misunderstandings. Lastly, some may become convinced that they can't learn without the support of the group.

Multiple Choice
1.d 2.a 3.b 4.a 5.d 6.c 7.a 8.b 9.e 10.b

CHAPTER 12 ANSWER KEY

Application 1: Teacher-Student Owned Problems
1. student 2. shared 3. teacher 4. student 5. teacher 6. student

Essay Questions:
1. Rather than engage in a public power struggle in front of the class where you have the potentiality of losing and appearing out of control in front of your class, it is best not to repeatedly tell him to take his seat. After the first time that you tell him to sit down and he refuses, you should change your strategy. Tell him to wait out in the hall and you will join him for a private talk as soon as you get the rest of the class started on a project. If he refuses to comply, send another student to the office for assistance so that you do not leave your class unattended. Whenever possible, try to defuse this type of situation as quickly as possible, but remember to stay calm and always stay in control, especially since the rest of the class is witnessing your ability to manage the problem.

2. Opponents of assertive discipline argue that it is a demeaning approach that utilizes threat tactics and public humiliation as a means for controlling students' behaviors. It is suggested that after a student's name is recorded on the board many times, the parents are informed and if the child's problem stems from a dysfunctional family, then what purposes have actually been served. It is argued that assertive discipline does nothing to enhance student self-esteem, self-worth, or responsibility and does not teach students the reasons behind moral behaviors, only that they should behave in a certain way because it is the rule. Proponents of the approach report that 78 to 97 percent of 8,700 teachers saw improvements in student behavior as a result of using the approach. Canter suggests that it is through making choices and learning to accept the consequences, that students learn to develop self-worth and responsibility. Others have suggested that it is the improper implementation of the approach that has given assertive discipline a bad name in some camps

Multiple Choice:
1.d 2.c 3.a 4.d 5.d 6.d 7.c 8.a 9.c 10.c

CHAPTER 13 ANSWER KEY

Application 1: Assessment Statements for Bloom's Cognitive Objectives
1. evaluation
2. comprehension 3. knowledge
4. application 5. analysis 6. synthesis

Application 2: Identifying Domains of Objectives
1. psychomotor   2. cognitive 3. cognitive 4. affective
5. cognitive 6. psychomotor   7. cognitive 8. affective

Essay Questions:
1. Research on effective teachers of low achievers has identified strategies consistent with direct instruction as beneficial to "at-risk" students. These basic approaches, i.e., break instruction into small steps, cover material thoroughly and at a moderate pace, give practice, feedback, praise, use whole group, avoid independent work, and emphasize short, frequent paper-and-pencil exercises, NOT games, discovery learning, or interest centers, which are less helpful for learning. Other effective approaches are to keep the level of difficulty consonant with guaranteeing success, ask convergent questions (only one answer), and avoid open-ended questions. The opponents of direct instruction object to these practices on the premise that they address only the lower level objectives from Bloom's taxonomy and that at-risk students are underestimated, unchallenged, and deprived of a meaningful motivating context for learning or for employing the skills that they have been taught. Opponents suggest that better approaches would be to provide scaffolding, embed basic skills within more challenging, authentic tasks, model powerful thinking strategies, and encourage multiple approaches to academic tasks. Furthermore, keep the level of the tasks high enough that the purpose of the task is apparent and makes sense to the student.

2. Planning takes the time that a teacher has available to him or her and transforms it into amount of classroom instruction, activities, assignments, and tasks for the day. Some teachers, especially at the elementary level, may have preferences or strengths for one subject area over another. I know of one teacher who feels weak in the artistic realm and as a result, her students spend little time in artistic endeavors yet great amounts of time in history-related activities, her personal favorite. These students will be much stronger in history than in art. The knowledge levels of educators plays a crucial role in determining planning also. The plans of beginning teachers sometimes don't work because they lack knowledge about the students or the subject. They may not know students' interests and abilities, how long it will take students to complete activities, or how to respond when asked for an explanation when they aren't real strong in a subject area. Effective planning is something that comes with experience.

Multiple Choice:
1.c 2.c 3.a 4.c 5.a 6.b 7.a 8.b 9.b 10.d

CHAPTER 14 ANSWER KEY

Application 1: Criterion or Norm-Referenced
1. norm 2. criterion 3. criterion 4. norm 5. norm 6. criterion 7. norm 8. norm 9. criterion 10. criterion

Application 2: Calculating Standard Scores
Student Math History English mean=80 mean=50 mean=34 SD=5 SD=10 SD=8
Todd X=85 X=55 X=50 Stephanie X=90 X=40 X=30 Carlos X=80 X=60 X=42 Terri   X=70   X=65 X=3 8

	Math	History	English
Todd	z= +1	z= +.5	z= +2
Stephanie	z= +2	z= -1	z= -1
Carlos	z= 0	z= +1	z= +1
Terri	z= -2	z= +1.5	z= +.5
Todd	T= 60	T= 55	T= 70
Stephanie	T= 70	T= 40	T= 40
Carlos	T= 50	T= 60	T= 60
Terri	T= 30	T= 65	T= 55

Essay Questions:
1. Critics of standardized testing state that these tests measure disjointed facts and skills that have no use or meaning in the real world. Test questions often do not match the curriculum and therefore cannot measure how well students have learned the curriculum. Because tests are best at measuring lower-level objectives, these tend to drive the curriculum. Teachers are pressured to produce high test scores and jobs, raises and the price of real estate is all influenced by test scores. Students become labeled as low-achievers on the basis of their test scores and teachers are adversely influenced by test pressure, alienation from the process, and the reduction to their teaching time. Advocates for standardized testing procedures state that standardized tests sample what is typically taught and cannot be expected to match every school's curriculum, but still provide valuable information. To use a test properly, advocates suggest that tests should not be used as the only basis for decision making. Don't use the test unless there is a good reason for testing. Know what the test measures, know our students and don't use test results to compare students or to foster competition.

Multiple Choice:
1. d 2. d 3. a 4. b 5. b 6. c 7. d 8 c 9. c 10. b

CHAPTER 15 ANSWER KEY

Application 1: Characteristics of Objective and Subjective Tests
1. objective 2. essay 3. essay 4. objective 5. objective 6. objective
7. essay 8. objective 9. essay 10. essay

Application 2: Tests of Tests
a. 2   b. 9   c. 4   d. 7   e. 5   f. 3 g. 6 h.   1   1. 8   The number is 15

Essay Questions:
1. Successful failure is actually beneficial to the student because successful or constructive failure involves teacher feedback. Students often need help figuring out why they are wrong so they can learn more appropriate strategies. Without such feedback, they are likely to make the same mistakes again.

2. When teachers impose grading curves for the sole purpose of masking poor student performance they are cheating the students in the long run. When a score of 54 on a scale of 100 becomes a C, the student is pacified but really possesses no comprehension of the material. Grading on the curve also implies a notion of limited good. Students are aware that only so many As will be administered which fosters student competition and resentment. Students would prefer that their classmates score poorly rather than succeed, bettering their own chances at a good grade. In actuality, there are not a limited number of As that teachers can give out. It should be the objective of every teacher to have their students be successful and master the material rather than guarantee certain failure before instruction has even begun. It is no wonder that some students suffer from a lack of motivation when they feel doomed to failure by the teacher's grading system. The classroom environment should be one that fosters achievement, success, and high self-esteem, not competition, learned helplessness, and lack of motivation. Given the right environment, all students can achieve as long as the environment includes the right methods of grading employed for the right reasons.

Multiple Choice:
1. b 2.d 3.a 4.c 5.b 6.a 7.b 8.d 9.c 10.c

My Personal Praxis Study Guide

The Teacher's Casebook: Praxis II Connections information at the end of each chapter of your Woolfolk *Educational Psychology, 10/e* text includes the key information from each chapter that is likely to appear on these exams. This Guide includes this information and some sample Praxis questions. Use this as a starting point to build a file that you may add and adapt to your own testing goals.

CHAPTER ONE

Praxis II recognized the role of reflective practice in the development of excellent teachers. Reflective practice includes contact with colleagues, membership in professional associations, and review of professional literature as resources, as well as the ability to understand the current views, significant debates, and research about effective teaching practices.

Sample test question

Expert teachers can best be described as those teachers
    a.   whose training has surpassed the undergraduate level
    b.   who have taught for many years
    c.   who are born with the natural ability for teaching
    d.   who possess elaborate systems of knowledge for understanding problems in teaching

Stop for a moment and consider why d is the best response. Jot your thoughts here:

CHAPTER TWO

Praxis II devotes much of its attention to an assessment of your knowledge of human development and its relationship to learning. Your understanding of theories of cognitive development and language development will help you design and implement instructional strategies that are appropriate for the developmental levels of your students and will aid you in understanding and interpreting the problems that they might have with learning activities.

Key Concepts to Know:

Piagetian and Vygotskian theories of development:
1. Basic assumptions of each
2. How students build their unique knowledge bases
3. How they acquire skills
4. Important terms and concepts related to each
5. Key steps, mechanisms, or milestones related to each theory
6. Limitations of each theory

Language:
1. Basic assumptions of major theories
2. Major accomplishments of language development of school age children
3. Relationship between language and literacy
4. Basic steps teachers can take to enhance literacy among students

Sample test questions

Teachers can help students develop their capacities for formal thinking by
    a. using direct instruction to provide them with as much factual information as possible
    b. putting students in situations that challenge their thinking and reveal their shortcomings
    c. teaching them the rules for abstract reasoning and problem solving
    d. encouraging them to attend to their physical environment

Stop for a moment and consider why b is the best response. Jot your thoughts here:

Which of the following is consistent with Piaget's notions of constructing knowledge?
    a. active experience should include mental manipulation of ideas
    b. students must be given a chance to actively experience the world
    c. students need to interact with teachers and peers to test their thinking, be challenged, and receive feedback.
    d. all of the above.

Stop for a moment and consider why d is the best response. Jot your thoughts here:

CHAPTER THREE

Chapter 3 reflects many of the professional standards created by the Interstate New Teacher Assessment and Support Consortium (INTASC). These standards form the basis of the Praxis II and state-created teacher licensure exams. The Praxis II will require you to be knowledgeable about the personal, emotional, social, moral, and physical development of students.

Key Concepts to Know:

Erikson's theory of psychosocial development
Paiget's and Kohlberg's perspectives on moral development
Gilligan's theory of caring

Design or choose strategies that:
- Support optimal social and emotional development of students
- Help students cope with major life transitions and challenges to safety, physical, and mental health
- Help students build a sense of self-concept and self-esteem

Sample test questions

A kindergarten student plays hide and seek by "hiding" behind a student desk. Although her face is covered, the rest of her body is not. This choice of hiding spot demonstrates the child's thinking is:
- a. adaptive
- b. within the zone of proximal development
- c. egocentric
- d. scaffolding
- e. gifted

Stop for a moment and consider why c is the best response. Jot your thoughts here:

The elementary/middle school child's struggle according to Erikson is to:
- a. Establish an identity regarding beliefs, abilities, drives, and future goals.
- b. Develop a sense of industry through performance of academic tasks.
- c. Develop a sense of trust for the adults who provide care for his well-being.
- d. Develop strong commitment to life choices after free consideration of alternatives.
- e. Accept parental life choices without consideration of options.

Stop for a moment and consider why b is the best response. Jot your thoughts here:

CHAPTER FOUR

Praxis II, like classroom teaching, will require you to make instructional decisions based on your knowledge of intelligence, academic ability, grouping practices, learning disabilities, giftedness, creativity, physical disabilities and state and federal legislation.

Key Concepts to Know:

Explain the effects of legislation on public education:
- American with Disabilities Act
- Individuals with Disabilities Act
- Section 504
- Individualized Education Plans (IEP)

Inclusion, mainstreaming and least restrictive environment

Understand views of intelligence and describe its measurement:
- Types of intelligence tests and their uses
- Multiple intelligences
- Interpreting intelligence scores
- Modifications to testing

Accommodate the needs of students with exceptionalities:
- Attention Deficit-Hyperactivity Disorder
- Visual, speech, and physical difficulties
- Learning disabilities
- Mental retardation

Sample test questions

Highly related to standardized IQ scores are measures of
   a. creativity
   b. scholastic achievement
   c. reflective/impulsive tempo
   d. midlife adjustment disorders

Stop for a moment and consider why b is the best response. Jot your thoughts here:

Preschool children who spend more time in pretend play
   a. have higher IQ scores
   b. possess greater self-control
   c. are more creative
   d. engage in a higher frequency of disruptive classroom behaviors

Stop for a moment and consider why c is the best response. Jot your thoughts here:

CHAPTER FIVE

In Praxis II you will be presented with scenarios and questions that will test your knowledge of the increasingly complex learning communities that teachers and students inhabit. You will be challenged to implement strategies and practices that foster learning for each of the varied students who are in that community with you.

Key Concepts to Know:

Recognize the influences that ethnicity, socioeconomic status, and community values may have on:
- Student-teacher relationships
- Parent-teacher relationships
- Academic achievement
- Attitudes, self-esteem, and expectations for success
- Opportunities for quality education experiences

Understand the influences that gender may have on:
- Teachers' attention to students
- Differences in mental abilities

Devise strategies that:
- Eliminate exist teaching practices
- Promote positive school-home relationships
- Support English acquisition in non-English speaking students
- Reduce or eliminate racial and ethnic stereotypes and biases
- Create classroom environments that provide equal opportunities for all students

Sample test question

When socioeconomic status and educational achievement are examined in research studies, results indicate that lack of income
- a. is the primary factor in determining lack of achievement
- b. is not related to decreased academic achievement
- c. is not as important for school achievement as family environment variables
- d. is strongly correlated with lack of support for children's learning

Stop for a moment and consider why c is the best response. Jot your thoughts here:

CHAPTER SIX

Look for Praxis II to test your knowledge of behaviorism to foster appropriate classroom conduct and to establish effective routines and procedures and to address many common classroom situations.

Key Concepts to Know:

Understand the basic assumptions and contributions of these behaviorists:
- Pavlov
- Watson
- Thorndike
- Skinner

Determine appropriate behavioral techniques to:
- Establish efficient classroom routines and procedures
- Roster appropriate classroom conduct
- Help students monitor and regulate learning

Understand basic processes of operant conditioning and their roles in learning, including:
- Antecedents and consequences
- Types of reinforcement and reinforcement schedules
- Punishment
- Shaping

Sample test questions

Which of the following is NOT a strategy used to decrease behaviors?
- a. satiation
- b. positive practice
- c. reprimands
- d. response cost

Stop for a moment and consider why b is the best response. Jot your thoughts here:

Mastery usually means a score of _____ on a test or other assignment.
- a. 80 to 90%
- b. 75%
- c. 100%
- d. none of the above

Stop for a moment and consider why a is the best response. Jot your thoughts here:

CHAPTER SEVEN

Knowledge of human memory and learning developed research based on the cognitive perspective has influenced nearly every aspect of classroom practice from the design of curricula and test to the design of textbooks and instructional software. Praxis II will assess your knowledge of the contributions of the cognitive perspective.

Key Concepts to Know:

Understand how memory and recall are affected by:
- The limitations, capacities, and capabilities of the various structures of human memory
- The manner in which humans process information
- Prior knowledge of a topic
- Metacognitive/executive control processes

Explain how students and teachers can enhance learning through the use of:
- Elaboration and mnemonic devices
- Organized presentations
- Study tools that organize information (outlines, concept maps)
- Meaningful learning and instructional activities

Sample test questions:

Learning is the result of our attempts to make sense of the world, and our existing knowledge influences how and what we learn. These assumptions are consistent with
   a. cognitive views of learning
   b. behaviorist approach
   c. metacognitive skills
   d. psychosocial theories
   e. none of the above

Stop for a moment and consider why a is the best response. Jot your thoughts here:

The single best method for helping students to learn is to
   a. organize the material for them
   b. make it meaningful
   c. provide them with mnemonics
   d. reinforce their learning with incentives and rewards

Stop for a moment and consider why b is the best response. Jot your thoughts here:

CHAPTER EIGHT

As you become more knowledgeable about teaching through experience, study, and reflection, you can expect to develop a sophisticated set of instructional strategies that you can use to address a variety of instruction challenges. Praxis II will test your understanding of instructional and learning strategies.

Key Concepts to Know:

Discovery learning and expository teaching:
- Basic assumptions
- Inductive reasoning/deductive reasoning
- Appropriate uses
- Principles of implementation

Problem solving:
- General problem-solving strategies
- The value of problem representation
- Heuristics and algorithms
- Factors that impede problem solving

Learning strategies:
- Basic principles of teaching these strategies
- Cognitive processes involved in various strategies

Transfer of learning:
- Types of transfer
- Steps that teachers can take to promote transfer

Sample test questions

A step-by-step procedure for solving a problem is called a(n)
  a. analogy
  b. heuristic
  c. means-ends analysis
  d. algorithm

Stop for a moment and consider why d is the best response. Jot your thoughts here:

When teaching concepts to your students, the most effective sequence is
  a. prototype, less obvious examples, nonexamples
  b. nonexamples, less obvious examples, prototypes
  c. less obvious examples, nonexamples, prototypes
  d. less obvious examples, prototypes, nonexamples

Stop for a moment and consider why a is the best response. Jot your thoughts here:

CHAPTER NINE

The Praxis II tests your knowledge of student-centered models of instruction and how you draw your students into active, meaningful learning. You will be asked to consider thoughtful learning activities about such topics as motivation, learning environments, evaluation, and instructional strategies.

Key Concepts to Know:

Explain the advantages and appropriate uses of major student-centered approaches to learning and instruction:
- Cooperative learning
- Inquiry method
- Problem-based learning
- Instructional conversations
- Cognitive apprenticeships

Understand important concepts related to student-centered models of instruction:
- Situated learning
- Critical thinking/Culture of thinking
- Complex learning environments
- Authentic tasks
- Multiple representations of content

Sample test question

Introduction of the fundamental structure of all subjects in the early years, revisiting them in more complex forms over time is called
- a. reciprocal teaching
- b. instructional conversations
- c. authentic learning
- d. situated learning
- e. spiral curriculum

Stop for a moment and consider why e is the best response. Jot your thoughts here:

CHAPTER TEN

Your level of self-determination, your expectations for success and support, and your goals are among the many factors that will influence your motivation to be a successful teacher. Now transfer these concepts about motivation to your students. The Praxis II will assess your understanding of the role of self-determination, positive expectations, and goal setting in the classroom.

Key Concepts to Know:

Describe the theoretical foundations of the major approaches to motivation.
Identify and define important terms related to motivation.
Use your knowledge of motivation to:
- Identify situations and conditions that can enhance or diminish student motivation to learn.
- Design strategies to support individual and group work in the classroom.
- Implement practices that help students become self-motivated.

Sample test questions

As a teacher, you give an assignment requiring students to go beyond the information given in the text by combining several ideas. You are asking students to use skills of:
   a.   memory
   b.   opinion
   c.   comprehension
   d.   authentic assessment

Stop for a moment and consider why c is the best response. Jot your thoughts here:

When students are required to engage in activities that have some connection to real-life problems and situations that students will face outside of the classroom this is aptly named:
   a.   inert knowledge
   b.   problem based learning
   c.   routine procedure
   d.   authentic tasks

Stop for a moment and consider why d is the best response. Jot your thoughts here:

CHAPTER ELEVEN

The Praxis II will assess your understanding of the effects of students' emotions, their interactions with you and each other, the ways in which educators manage classrooms and schools, and the values that teacher emphasize in their classrooms and curricula.

Key Concepts to Know:

Focus on these major topics:
- Strategies for building a community of learners
- Cooperative Learning Structures
- The role of the school in the community.
- Community environments and conditions that affect students' lives and learning.

Sample test questions

Positive interdependence, needing each other for support, explanations and guidance, are characteristic of what form of learning?
- a. cooperative learning
- b. situated learning
- c. inquiry learning authentic learning
- d. group learning

Stop for a moment and consider why a is the best response. Jot your thoughts here:

As a teacher, you will undoubtedly use group learning. Without careful planning and monitoring, group interactions can hinder learning and reduce, rather than improve, social relations in classes. Which of the following is a potential disadvantage of group learning?
- a. Students value the process or procedures over the learning.
- b. Students use each other for support, explanations and guidance.
- c. Students give each other constructive feedback, reaching consensus.
- d. Students are individually assessed.

Stop for a moment and consider why a is the best response. Jot your thoughts here:

CHAPTER TWELVE

As a teacher, you are responsible for creating a classroom climate where all students can learn in an environment in which they feel safe, respected, and accepted. The Praxis II will test your knowledge of strategies and techniques used to create classroom climates that are conducive to learning and academic risk-taking.

Key Concepts to Know:

Understand principles of classroom management that promote positive relationships by:
- Establishing daily procedures and routines
- Responding effectively to minor student misbehavior
- Implementing reasonable rules, penalties, and rewards
- Keeping students actively engaged in purposeful learning
- Diagnose problems and prevent or reduce inappropriate behaviors by:
- Communicating with students and parents
- Addressing misbehaviors in the least intrusive way possible
- Confronting disruptive behaviors in an effective, efficient manner.

Sample test question:

An essential goal of classroom management is to expand the sheer number of minutes available for learning. This is called:
    e. academic learning time
    f. engaged time
    g. time on task
    h. seat to seat time

Stop for a moment and consider why c is the best response. Jot your thoughts here:

CHAPTER THIRTEEN

Recent policy changes in many states, as well as the federal Leave No Child Behind Act, will probably have a strong influence on your new career as a teacher. The test scores of your students will receive increased scrutiny from administrators, boards of education, and state education departments. Many newer tests emphasize skills and knowledge that are learned most effectively through a variety of student-centered instructional strategies that you have encountered in you textbook. The Praxis II will evaluate your understanding of these important student-centered instructional strategies.

Key Concepts to Know:

Develop plans for instruction and consider:
- The role of objectives in instruction
- Writing behavioral cognitive objectives
- The use of educational taxonomies to design effective objectives and plans
- The role of independent practice (seatwork and homework)

Understand the basic principles of teacher-centered and student-centeeed forms of instruction, including:
- Appropriate uses and limitations
- The role of the teacher
- Effective questioning techniques
- Whole group discussions
- Recitation
- Cooperative learning
- Thematic/interdisciplinary instruction

Sample test questions

The best way to evaluate a student's performance in the psychomotor domain is to
  a. grade on effort and perseverance since this domain addresses inherited abilities
  b. observe and rate the student's proficiency in producing a product or performing a skill
  c. select a panel of unbiased judges as in professional competitions
  d. allow the students to rate their own performances

Stop for a moment and consider why b is the best response. Jot your thoughts here:

Which of the following is consistent with the constructivist approach?
  a. a.teachers and students together make decisions about content, activities, and approaches
  b. teacher has overarching goals that guide planning
  c. the focus is on students' process of learning and thinking
  d. all of the above

Stop for a moment and consider why d is the best response. Jot your thoughts here:

CHAPTER FOURTEEN

The Praxis II will assess your knowledge about the various types of standardized tests, results of these instruments, purposes of specific tests and the strengths and limitations of those tests.

Key Concepts to Know:

Understand the major concepts related to measurement theory, including:
- Norming samples
- Percentile rank, grade-equivalent scores, stanine scores, T and z scores
- Standard deviation, mean, mode, median, standard error of measurement, and confidence intervals
- Reliability and validity

Describe the characteristics and purposes of the major types of tests:
- Criterion-referenced and norm-referenced tests
- Achievement, aptitude, diagnostic, and readiness tests

Explain the major issues related to concerns about standardized testing, including:
- High-stakes testing
- Bias in testing
- Test-taking programs

Sample test questions

When teachers attempt to address the relatedness between testing and teaching, they are trying to ensure that their teacher-made tests have
- a. content validity
- b. criterion-related validity
- c. external validity
- d. extreme validity

Stop for a moment and consider why b is the best response. Jot your thoughts here:

In which of the following scenarios would norm referenced tests be most useful?
- a. to tell whether students are ready to move on to more advanced material
- b. to measure affective and psychomotor domains
- c. to foster cooperation and collaboration
- d. to select the top candidates when limited numbers can be admitted to a program

Stop for a moment and consider why d is the best response. Jot your thoughts here:

CHAPTER FIFTEEN

A useful grading system is fair, manageable, and supportive of learning. The Praxis II will evaluate your understanding of the complexities of classroom assessment.

Key Concepts to Know:

Understand major concepts related to classroom assessment and grading:
- Formative and summative assessment
- Reliability and validity
- Criterion-referenced and norm-referenced grading

Describe the characteristics, uses, and limitations of major assessment techniques, including:
- Multiple-choice items
- Essays
- Portfolios
- Exhibitions

Design a scoring rubric for an authentic learning task that possesses:
- Validity
- Reliability
- Generalizability
- Equity

Sample test questions

Which of the following is NOT an example of criterion-referenced grading?
- a. portfolios
- b. percentage grading
- c. grading on the curve
- d. exhibitions

> Stop for a moment and consider why c is the best response. Jot your thoughts here:

Sometimes, teachers form a general impression about a student and that impression may positively or negatively influence the teacher when assigning the student a grade. This effect is called
- a. self-fulfilling prophecy
- b. dual marking effect
- c. halo effect
- d. error of measurement

> Stop for a moment and consider why c is the best response. Jot your thoughts here: